Simon Lister

FIRE IN BABYLON

How the West Indies Cricket Team Brought a People to its Feet

YELLOW JERSEY PRESS
LONDON

1 3 5 7 9 10 8 6 4 2

Yellow Jersey
20 Vauxhall Bridge Road,
London SW1V 2SA

Yellow Jersey Press is part of the Penguin Random House
group of companies whose addresses can be found at
global.penguinrandomhouse.com

Penguin
Random House
UK

First published by Yellow Jersey Press in 2015

www.vintage-books.co.uk

A CIP catalogue record for this book
is available from the British Library

ISBN 9780224092227

Typeset by Palimpsest Book Production Ltd, Falkirk, Stirlingshire
Printed and bound in Great Britain by Clays Ltd, St Ives plc

Penguin Random House is committed
to a sustainable future for our business, our
readers and our planet. This book is made from
Forest Stewardship Council® certified paper

MIX
Paper from
responsible sources
FSC® C018179

For Madeleine, who makes everything possible
– and everything worthwhile.

Contents

Foreword

by Clive Lloyd

When I read this book, a lot of powerful memories returned. I recalled places and events and fragments of conversations that hadn't entered my mind for years; I remembered long-forgotten scenes from dressing rooms, airport lounges, hotel lobbies. Bus journeys through Pakistani mountain passes and slightly less terrifying coach trips from Nottingham to Swansea. Once again I heard Joel Garner's deep laugh and the infectious chuckle of Alvin Kallicharran. Once more I saw that look in Viv's eyes when he knew it was going to be his day. I glimpsed Desmond Haynes's mischievous raised eyebrows, which were the sign that some kind of horseplay was around the corner.

Small moments from big games came back to me too: taking guard in a Test match at Melbourne and looking up through the heat haze and the din to see Dennis Lillee in the distance, ready to do his worst. I remember leaning on my bat at the non-striker's end at the Oval and inhaling the exuberant buzz that only a West Indian cricket crowd far from home can create. A small moment that brought me great pride. How could we not try to do our best with that kind of support?

Sitting at my desk as I write, I can almost feel my soaked shirt sticking to my shoulders again as I slumped on a dressing-room bench after a game. Time and again over ten seasons that sensation was often accompanied by dizzying elation – a Test win, a series victory and twice a World Cup. Of course, there were also times when sitting on that bench all I felt was frustration or a disappointment so heavy that it could have overwhelmed me. Reading *Fire in Babylon* has reminded me that being captain of the West Indies brought so many privileges – and so many emotions.

With the hindsight of nearly 40 years, I believe two words sum up those days: joy and hope. The joy came from sharing a field with a very special group of sportsmen, and the hope came from our belief that tomorrow could be even better, that there was more excellence to come, that the job was not complete.

From my first Test as captain at Bangalore in 1974, through the adventure of World Series Cricket, to my last Test in Sydney in 1985, I played alongside 45 other West Indian cricketers. Some, like Arthur Barrett and Rangy Nanan, I captained just a couple of times. Others, such as Vivian Richards and Michael Holding, seemed to walk on every step of the same path. But whether these men were there for a pace or a mile, we all achieved something memorable. It was an unforgettable decade. Building on what had been patiently laid down, we turned the West Indies into winners and brought joy and respect to the region. It sounds simple, unremarkable even, but when you consider our painful history, the bitter impositions forced upon those who came before us and the particular ordeals that the inhabitants of the Caribbean have had to overcome each day of their lives, you can begin to understand why winning cricket matches for the West Indies meant so much to us all – those at home and those making their way around the world. Excellence had arrived. Our collective and individual skills had at last been recognised and could not be denied any longer. We represented a people who could make a difference. As the great writer C. L. R. James put it, we had entered the comity of nations.

What I particularly like about *Fire in Babylon* is the way it explains how the tradition of West Indian cricket developed. At the end of the book – and I hope I'm not giving anything away here – the author writes that the teams led by Vivian Richards and me did not fall from passing comets, ready to go. He's right. We had to fight hard to get to where we did. We had battles with our own administrators. We took on those less discerning people who believed that men and women from the Caribbean had nothing good to offer. We stood firm against those inside the game who tried to blunt our talents by changing the laws of cricket. The players came through it all, but at times it was very tough. There are many revealing interviews in this book but, believe me, there are other things that we haven't shared, things that will stay private. It wasn't always easy. Yet even in the midst of disappointments, disagreements or setbacks, I knew that we could draw on the great men of our past for inspiration. In my playing days I always felt the shade from the branches of our cricket family tree. I believe its roots are deeper and stronger than those of all the other cricket-playing nations. I knew that Rohan Kanhai and Garry Sobers had learned from Frank Worrell and that he in turn had taken good things from the example of George Headley and Learie Constantine. When it was my time to lead the side, the knowledge that there were links in the chain to which I was connected was an invaluable source of strength.

My great hope is that today's West Indian cricketers can somehow absorb that strength too. We all know that the sides written about in *Fire in Babylon* enjoyed very different fortunes to those of the past few years. I am now in my sixth decade with West Indian cricket. I have been a player, captain, coach, manager, board member and selector. I will never give up trying to get us to where I know we can be. The joy may have been rationed in recent years, but we must always have hope. Always. Just to read about fellows like Charles Ollivierre in this book fills me with hope. Here was a young man setting off into the unknown more than a hundred years ago, unsure of the outcome. A pioneer for West Indian cricket. A man with determination and a dream. I know there are young cricketers with similar strength of character in the Caribbean today. They must be protected and encouraged.

This is a fine book indeed. I doubt there will be a better book written about this period in West Indies cricket history. We have been blessed with writers who have understood what the game has meant to the people of the Caribbean – C. L. R. James, Michael Manley, Hilary Beckles, Tony Cozier and Tony Becca. I know that the author is from London town and not Georgetown, but *Fire in Babylon* has added to that long tradition.

Clive Lloyd CBE
April 2015

Cricket is more than a sport, it is a political and social process that requires detailed investigation.

Sir Vivian Richards

For some folks it was more exciting that they were going to meet their cousin from Birmingham rather than anything Viv might do. It was about having a good day out.

Colin Babb

Prologue

Michael Holding was crying.

Crying on a cricket pitch.

He was a young man, just 21 years old, who still lived at home with his parents on the Caribbean island of Jamaica. He worked as a government computer programmer at the Central Data Processing Unit on East Street in Kingston.

He sat on his haunches and stared down at the grass as the tears came. He wasn't alone. Far from it. He was in Sydney in Australia. He was representing the West Indies in a Test match, and roughly 39,000 people inside the Sydney Cricket Ground were watching him weep. It was just after tea on Sunday 4 January 1976.

Holding was a fast bowler. Really very fast. But he hadn't played Test cricket before this tour. He had been chosen by the captain of the West Indies, Clive Lloyd, for his promise, not his results.

The West Indies were in Australia to play six Test matches. This one in Sydney was the fourth. Lloyd's side were behind in the series but it was still close. It was the toughest cricket Holding had known, but they could still win.

First ball after the tea break on the second afternoon, Holding had got the wicket of the opening batsman, Ian Redpath. Caught behind by the wicket-keeper, Deryck Murray. That brought Ian

Chappell to the crease, the former Australia captain. The West Indies were getting back in the game.

Chappell had given up the skipper's job earlier in the year, worn down by the grind and determined not to endure the fate of his predecessor, who had found out he'd been sacked from teammates told by a reporter. 'The bastards won't get *me* that way,' Chappell had promised his wife when he accepted the captaincy. Anyway, it wasn't his problem any longer; the responsibility of leading the country's cricket team now lay with his younger brother Greg, who was padded up in the dressing room, next in.

Ian Chappell was an articulate, thoughtful, intelligent man. He could also be opinionated, caustic and had a visceral disregard for bullshit. As he said himself, there were more opinions around the Chappell family breakfast table each morning than there were glasses of orange juice. 'Aw, you're just like your old man,' the South Australia wicket-keeper Barry Jarman had once taunted the young Chappell on the team bus. 'You think you know everything.'

Chappell walked from the Sydney Cricket Ground dressing room to the middle of the pitch. Collar pointing up, moustache pointing down. Shirt unbuttoned almost to the nipples. Sleeves rolled up to the elbows. His articulacy, thoughtfulness and intelligence weren't evident at this exact moment; he just looked like what he was – a bloody tough cricketer.

First ball, Michael Holding bowled him a beauty. It was fast – short but not too short – on the line of the off stump. It moved away just a little after it bounced. Chappell had to play at it.

'Oh yeah, and I hit it,' he says. 'Because it was short, I edged it right next to my ear, playing a defensive shot, so to me it sounded like a bloody gun going off.'

Behind the stumps Deryck Murray took the catch. His second in two balls.

'It was about the only time in my career that I thought about walking,' says Chappell. 'I actually did a little shuffle towards the gate because I was batting at the Bradman–Noble end so the dressing rooms were off to the right. I took a pace but then my natural instincts took over and I stood there. I couldn't believe it when Reg Ledwidge didn't give me out.'

Murray was holding the ball above his head in his glove, shouting the appeal. At first slip Alvin Kallicharran threw his hands high. Lawrence Rowe at second slip joined in, and Clive Lloyd at third jumped off the ground. But umpire Ledwidge said no. He decided that the ball had not touched the bat. Ian Chappell was not out.

By now Michael Holding had run to the fielding position of extra cover as his celebration turned to dismay. He crouched down and he began to cry. The tears were caused not just by the injustice of the moment. At that instant Holding had been overwhelmed by the potency of his emotions during the past two months; the peevish, disagreeable and ill-humoured atmosphere that had polluted the West Indies dressing room. The lack of respect shown by some teammates to Lloyd and to the tour manager, who was a friend of Holding's father. The inability of his captain to provide harmony away from the ground and tactical acuity on it. The cutting comments of the Australian players and the hooting vulgarity of the spectators. He missed his family and had spent Christmas apart from them for the first time. Sitting in a crappy three-star hotel room eating rum-flavoured fruit cake sent by his mother was no substitute. And apart from all that he was being paid about £350 for the whole damned tour. If this was Test cricket, you could forget it.

'We were playing against a very good team, highly motivated with some great fast bowlers under conditions that most of us were unfamiliar with,' says Holding. 'Big grounds, huge crowds, very partisan. Yes. It was like a war. Eventually you get to realise what Test cricket is all about, and it is not as simple as it may seem.'

Holding's room-mate, Andy Roberts, was the first player to console him and help him to his feet. Lance Gibbs ran over to offer solace. Holding went back to his bowling mark but was so distracted that it took him nearly ten minutes to complete the eight-ball over. The crowd jeered and mocked. Chappell was sufficiently embarrassed by the umpire's mistake to consider giving his wicket away. The temptation passed. Instead, he hooked the last ball of Holding's over for four.

1

'Our business was to admire, wonder, imitate, learn'

The West Indian side which had landed in Australia towards the end of October 1975 was a mix. A mix of those who had seen much and those who understood very little. The opening batsman Roy Fredericks from Guyana had played 39 times for the Test team; his partner Gordon Greenidge from Barbados had played five times. Lawrence Rowe from Jamaica had scored a triple, a double century and a century in Test match innings since 1972; Vivian Richards from Antigua had yet to make that many runs combined in all of the Test matches he had played. Michael Holding didn't know the feeling of taking a Test match wicket, yet Lance Gibbs had experienced it 293 times; the Guyanese off-spinner needed just 15 more wickets to break the world record total. Clive Lloyd was older than 12 of the squad and younger than four of the men he captained.

Lloyd had been in charge of the side for 18 months. He was 31 but had known the challenges of taking decisions on others' behalves since he was a teenager. His life had changed the night he climbed on his bicycle and pedalled through a tropical storm whipping Georgetown, the capital of British Guiana on the South American mainland. He was 14 and was delivering the news to relatives that his father was dead.

Arthur Lloyd was a driver who liked to drink. He was chauffeur to an Indian doctor and had been warned many times that the amount of alcohol he drank would shorten his life, but in 1950s Georgetown a man's options for entertainment were pretty limited. There was the dance hall, the cinema, the race track and not much else. As Clive Lloyd lay in his bed, he would often hear the chink of glasses and the laughter of the jockeys from Durban Park who drank at the Lloyds' house. In the mornings he looked on aghast at his father standing in the bathroom, coughing blood into the sink. The death of Arthur Lloyd – and the manner of it – traumatised the teenager.

Lloyd had no choice but to leave school as soon he was able in order to support his widowed mother and his four younger sisters. He became an administrative clerk for the Ministry of Health, and that was his lot. Lloyd was from the black lower middle class, towards the bottom of colonial society, and he was expected to stay there. His formal education had ceased and there was no practical way of it continuing. British Guiana was a stifling place in the 1950s, where an enveloping stasis of education, the law, religion and above all class and race kept people such as Lloyd pinned in their place.

But he did have cricket.

The colony had produced few outstanding players before Lloyd was born, but then, in the 1950s, there came a flourish of talent: Rohan Kanhai, Joe Solomon and Basil Butcher. And Lance Gibbs. The off-spin bowler playing his final Test matches on the Australia tour in 1975–76 was Lloyd's older cousin. The teenager adored his cricketing relative. Gibbs had always been a talented spinner – he had to be to get recognised. When he first went for trials with the British Guiana side, he had to perform as a leg-break bowler because there was another off-spinner called Norman Wight – a light-skinned Portuguese. He wasn't as good as Gibbs, but because of the colonial structure, the enveloping stasis, he was the chosen player.

Gibbs's success brought hope to Lloyd. And he needed hope. 'In an outpost of colonialism where a young man's only capital is his body,' wrote the American sports journalist Robert Lipsyte, 'cricket heroes offered promise and possibility.' Lloyd himself would only say it was a 'rough, rough scene' and that his life was not easy. 'After my father died, I knew that I had to be somebody. Most of the decisions I made for my family, I made on my own.'

By the end of his teenage years, Lloyd had become a batsman to watch at the Demerara Cricket Club. He was developing athletic skills that would transform his life, his talent the ejector seat that flung him away from his constraints. Even so, this new trajectory was informed by the values he had learned in his early years. Like millions of other Caribbean boys born around the time of the Second World War, Lloyd experienced what they called in Georgetown a British Christian education. Sitting in a classroom in South America, he was drilled in the history, literature and moral code of a tiny distant country that had a claim over the land he lived in. He knew about Shakespeare, the rivers of England, Trafalgar.

'It was only long years after', reflected the cricket journalist and Trinidadian intellectual C. L. R. James, 'that I understood the limitations on spirit, vision and self-respect which were imposed on us by the fact that our masters, our curriculum, our code of morals, *everything* began from the basis that Britain was the source of all light and leading, and our business was to admire, wonder, imitate, learn; our criterion of success was to have succeeded in approaching that distant ideal – to attain it of course was impossible.' Lloyd himself puts it simply: 'Given where I came from and given my personal history, why the hell was I taught about the Battle of Hastings?'

Yet an unintended consequence of Lloyd's education was that the values it imparted – a commitment to excellence, the idea that knowledge brings reward, the authority of the teacher, the particular dynamics of male company – helped to make him into the sort of man who could cope intellectually with the complex challenge of captaining the West Indies cricket team. In short, his experiences in his home and his classroom informed his leadership.

The Australian summer of 1975–6 was to test it in new and unpleasant ways.

* * *

A fast bowler from Antigua, Andy Roberts, had delivered the first ball of the West Indies' tour. Not in Australia but in Papua New Guinea. This new nation was only five weeks old and the West Indies were happy to assist with its independence celebrations. Up in the north, by the muddy waters of the Markham River, Clive Lloyd tossed up on a concrete wicket covered by a canvas mat at a ground in the small administrative city of Lae. Cricket had been known in the region for almost a century since Protestant mission-aries had used the game as a tool to distract the Papuans from their supposed sexual profligacy. Alongside the Bible, the evangelists prayed the sport would turn the islanders into 'obedient, chanting, cricket-loving Christians'. They had had some success. An Australian expedition in the years before the First World War noted that it was impossible to raise a team of porters for a trek into the interior until the village match was completed.

The game versus the West Indies in October 1975 was short, just 25 overs per side, but it caught the attention of the people who lived there. Bob Turnbull was 22 at the time, working as an accountant. In his spare time he was secretary of the Lae Cricket Association. 'It was the sort of place where you tended to drink a lot,' he recalls. 'Australian men who were posted there with their wives were told by older expats that the experience would either make or break their marriage.'

Bob and other volunteers had made sure that the grass around the concrete wicket had been cut short and had put up parasols along the boundary. But there was no pavilion, no tent, and nowhere for anyone to get changed. So the West Indies got into their whites at the nearby Melanesian Hotel and were driven to the ground in locals' cars. Well over half the city came to the match. Children were given the day off school and sat on the grass around the outfield. Under the shade of a tree, perched on a small blue plastic chair, Clive Lloyd signed autographs.

The journalist Jack Fingleton, who had played for Australia under Don Bradman in the late 1930s, was on the trip and was asked to predict the fortunes of the West Indies and their captain over the next three months.

> Anything could happen at all. The West Indians are unpredictable cricketers. And they're likely to do anything. It's a big ordeal for Clive Lloyd. Whether Clive will be as good a skipper as Frank Worrell, well, he's got a lot to do. Frank Worrell was a great man, a great leader. But Clive Lloyd has now had a lot of experience in England, and he was the hero of that great game, remember at Lord's when they beat us in the cup final? And that has led a lot of people to say that they are the champions.

The rough outfields of Lae and Port Moresby were a long way from the manicured splendour of Lord's and London. On the longest day of the summer in June 1975 the West Indies had beaten Australia in the first World Cup final. Almost until the end, at a quarter to nine at night, either side could have won. It was so exciting that in Australia hundreds of thousands of people stayed up through the night to watch, causing a surge in the nation's electricity supply system. Never before had a match from overseas been televised in Australia from first ball till last. Clive Lloyd had made a hundred. Vivian Richards had run out three Australian batsmen, and yet with their last two players at the crease Australia could still have lifted the cup. After nearly nine hours of cricket, when Deryck Murray ran out the fast bowler Jeff Thomson, there were only 17 runs between the two sides. The West Indies became champions of the world.

Now, four months on, Australia wanted to contest that accolade. Their new captain, Greg Chappell, believed that winning a competition in which the cricket began and ended in a day was one thing. An unremitting examination of skill, technique and ticker over five days – Test cricket – was much more likely to show who was the best side in the world. And he was clear as to why – despite the defeat at Lord's – his side were better. 'Fast bowlers all through Test history have been the difference between a good side and a great side,' he said.

Australia had two very fast bowlers. Dennis Lillee and Jeff Thomson. They were from opposite sides of the country – Lillee was from Perth and Thomson from Sydney – and they bowled very differently too. But they both had extreme pace and a loathing for batsmen that couldn't be extinguished.

Thomson had been able to bowl fast since he was a kid in New South Wales. When he was 12, he played for the Saturday boys' team in the morning, then the under-16s until lunch and then the men's side in the afternoon. If his dad wasn't around to pick him up, he'd run between the three grounds. At the Bankstown club as a teenager, his pace accelerated from slippery to dangerous. He once had an argument in a shopping centre with his school friend Lenny Durtanovitch, also a good bowler, about which one of them had broken more batsmen's fingers (Durtanovitch would later change his surname to Pascoe and play for Australia alongside Thomson). He could remember the first time a ball he bowled hit a batsman in the face. 'It reared and smashed him straight in the eye. It was frightening to see this bloke just screaming and shaking and the pitch was spattered with blood.'

When England had played the 1974–75 Test series in Australia the summer before the West Indies, Thomson had never bowled faster and had never been fitter. He showed off for TV by chasing wild pigs through the bush. It may have been a stunt but it looked impressive. After jumping from a moving jeep, Thomson sprinted and sidestepped before rugby-tackling the grunting animals to the ground. 'I hope none of the Pommies can run as fast as this thing,' he panted at the camera, smeared with orange bush dust while holding his latest victim, squealing and shaking, upside down by the back legs.

Away from the cricket field, Dennis Lillee promoted himself in a slightly more urbane way, modelling summer suits for the David Jones department store. Pure wool blend fabric in silver-grey, blue-grey or beige, the Townsman Celsius 30 could be hanging in any Australian man's wardrobe for just $120. He may have exuded a brand of nascent Aussie metropolitan sophistication in his adverts, but Lillee was no less a hard man than his hog-wrestling bowling mate.

What did he hope to do to a batsman?

'I'm trying to scare him,' Lillee answered. 'Trying to hurt him, perhaps in the ribs or the leg or something like that so that he at least knows you're around.'

'Dennis Lillee was a self-made bowler and athlete,' says Greg Chappell. 'I've seen him try to play tennis and golf – it wasn't natural for him. He made himself into a great fast bowler through hard work and willpower. Whereas Thommo was just born to bowl fast – he was born to do most things fast. He was blessed with a natural athleticism and a beautiful build.'

Lillee was 26, a year older than Thomson, and had been around Test cricket for a year longer. He was beloved by Australians because he had rid them of their fear, which had been growing fast by the end of the 1960s, that the country had run out of quick bowlers. When he bowled, he had the concentration of a batsman. He had self-discipline and a capacity for reflection. As a young Test bowler, he could deliver little more than an outswinging ball, albeit a rapid one. But after being told he had three fractures in his spine in 1973, he recovered when many thought his international cricket career was over and taught himself several other ways of getting batsmen out: balls which cut off the seam towards and away from the stumps, bouncers that were fast, bouncers that were slower.

'The first thing a batsman had to do with Dennis was to overcome his skill and courage,' says Ian Chappell. 'Then you had to overcome his iron will. He was always the last guy in our side to concede that the match couldn't be won. He never, ever asked me for a defensive fielder. If he wanted someone in a different position, it was to get a wicket. It was a hell of a help for a captain that he was never wanting men back to save boundaries. The best way of summing him up is that he was a captain's dream and a batsman's nightmare.'

The thing Jeff Thomson did best – some days at nearly 100 miles per hour – was to bowl a ball which would bounce from the pitch and then head straight for a batsman's throat. The combination of angle and velocity to make that happen was unusual. Batting against such a ball was very difficult.

Ian Chappell reckoned he could hook any bowler in the game except Thomson. No point trying. The ball that was short enough

8

to hit would go way over your head, and the one that was at the right height wasn't short enough. Thomson's bowling style – he released the ball from behind him as if it came from the arm of a catapult – enabled him to get the bounce of a man three or four inches taller. Deliveries that a cricketer would recognise as being almost a 'good length' could not be driven off the front foot because they passed the batsman at chest height.

He also had a fantastically strong arm. During the England series the Australia wicket-keeper Rod Marsh would often yell 'No, don't!' at Thomson as the bowler picked the ball up from the deep and prepared to fizz it at him as he stood over the stumps 60 yards away. Marsh had learned that he was either about to experience a burning pain in his palms or watch the ball flash over his head.

'Thommo was the most lethal bowler I've seen – certainly for those two and a half years in the mid-70s,' says Ian Chappell. 'He is also one of the funniest men I know. Often very funny without trying to be. He would just say whatever was on his mind – not a loudmouth, just says what he thinks. That's Thommo. If he didn't like you, you knew about it pretty quickly.'

Aside from his bowling skill, Thomson was a superb artist, draughtsman and designer. His mother had taught him the botanical names of dozens of Australia's plants, and he was a fine gardener too. Years after he retired from cricket, he would add tens of thousands of dollars to the value of Greg Chappell's house by planning and building a landscaped outdoor living area, with decking, a thatched roof, flower beds, floodlights on the tennis court. No, he wasn't stupid, but he liked to play up to the preconception of the brainless Aussie fast bowler.

'We were standing in the pub once and he was speaking,' says Ian Chappell, 'and I said facetiously, "Jesus, Thommo – that's a big word for a fast bowler." And he said, "Yeah, mate, I'm a lot smarter than you bastards know, but I'm quite happy for you to think I'm dumb.'

* * *

After the little adventure in Papua New Guinea, the West Indies had a further month to prepare for the first Test match in Brisbane, which would begin on 28 November. They would play against four Australian states as well as take on local sides upcountry. These were light duties. In Adelaide Clive Lloyd oversaw net practice and played squash. They made a TV advert for men's toiletries. To the tune of a tacky calypso, they sang,

Sweat all day in burnin' sun,
Aussie pacemen not much fun.
Batsman wear Brut 33,
He got hundred runs by tea.

In one sequence Ian Chappell batted against Lance Gibbs, only to be fooled by the spinner, who had him stumped. They filmed the take again and again; each time the wicket-keeper knocked off the bails with Chappell stranded out of his crease.

'You must have that fuckin' world record by now, haven't you?' Chappell asked Gibbs.

In Melbourne the West Indies team were guests of the Victoria Racing Club and watched Think Big retain the Melbourne Cup. At the Queen Elizabeth Oval in Bendigo the local sewerage department was given the afternoon off so staff could watch the West Indies defeat the Victoria Country XI. In the game at Dubbo, five hours' drive from Sydney, children searched for cricket balls spanked by Vivian Richards beyond the war memorial in Victoria Park and people bought prize raffle tickets for a pig and two autographed bats.

*   *   *

Both captains looked hard at the Woolloongabba pitch in Brisbane, on which the first Test match was to be played. The Queensland wicket had too little grass and had seen too much water. Heavy rain had got underneath the covers protecting the square and the lord mayor of the city was getting the blame.

Alderman Clem Jones was both a politician and a groundsman. One of the reasons he was mower-pusher-in-chief at the Gabba was that he had sacked the ground's previous curator. Jones stood towards the left of Australian politics and as a boy had stood at the family piano to sing the Internationale. It was on account of his membership of the Labor Party that Sir Donald Bradman had once informed him that the two men could never be friends. Undaunted by this impediment, Jones had, during his many years in office, provided the city with its first proper sewerage system and its first tarmac roads. In gratitude, a stand at the cricket ground was named after him. Horticulture though was more of a challenge.

'They tell me he was a fine lord mayor,' says Ian Chappell. 'I'm sure he was. But he was a bloody awful groundsman.'

'The only bloke in Queensland who couldn't grow grass,' adds his brother. 'The wicket at Brisbane was just rolled mud with a lot of grass clippings mixed in.'

The alderman was not the sort of man to be put off by criticism or excessive dampness. He stabbed his Test wicket with a kitchen knife to aid ventilation and then brought in a heat lamp used to hatch chickens to dry the wicket out. 'It should be an extremely interesting pitch,' he concluded.

Having seen it, the captains of both Australia and the West Indies thought it would be a spinners' pitch and so for the only time in the series four slow bowlers played in the same Test match. But after three balls it was a fast bowler who took the contest's first wicket. Dennis Lillee got Gordon Greenidge out for nought, just as he had been against the amateurs of Papua New Guinea a month earlier, and just as he would be in the second innings. But as the Australia players gathered to slap Lillee's back, Greg Chappell realised that he had made a serious tactical mistake. In his first Test as captain he'd committed the elementary error of not putting a fielder in front of the wicket on the off side for his opening bowler.

'I had four slips and a couple of gullys and a bat-pad. I remember Ian saying to me at the beginning of the series, "I'm not going to interfere, but if you need any help I'll be there." He must have been biting his tongue when I set that field.' As the new West Indies batsman, Lawrence Rowe, took guard, the captain quietly moved a man to the correct position.

Almost all of the other mistakes on that first day came from the West Indies. They hit sixes and fours but quickly lost wickets. In a match that could have lasted for 15 two-hour sessions over five days, they had appeared to lose it by lunch at the end of the first session. Their spendthrift batting – all out for 214 – reminded one Australian reporter of the nonchalant participants in an annual office match. By the end of the first day Australia were already building their own total.

Before he left the ground that evening, Greg Chappell took a look at the pitch. The grass clippings glued in place by the lord mayor's mud had dried up, and those that hadn't blown away looked like desiccated shreds of tobacco. The top crust of the mud was starting to break off. That night Chappell woke several times to fret about batting last on such a poor wicket. If it looked like this after day one, what would the bloody thing be like by the fourth innings?

As soon as he arrived at the ground on the second morning he walked out to look at the pitch again. It didn't have a mark on it.

Christ, what's happened here? he thought. Under the laws of cricket, titivating a Test match pitch once the game had started is a serious crime.

So I knocked on the West Indies dressing room door and asked for Clive. I said, 'Have you seen the deck?' And he said, 'No – do you think I should?' 'I think it's probably worth the walk,' I said. Well, I thought Clive would blow his top because the wicket had so obviously been touched up. He walked up and down the length of the track and looked at the alterations. After a while I said, 'What do you think?' and he said, 'Well, it wouldn't have been much of a game without them,' and walked off. Had it been 12 months further into Clive's captaincy I think there would have been an international incident because there was no doubt that Clem Jones had been out there and used the hose and the roller and done a bit of midnight repair work, which was obviously illegal.

The alderman's intervention flattened out the pitch and killed it. Greg Chappell's fears about batting on it also disappeared. He scored a hundred in each innings, which helped his team to win the first Test with a day to spare. In the dressing room at the end of the game his older brother lit him a celebratory cigar, and the next day, wearing an Arsenal football shirt, which he had picked up in London that summer, he was relaxed enough to be photographed at home in Kenmore, posing with his baby son and wife.

In his first Test match Michael Holding didn't take a single wicket.

*   *   *

There were no doubts about the pitch for the second Test at Perth on the west coast. It was the hardest, fastest wicket in the cricket world. Made for quick bowlers. Since the 1930s the grass on the WACA (Western Australian Cricket Association) square had sprouted from mud scooped out of the banks of the Harvey River. Tonnes of alluvial soil full of clay, which set fast in the sun like cement, were carried 70 miles north to the ground from a site near the town of Waroona. A groundsman could turn a stump by hand into the dampened earth in the afternoon, but if he tried to do the same in the evening the wooden spike could barely make a dent.

Jeff Thomson bowled the fastest ball that cricket had recorded – 99.68 miles per hour – during this game. Roy Fredericks was the batsman, not that he was greatly inconvenienced. On the second day, after Australia had made 329, Fredericks scored one of the best hundreds seen at the WACA ground. He hooked the second ball of his innings, a bouncer from Dennis Lillee, for the finest of sixes into the river end. It would have crashed into the back of the newly built police headquarters on the corner of Hay Street if its withering swiftness hadn't been halted by the seats of the southern stand. Within three quarters of an hour Fredericks had reached 50, and his hundred came in less than two hours.

Watching at the northern end of the ground with his mother was a 17-year-old schoolboy called Charles Maskell-Knight. He was a junior member at the ground and that meant he could sit anywhere he wanted in the Members' Stand. Charles's favourite spot was somewhere in the first ten rows or so behind the bowler's arm.

'There was a lot of anticipation,' he remembers, 'because the English had been well beaten the year before. So we'd got rid of the Poms, and the Pakistanis, who were due to come the next season, didn't really count, but we knew about and were excited by the West Indies.' Charles and his mother observed Fredericks's extra-ordinarily bold innings as the batsman hooked and drove and cut at Lillee and Thomson, and then Gary Gilmour and Max Walker. 'He just seemed to go berserk. There was disbelief to start with because our bowlers were thought to be so dominant. Then there was a hush as we all took it in and, finally, applause every time Fredericks played a shot.'

Twenty runs came from one Thomson over, 22 from another bowled by Gilmour. Fredericks was a small man but strong and quick. As a teenager his fast reactions and early sight of a moving ball had won him a place in British Guiana's table-tennis team. Yet only when he was seen stripped, revealed the cricket correspondent of *The Times*, was it possible to tell from where his power came. Fredericks had forearms like ten-pound trout, wrote John Woodcock – and wild ones at that.

'I don't want to denigrate Roy's innings,' says Greg Chappell, 'but that was some of the least intelligent bowling that I have ever seen. At least two of our bowlers were just intent on trying to knock Freddo's head off, so the length was way too short. I had no success in trying to rein them in and get them to pitch the thing up.'

It certainly wasn't just bad bowling. This was one of *the* remarkable attacking innings of modern Test cricket. Fredericks had the attention of the whole ground. All of Perth seemed to be represented.

'In the Members' Stand there were the sort of people I went to school with,' remembers Charles Maskell-Knight.

There was old Perth money, those well enough off to send their kids to private school. There were academics from the university, doctors, retired school teachers. Then the Test Stand – what became the Inverarity Stand – which was ticketed, so people who were upper working class – the decent and the decorous – out for the day with their families. Then round to the Southern End, where you had the big bar. That was your brickies, labourers, concreters. The home of the all-day drinkers, where the chants of 'Lil-lee, Lil-lee, Lil-lee' came from. It was a sort of well informed rowdyism. Australian humour. Not meaning to wound.

Standing in the back bar with his mates and holding a can of Swan lager was Scotty Mitchell. He was 19, an apprentice mechanic and had driven for three hours from the family farm to get to the WACA. He could make out the members across the ground with their binoculars and white shirts. Where Scotty stood, there was much to see and hear apart from the cricket. There was heckling and shenanigans, repartee and smart-aleckry. A favourite crowd trick was to make a large lasso and lay the loop in a walkway until a woman walked over it. If she was snared, only a kiss for the holder of the rope would set her free. Every so often Scotty would make his way from the bar with another soft drink for his younger brother Glenn, who refused to move from his spot at the front of the crowd by the boundary edge.

On their way in they had watched Clive Lloyd in the nets smash a ball straight over Nelson Avenue and into the car park of the Gloucester Park Trotting Ground, where it hit the windscreen of a parked car. 'You'd better find out whose that is,' they heard Lloyd say. 'I might owe him an autograph.'

Scotty brought Glenn another drink. Fredericks was still batting. 'Come on, Lillee. Bowl him out!' someone bellowed at the local fast bowler, who was walking towards them to get to the end of his run.

'Do you wanna try?' Lillee asked, holding the ball out to the laughing crowd.

Lillee got him eventually. Roy Fredericks's innings was ended by the first ball bowled after the tea interval. He had scored 169. Charles returned home that evening keen to tell his father about what he had seen, but Mr Maskell-Knight was grumbling. He had missed the innings, missed the whole day out, because he'd been stuck volunteering at a polling station in the Swan Valley.

Australia was having a general election. About the same time that Charles's father arrived home in the Perth suburb of Greenmount, the Labor Prime Minister Gough Whitlam was conceding defeat across the other side of the country at a school hall in Canberra. Charles had been as fascinated by the election campaign as he was by the touring West Indies. In November the governor general, who acted as Australia's head of state on behalf of the Queen, had taken the extraordinary step of dismissing Whitlam from office. The dismissal was the greatest constitutional crisis Australia had known.

'The bastard's sacked us,' Whitlam told his stunned cabinet colleagues half an hour later.

His centre-left government had come to power in 1972 on a platform of social reform. Australian troops came home from Vietnam; the voting age was lowered; communist China was recognised; and free university education was introduced. However, the Labor Party didn't control the upper house of Australia's legislature, and in 1975 the Senate refused to pass a budget bill. As the impasse became more intractable, the prospect of the government's money supply drying up increased, and the governor general acted. Whitlam was dismissed, and had now been walloped by the Liberal-led coalition at the election which followed.

By the Monday rest day of the Perth Test, the extent of Labor's defeat was evident. Australia's cricketers were feeling almost as glum. The West Indies had made a huge 585 in their only innings, and with Andy Roberts bowling as fast as anyone had seen him (Deryck Murray stood further back from the stumps than Rod Marsh did for Thomson) his team were soon to win by an innings. The *Sydney Morning Herald* noted that Gough Whitlam had been 'donkey-licked'. So had Australia.

On the day after the election, with the West Indies heading for a win, a wag had stood up in the Southern End and shouted at the ragged Aussie batsmen, 'You're stuffed! Four wickets down, 200 behind, and the Libs have got back in!'

* * *

The Test series had been promoted by Australian television as a virility contest between fast bowlers: Roberts and Holding versus Thomson and Lillee. It was to be thrilling, gladiatorial, unpredictable, possibly dangerous. The Australia pair was spoken of on TV as 'the most talked-about cricketers in the world – the underlying point was controversy – controversy about bouncers or bumpers – deliberate intimidation aiming to hit the batsman'. But that was hyperbole. There was no Bumper War. Skirmishes perhaps but no bloody battle.

'I've heard we bounced the West Indies out in '75–76,' says Greg Chappell. 'We didn't. I didn't want Thomson bowling bouncers at their blokes because his pace and the pace of the pitch meant they went way over the batsman's head and sometimes over the wicket-keeper's too. That's what I was trying to get into them at Perth. The bouncer itself was redundant.'

That's not to say that the pace of the Australian bowlers – and the damage they could do – wasn't a real concern inside the West Indian dressing room. The team talked about it and worried about it. And it was true that Alvin Kallicharran had hooked a ball into his own face and broken his nose during the second Test. But so far the most damage done by Dennis Lillee since the West Indies arrived had been to an Australia teammate. Playing for Western Australia against Victoria, Lillee had dropped one short to Max Walker, fractured the swing bowler's cheek below the eye and then watched as the Victorian was removed from the pitch on a stretcher and taken to hospital.

After the second Test at Perth, where Thomson had the fastest ball in the world recorded by academics from the University of Western Australia, journalists wondered if, with only four wickets taken and the fire and the direction missing, he should be dropped for the third Test at Melbourne.

The Bumper War really wasn't happening.

Not that Thomson cared much. He had been distracted by some dreadful news. In the tea interval on the second day the Australia selector Sam Loxton had walked into the dressing room to tell him that his flatmate from Brisbane had been killed.

Like Thomson, Martin Bedkober was a cricketer from New South Wales. He had moved to Queensland because he thought he would have more opportunities to play the first-class game. He was a 23-year-old wicket-keeper and a good batsman. The third young cricketer in the flat was Ian Davis. While Thomson was at the Test, Davis and Bedkober were playing in a local Brisbane match for the Toombul District club. Davis was out and back in the pavilion when a short ball from a medium-fast bowler hit his friend in the chest, near the heart. Bedkober collapsed very soon afterwards. Players on the pitch tried to save his life, as did the ambulance crew which rushed to the field and then took the cricketer to the Royal Brisbane Hospital. Davis went too and was the first to be told of the death. He had to post a parcel of his mate's unwashed clothes back to his grieving mother in New South Wales.

In the week between the second and third Tests Jeff Thomson returned to Sydney for Martin Bedkober's funeral. He now felt differently about the thing he did best. He still wanted to bowl as fast as he could, but he didn't particularly want to knock blokes over any more.

* * *

Thomson wasn't dropped for the third Test match at the Melbourne Cricket Ground; instead a huge crowd saw him take six wickets.

Never before on a Boxing Day had so many people been in one place to watch a Test match. Queues had started at about six o'clock in the morning, and by 9.30 most of the seats had gone and the standing areas were jammed. People were even sitting on the flat roofs of the small club offices built on top of the stands. Somebody counted 85,661 spectators inside the MCG, but the club secretary reckoned the temperature of 33 degrees Celsius was too much for some and had cost the Melbourne Cricket Club the price of up to 15,000 tickets. Even so, the lines for drinks were an hour long for those who hadn't brought their own beer. Those who did were asked by the ground authorities to stick to the local limit of 24 cans per patron. One senior police officer on duty that day reckoned there was a 'car fridge' for every bloke in the ground.

No great surprise then that by the late afternoon some spectators in the southern stand were lobbing open cans full of beer (or perhaps their own piddle) at each other. Ice cubes were flung. Fights started. St John Ambulance staff treated about 200 people who had either cut themselves, were suffering from sunburn or had fainted. Three streakers were taken by police to the City Watch House to be charged, along with 11 other spectators accused of offensive behaviour or of being drunk and disorderly.

A feature writer from *The Age* newspaper printed some of the interviews he'd recorded with spectators that day.

'It's good to see this at the cricket,' said a man called Barry Howson who'd come from the suburb of Lilydale. 'It's getting more like the football.' Further along the stand other people were less happy with the exuberance. Two well-dressed ladies who had journeyed with their husbands from Traralgon, two hours' drive away along the south-eastern freeway, had to keep moving the blanket they were sitting on to avoid the rivulets of beer and urine flowing down the terraces. Neither husband was drinking. 'We come from the country and we think this is disgusting,' they said. 'It makes you ashamed to be Australian.'

If their blanket had remained dry and if they'd had the fortitude to remain, the sober folk of Traralgon would have witnessed Lillee and Thomson bowling as well as they had the previous summer against England. They took 9 of the 10 wickets to fall on the first day, and the West Indians could not get back into the game. By the fourth afternoon they had been beaten.

The West Indies were now two–one down in the six-match series. They could still win it, but that was unlikely. Clive Lloyd had a side with talent – the huge win at Perth proved that – but it was weighed down by a collective temperamental fragility which the captain was too inexperienced to correct. Winning was a treat, not an expectation. The side was also shy of one more outstanding bowler and another fine batsman. These realities impaired Lloyd's leadership. His belief that men who were good enough to play international cricket should have the emotional maturity to work out their own shortcomings was reasonable enough; it just didn't work with some of these players. Resentment over selection was also evident, particularly in the case of Gordon Greenidge. He was in poor form – a pair of noughts in the first Test, dropped for the second, brought back for the third, in which he made three and eight, then dropped again. Sure, he couldn't get a run, but the humiliation he felt was compounded by the manner of his replacement. Bernard Julien was a lower-order all-rounder who was asked to open the innings, and Greenidge believed the reasons for the switch were never adequately explained to him.

Players began criticising each other. At the Hotel Windsor in Melbourne a row between Alvin Kallicharran and Keith Boyce at a team meeting about whether or not they should play the hook shot ended up with Michael Holding chasing after Kallicharran to plead with him to return to the room. Aside from all of this, there was a dressing room sense that the umpiring was pretty ordinary.

Lloyd complained about decisions made at significant moments of the game at the MCG. He was not squealing, he said, but it was important for the officials to be familiar with the laws of cricket.

Then came the Sydney Test.

Dennis Lillee was unable to play because he was ill, but very fast, accurate bowling disrupted the West Indies once more. Serious concentration was needed to bat against Thomson's pace. In the first innings Vivian Richards was unsettled by how quiet his batting partner Lawrence Rowe had become. Rowe usually whistled when he batted, and of late his chosen tune had been 'Games People Play' by the Spinners. But in Sydney Richards at the non-striker's end heard nothing.

'What is it, Yagga?' he said at the end of an over. 'Why aren't you whistling?'

'I'm not doing that when this guy is bowling,' replied Rowe, nodding towards Thomson. 'He hides the ball in his run-up – you can't see it except from between his legs at the last minute – and whenever he rips a quick one, there isn't enough time for you to whistle anything.'

During this match Thomson hit Lloyd on the jaw, Bernard Julien had his right thumb fractured, and Michael Holding hit the ball into his own face. More damagingly, several West Indians again played thoughtless attacking shots – hooks – and lost their wickets. The offenders should be laid out and flogged on their backsides, suggested the *Jamaica Star*. To amplify the West Indian batsmen's shortcomings, Greg Chappell, hooked beautifully to make one of the best hundreds seen on the ground. The West Indies' bowling had been listless, wrote the cricket reporter of the *Sydney Morning Herald*, the fielding poor, and the batting as unreliable as ever. In his column in the same paper Ian Chappell revealed he had been surprised by some of Clive Lloyd's tactical decisions, while Bill

O'Reilly – who had played for Australia in the Bradman years – called the West Indian captain clueless.

Australia had been rescued by its captain, commented John Woodcock in *The Age*; the West Indies not led by their own. Lloyd was a super cricketer, he went on, but not an assertive captain. Then there were Michael Holding's tears on the Sunday afternoon. 'What would Frank Worrell have said?' wondered Woodcock. 'No excuses would have done for him. That is what all West Indian sides need, the moderating influence of a Worrell.'

Australia won the Sydney Test by seven wickets. The widow of Sir Frank Worrell was soon to fly in to present the trophy named after her husband, for which the two sides competed. The silver prize would be staying in Australia.

* * *

Clive Lloyd was damaged by what was said and written about his captaincy. He was aware too that the spirit of the side was un-developed and that he had not been able to cheer those who needed support. This tour was getting more difficult the longer it went on. 'On and off the pitch,' he would say years later, 'I was still working it through.' One report suggested that Deryck Murray would become the skipper once the tour was over.

Lloyd had not quite lost the dressing room but he had certainly misplaced it temporarily. Back in Melbourne for the final Test of the series – after another defeat at Adelaide had made the score four–one to Australia – a teammate from Lancashire, where they both played county cricket, paid a visit. David Hughes popped into the pavilion to say hello, but Lloyd was batting in the middle. Instead, he registered the dismal sight of a team getting hammered but the men in the dressing room seeming disinterested. They played table tennis out the back and weren't even watching the game. This final Test match would end in defeat too, the series lost by five matches to one. The West Indies knew they had been subdued and just wanted to get home.

In fact, the West Indies had been thrashed. Humiliated. Undone by a better side playing better cricket. They had been cowed by the fast bowling of Dennis Lillee and Jeff Thomson, who between them took 56 West Indian wickets, while Roberts and Holding hadn't bowled well enough or stayed fit enough to return the threat. The AUS $500 bet that Thomson had made with a businessman from the Caribbean that he would get more men out than Roberts was collected.

Lloyd's intention – to captain a side that had pride, judgement and discipline, that would not capitulate – had been stillborn. This defeat – and the style of it – meant that the world was still satisfied, even justified, to regard the West Indies as 'calypso cricketers'. It was a phrase detested by West Indians. 'It meant we were just all fun, frolic but no real substance, entertaining the crowd and then losing,' says Michael Holding. Correspondents, commentators, desk subs and Australian players used the term throughout the tour.

What was harmless journalese to Australians was a pejorative put-down to a West Indian. 'Our visitors of course are renowned for the relaxed attitude they appear to have towards their batting responsibilities – this is what makes them so popular with the paying public,' wrote Bill O'Reilly.

'It was patronising,' says Lloyd. 'The suggestion was that we had always been slap-happy, unthinking – players who only hoped for the best. There was a lazy way of looking at the West Indies and West Indian cricket in those days. And "calypso cricket" was a big part of it.'

This team knew that their predecessors had frequently illustrated collective endeavour and application as well as personal enterprise.

The sides led by Frank Worrell and Garry Sobers beat Australia and then England and India twice each between 1962 and 1967 to become the unofficial, yet undisputed, world champions. Further back, it was possible to recall the determination of the all-rounder Learie Constantine. He trained for months to develop into a specialist slip catcher in order to complement his batting and bowling before the 1928 tour to England so he would be noticed and asked to stay on as a professional player. His determination involved hours of labour on the slip machine, gymnastic exercises and hard thought. 'No cricketer has worked at his cricket and studied it more than this so original and creative of cricketers,' commented his biographer C. L. R. James. 'So much for the persistent illusion of West Indian spontaneity.'

Fifty years on, the spontaneity myth remained, and what infuriated the players was that they had nothing with which to counter the stereotype. Their cricket on this tour had been the poorest of rebuttals.

Yet despite their defeat – as well as because of it – the West Indians had been a lasting attraction. They were marketable. Cricket in Australia was now as popular as it had been in the years after the Second World War. Almost three quarters of a million tickets were sold to watch the six West Indies Test matches in five Australian cities that summer, and millions of people watched at home. Only in the previous five years had international cricket series been broadcast live across Australia – and if you lived in the city where the game was being played, only the last session of the day was televised. Around this time the national broadcaster, the ABC, reported that one in four citizens was watching their coverage at some point on the day of a Test match.

All across this vast country Australians wanted to enjoy Test cricket.

* * *

All summer Paul Newman had been fiddling with his TV aerial – a wire coat hanger stuck in the back of the family set – to get the best picture of the cricket.

Paul lived near Wellington, a small town in rural New South Wales. He was 14 years old and a very good cricketer – probably the best of his age in the area – an all-rounder who opened the batting. Even though he was a teenager, he played senior cricket. In the country, where there was nothing much to do, the game helped him to keep busy and stay out of trouble. If the TV reception was no good, there was always the portable radio. Paul kept in touch with the Test score by listening to the commentary while he played outside. He had his favourites. Not Jeff Thomson, Greg Chappell or Gary Gilmour, but Lawrence Rowe, Vivian Richards and Clive Lloyd.

Paul supported the West Indies.

'In a typical town like Wellington they had what they called a mission,' he says. 'That was where the Aboriginal people were segregated from the white population, and you actually lived outside of the town. The white people liked to call it a mission because it sounded religious, but actually it was a reserve.' Paul was from the Wiradjuri people on his father's side; his mother was descended from the Darug and the Murrawarri. 'So really Aboriginal people and non-Aboriginal people didn't mix, you know? When I was growing up, there were only certain shops that we could go in to buy our groceries – places where blacks were allowed. But because I could play cricket really well, I was accepted. I had a talent. To be an Aboriginal person in my neighbourhood and be in a cricket team with white kids was a big thing back in those days.'

This was the late 1960s and early 1970s, not the 1930s.

'[The Aboriginal people] are, without doubt,' wrote the essayist

Craig McGregor in his *Profile of Australia* in 1966, 'the most depressed and under-privileged minority in Australian society. Poverty-stricken, barely educated, degraded by white prejudice, disoriented and with little hope for the future, they expose the seamy side of Australian egalitarianism.'

Another writer, the Aboriginal activist and playwright Kevin Gilbert wanted to show Australia what 'really existed in these outback towns'. *Because a White Man'll Never Do it* recorded the testimony of people around from the country.

> For example, in those days, in Moree, black kids weren't free to go in the swimming baths. Blacks couldn't go where they chose in the picture show. At Walgett they weren't allowed to drink out of the glasses in a local milk bar. Young girls weren't allowed to try on dresses in a frock shop there. And, of course, there was the pub discrimination. These were the things that we were trying to pick up, the grassroots discrimination that we were trying to bring out into the open.

'Don't forget,' says Paul Newman, 'that when I was born, I was invisible. I didn't exist as an Australian. Let me explain that to you. The constitution which set up federal Australia in 1901 – the modern Australia if you like – had a preamble about what the nation would achieve, and it excluded Aboriginal people. The referendum that changed all that wasn't until 1967.' That 1901 declaration was not just a legislative document, it was Australia's symbolic birth certificate. It created the identity of the nation. It read, 'In reckoning the numbers of people of the Commonwealth or of a State or other part of the Commonwealth, aboriginal natives shall not be counted.'

From the very beginning of Australia's national life, there was a profound and lasting fear that racial contamination, principally from Asia, would pollute and corrupt the new democracy. Australia's first prime minister, Edmund Barton, told colleagues in the House of Representatives in 1901 that he didn't believe 'the doctrine of the equality of man was really ever intended to include racial equality . . . These races are, in comparison with white races – I think no one wants convincing of this fact – unequal and inferior.'

For indigenous Australians, the consequences of such attitudes were calamitous. Until well after the Second World War there were large areas of the country where Aboriginal people weren't allowed to vote, buy alcohol, travel unmolested or marry a white Australian. Half a century of legislation had ensured that most of the people whose ancestors had been on the land for at least 50,000 years were forced by law to live on reserves under strict white control.

One of those people was Eddie Gilbert, a first-class cricketer from Queensland. He was an extremely quick bowler, whose pace knocked the bat from Donald Bradman's hands against New South Wales in 1931. In the same over he had Bradman caught behind for nought. Bradman would later say that this spell of bowling was the fastest he had faced in his career – including batting against England's Harold Larwood. The romantic version of Bradman's dismissal has the ball smashing through the stumps, breaking the white picket fence at the Gabba boundary and killing a dog named Churchill.

Gilbert's life was not romantic though. An Aboriginal man playing first-class cricket was almost unheard of. He needed written permission from an official called the Aboriginal Protector to leave his reservation to play in other states. Some members of the Queensland side tolerated him; others refused to speak to him or travel with him. When he died in 1978 he owned nothing and had been tormented for years by alcoholism and mental illness.

Paul Newman was born in 1961. At the time his family lived in a small shack with a tin roof, dirt floors and no mains water or lavatory. It was the year that the West Indian cricket side led by Frank Worrell departed Australia after a thrilling Test series played in a great spirit. Worrell had written in the days before he left, 'We've had open-hearted hospitality, the red-carpet treatment, without prejudice or patronage . . . the colour question has never arisen.' On the day Worrell's team left Melbourne, ten open-topped cars drove the players to a reception at the town hall organised by the city's lord mayor. Hundreds of thousands of Australians cheered them along the way.

The affection Australia showed for these dark-skinned visiting sportsmen was genuine; the relationship the country had with its own black people was much more complicated. Two months after Worrell's side left, the Australian parliament recommended that Aboriginal people should be expected to 'live as members of a single Australian community . . . accepting the same responsibilities, observing the same customs and influenced by the same beliefs, hopes and loyalties as other Australians'.

By the time Paul Newman was following the West Indies during the 1975–76 tour, official attitudes were changing, albeit slowly. Portions of the most discriminatory legislation, for instance that regarding land rights, were being repealed in some parts of the country. There had been a few isolated examples of Aboriginal sporting success: the boxer Lionel Rose, the tennis player Yvonne Goolagong and Harry Williams, who played football for Australia at the 1974 World Cup finals. But the traditional notion of what it meant to be Australian more than lingered.

'It didn't work for me,' says Paul.

When I was watching the cricket, I couldn't barrack for Australia. Aged 14, it was an instinctive reaction. Nowadays I can reflect that what I was working out was the sensation that I hadn't ever been valued within mainstream society. I didn't feel Australian. If I had, would my mum have needed to warn me about going outdoors after dark? When I was growing up we were told by our parents to stay at home. If you were a black person on the street at night, it was not unknown for the police to pick you up and bash you.

Paul's allegiances were formed by what he calls the 'overt prejudice and covert racism' he saw when he was growing up. 'For me, that was typical of country New South Wales in the early 1970s. That was life, you know?' But when he watched the West Indies on his black and white TV in Wellington he saw something fresh. For the first time in his life he was looking at a group of black people who excelled.

They were so talented. They were able to perform on the field, and from where I was standing, that was one way of getting around the racism that I was experiencing. These were men who could go out there and do something well. Score the runs, get the wickets. We could connect to their humour, the way they carried on when they got a wicket – that was black people's humour. The way they spoke and the things they thought when they were interviewed on the TV or radio – we could connect with that.

It was a connection appreciated by some of the West Indian players. Vivian Richards remembers visiting Aboriginal reservations to give away match tickets for West Indies games.

We knew that these indigenous people were on a suffering path. I saw a whole lot of racism in Australia concerning Aboriginal people, and I would see it again when I signed to play with Queensland in 1976, so I can identify with that. There were people here who needed representing. I felt it, I can't lie about that. So the times that we were able to touch up Australia in Australia, it wasn't just a sporting victory – it brought pride to the people who had been oppressed and a feeling that 'Hey, these other people can be beaten.' That was one of the more serious messages that the West Indies team could have sent to these indigenous people.

Richards's phrase 'a suffering path' is an apt one. Between 1910 and 1970 thousands of Aboriginal children were forcibly removed from their families by law. It was part of Australia's policy of 'assimilation'. For the politicians it was an effort to absorb indigenous people into white society. For Paul it was nothing less than a campaign of deliberate cultural extinction. In his state of New South Wales indigenous children who were ruled to be 'neglected, destitute or uncontrollable' could be taken.

I am one of those Stolen Generation kids. I had seven brothers and sisters and I have memories of the police and the welfare coming to the mission. They took us away to Coonamble police station. I can still visualise being put in that police cell at five years of age. I was fostered, then ended up in a boys' home until my dad was able to get us back. This country has never used the word apartheid, but my view was that it was apartheid in action. I know everything I've told you may seem pretty complicated, but it's really the only way I can answer the question 'Why did I support the West Indies?'

Everything that I've described helped to form my life experiences. As I said, people like me were invisible. We always had been. That's why I had an affiliation with these black people from other countries. We saw those West Indies cricketers as brothers. They were my cricketing mob.

* * *

'Yeah, I think it's fair to say that Australia had a pretty unattractive track record when it came to racial tolerance in the seventies, reflects Ian Chappell.

It doesn't make me very proud. I had plenty of discussions with people at the tennis club along the lines of 'How would you feel if your daughter came home with a black man?' My response was always this: 'First, I trust my daughter's judgement, so if she likes someone, there's a good chance I will too. Secondly, I've played against a lot of boys from the Caribbean who are really good guys and I'd be happy for her to go out with any of them. So don't give me that shit.'

The sort of conversations Chappell had at his tennis club were being held across Australia in the 1970s. The 'dangers inherent in attempting to achieve a multi-racial society too quickly are apparent from a recent survey,' the *Sydney Morning Herald* reported in August 1971. A thousand people in Sydney and Melbourne were asked for their views on different types of potential immigrant. Thirty-four per cent said that 'Negroes' should be kept out of Australia entirely; 32 per cent believed that 'only a few' should be let in; 29 per cent wanted no restriction, while 3 per cent thought they should be actively encouraged to come to Australia. When the same question was asked in 1964 – three years after Frank Worrell and his side had been joyfully waved off – 47 per cent of those who answered wanted no 'Negroes' to be allowed into Australia. In 1948 that figure had been 77 per cent. The disarmingly honest headline above the 1971 survey was WE ARE LESS RACIST.

The following year Ian Chappell was preparing to lead Australia in two Test series, at home against Pakistan and away in the West Indies.

It must have crossed my mind that one of the blokes might come out with something racial and I didn't want that on my conscience. So in Adelaide in the dressing room before the first Pakistan Test, I said to them all, 'If I hear any comment prefixed with the word "black" you'll have a problem with me. If you call someone a "lucky bastard", that's up to you, but I've never heard any of you call someone a "lucky white bastard" and I don't expect to hear the word "black" used. If I do hear it, there'll be a problem.'

When I was growing up, this sort of language just wasn't used around our house. If you do use those words a bit in your life, they will come out at some point on the field. You can't turn it on and off like a tap. It offends me when I hear it. Life is not about your skin. You're either a good bloke or a prick, and colour's got bugger all to do with it.

*   *   *

The newspaper for which Chappell wrote throughout the 1975–76 series, the *Sydney Morning Herald*, welcomed the West Indies players to Australia like this. They were 'dusky revellers in white. Not the Black and White minstrels, but entertainers to delight the hearts of a nation . . . Calypso cavaliers, drawn from a dozen tiny islands nestling in the Caribbean, they play their cricket in the life-style of their sun-drenched islands, with the rhythm of a steel band, with a grin and for the sheer joy of scampering around an oval.' And as the series went on, a particular theme regarding West Indian athleticism developed. Bernard Julien ran like a gazelle. When he wasn't bowling, Andy Roberts was a sleepy cat. Michael Holding seemed in good enough condition to enter for the Melbourne Cup – a horse race.

None of this was surprising – such metaphors were well-established journalistic devices which had accompanied the West Indians for as long as they had played international cricket. Neville Cardus of the *Guardian* once described the batting of Learie Constantine against England as 'the attack and savagings of a panther on the kill, sinuous, stealthy, strong and unburdened. The batsmanship of the jungle, beautiful, ravaging, marvellously springy, swift as the blow of a paw.' Cardus also made this observation of the 1928 West Indies team fielding at Lord's: 'There are six of them black as ebony, and three with faces of chocolate brown. When they smile they are loveable; we see white teeth and we think of melons and the dear humorous friends of our nursery days in a hundred tales of the old plantations.'

By 1975 the *Herald* had Andy Roberts doing 'galley slave work' when he bowled nine overs in a row, while the spectator dressed in a gorilla suit and dancing on the boundary edge during the Sydney Test was making a 'fancy-dress contribution to calypso cricket'.

The West Indian players could read these lines with little more than a shrug of the shoulders; they were less tolerant of the explicit racial abuse they received off the pitch throughout the tour, including notes slipped under their hotel-room doors and postcards written by bigots disguised as correspondence from children. They also had to cope with racist comments from spectators.

'Half of Australians are as wonderful as you could get, down to earth, and then there is that other side,' says Vivian Richards. 'People get angry and call you a black bastard. And I get rather annoyed that someone is going to call me a black bastard. Because I am not. So I take offence to that and I would be confrontational.'

'There was always someone in the crowd who would happen to think it was funny,' remembers Scotty Mitchell.

Particularly in those days and particularly after a few Swan lagers. Back then about the only black-skinned people were the local Indigenous people, and there would have been very, very few who went to the cricket. So for most people in the crowd I reckon their contact with black people was minimal. To see in the flesh such well-built athletic men who were black would have been something most people from Perth wouldn't have experienced before.

'The whole thing where the colour of your skin came into it was something that you had to overcome. I wouldn't want to go into the variety of things that were said because I don't think I need to repeat them,' says Gordon Greenidge. 'It wasn't healthy because it wasn't something that you expected, it wasn't something you wanted, it wasn't something that you were briefed about, so when it came it hurt, and yes, it left a bit of a scar for a while. These people were ignorant – they didn't know about black people, they hadn't had a friendship or a relationship with a black person. They don't know about the Caribbean.'

Greenidge makes a distinction between the specifically racist abuse he heard shouted by spectators and the aggression transmitted by Australian cricketers. 'I had never experienced anything like this,' he recalls. 'This was something very different again, and it was like a war. We have Australians against West Indians, you have the black against white, and you're thinking, *Well, you know, there can't be a lot of love going on here*. They didn't let up. They let you know: "We're in charge and you're not coming on our patch to do well."'

'I'm sure Dennis Lillee may well have told a batsman he would knock his fuckin' block off. That's standard fare for fast bowlers, and I heard it plenty of times myself,' recalls Ian Chappell.

'Ian Chappell – aggressive,' says Vivian Richards.

Dennis Lillee – in your face. Sure, they would say the odd thing, but it wasn't racial. No. Just the normal Aussie bravado. Heavy stuff at times which would sometimes blow your ears out. Now, in the crowd there was a different tempo when it came to this race stuff. There were a few rotten apples in the sack, and even though you could smell them, you mustn't let it ruin the rest of the crop. These guys were struggling to get to grips with the fact that there was plenty of space on the earth for everyone.

'I can tell you – hand on heart, hand on Bible, wherever you want it – there was no racial abuse from our team during that series,' insists Greg Chappell.

My brother would never have accepted it and neither would I. We were tough and aggressive, we swore at different times on the cricket field but we never abused anyone. And I know, having spoken to some of the opposition from those times, that they were very disconcerted by it. Particularly if they had perhaps come from a culture of deference, to go up against this aggressive, snarling bunch of blokes. But at no stage did any of our players racially vilify anyone. What is worth saying is that there was every chance that there was racism coming from over the fence, from someone in the crowd.

'It didn't happen on the field,' says Clive Lloyd. 'I was a big guy in those days and I carried a big bat. Do you think I would just stand there and let it go on if I was hearing that sort of thing from first slip?'

Michael Holding says he is 'extremely grateful' that he never heard racial abuse on a Test match pitch. 'Yes, you would hear it from people in the stands. They have paid their money so let them say what they want – I don't care. On a cricket field I never came across any racial abuse because if I had my career wouldn't have lasted as long as it did. I wouldn't just have listened and walked away.'

Throughout the series the two sides drank in each others' dressing rooms after the day's play had ended. There were rounds of golf together on the rest days of some of the Test matches. In the pavilion at Sydney Michael Holding introduced his father to Ian Chappell. After the West Indies victory at Perth Chappell wrote, 'If we had to lose a Test, it couldn't be to a more pleasant and entertaining bunch.' On a later tour Chappell would take Clive Lloyd's children on a day out to the Luna Park fairground in Sydney and carry Lloyd's daughter on his shoulders for the afternoon. Lloyd says he would not have allowed this to happen if he had had any doubts about Chappell's character.

* * *

It had been a terrible tour for the West Indies. The Jamaican cricket journalist Tony Becca was there throughout.

> I spoke to George Headley and Garry Sobers before I left, and Garry predicted that the West Indies would get clobbered. Lose and lose badly. Now the team that went there was the best team, but it was too young, too inexperienced. George said that if the wickets were as fast and as bouncy as they had been when he was there in 1930–31, then the Australians would rip us to pieces. The West Indian batsmen were just no match for them – Lillee and Thomson. It hurt me to see them. I had never seen a bowler like Thomson. He was fast like the wind.

'It was dreadful,' says the middle-order batsman Alvin Kallicharran. 'A lot of youngsters in Australia for the first time and we got a walloping. We didn't have the weapons and they really came at us. It wasn't easy. But even after the taste of the beating we got, we still thought we could be a good team.'

'Oh, we were completely demoralised by the end,' admits Vivian Richards. 'Australia was like a lion's den, and we didn't know how to get out. We were a young side, but what it showed to us was that we needed to find some people who were as sharp and as aggressive as they were. Individuals who gave as much as we had been getting.'

The only hope that Clive Lloyd retained from his experience in

Australia was the memory of the crushing win in Perth. West Indian batting and bowling at its very best – powerful and authoritative. But it was only a speck of solace. Lloyd's team had been routed, and he had been accused publicly of inadequacy. There was no way he was going to throw it away though. No way. Lloyd was dogged. He had a resilient streak that had almost certainly been passed down to him by his Barbadian mother.

'We were in a bar at the end of the tour having a drink,' says Vivian Richards, 'and Clive said to me, "Never again." "What do you mean?" I asked him. "The next time we come back here," he replied, "we'll be winners."'

2

The England captain had something wrong with his mouth

Martin Adrien was at school in the summer of 1976. He had been in England for five and a half years. He first saw London through the window of an aircraft three days before Christmas in 1970. He was 11 and had left the Caribbean island of Dominica in a short-sleeved shirt. Somewhere down there, at a place called Gatwick Airport, his dad was waiting for him. Martin had come to England to get an education. His dad, who in Dominica had been a farmer growing bananas, yams and sweet potatoes, had been living in east London since 1959. Now he had sent for Martin and his sister.

'He was looking for better-paid work and so he retrained as a welder,' says Martin. 'There was an open invitation to come over, a shortage of manpower. He was wanted and now we were joining him. I'd read about this great country, and yes, I was very excited.'

Martin bowled fast and he could bat. He had played his last game of cricket in Dominica the day before he got on the plane.

Any village of any size would have a cricket ground. My village was Dublanc. Only about 400 people lived there but we had a pitch that was used every Saturday and Sunday. We had a bag of shared kit. You were very fortunate if somebody you knew from England sent over a bat, gloves or some pads. We would usually make bats from

39

coconut-tree branches and would burn plastic and melt it into the shape of a ball. So being hit by a cricket ball meant nothing. A plastic one was far more painful.

In east London Martin went to a school in Canning Town, which took a bit of getting used to. In his father's house there was discipline. Strict rules. No TV, no playing until homework was done, but at school he was surprised at how the pupils spoke back to the teachers. When spring came, he played cricket for the school and bowled well but was taken off if he picked up too many wickets. That wouldn't happen in Dominica. In the playgound he was told by other kids that his colour was a problem. He hadn't been prepared for that.

'At home the white people were just other Dominicans. I'd just assumed everybody was the same. Now there were other black kids in my school but a pretty strong element of racism too. It took me two years to find what I would call a "white friend" because of my first experience of white boys and girls.'

*   *   *

Vivian Richards had also been sent to England to further his education. The school he went to in 1972 was the Alf Gover cricket school in Wandsworth in south London. Richards was 20 then, and Andy Roberts, who was a year older, went with him. It was the first time that two young sportsmen from the island of Antigua had been given such a chance. Their fares and fees had been paid for by the local voluntary coaching committee, the money raised by holding jumble sales, dances and barbecues.

Richards and Roberts hated England in November. They lived in a freezing guest house in Putney, and Richards soon lost all his money. It had been folded carefully into the back pocket of his trousers. Had it been stolen?

'Well, that was my excuse,' says Richards.

I had no wallet, and my fingers were so cold that perhaps I pulled the roll of cash from my pocket and had no feeling of it going missing. It was a rude awakening. What is this place? How can we play cricket in these temperatures? It seemed to be dark all day, midday looked more like midnight. Ah man, that guest house was crazy stuff. Every night before we went to bed we had to make sure that we had enough ten-pence pieces to stick into the machine to give us the necessary juice – the electric and the heat. We would go to the pub. Andy didn't drink, but if I had a few pints, and then we'd get home and realise 'Oh wow – no ten-pence pieces!' so sometimes we had to man it out, you know?

During the six weeks they stayed the highlights were a visit to Highbury to watch Arsenal beat Leeds United two–one in the football first division and moving to Hackney, where Roberts's sister rented a flat. It was warmer there and they ate food that they were used to. During the day Richards was told by Alf Gover to close his batting stance to make his defence stronger and Roberts was made to run between a pair of wooden stools lined up at the bowling crease to stop him from falling away as he released the ball.

'Before I went to Alf Gover I was a brash cricketer,' reflects Richards now. 'It was all about going after any- and everything, but with Alf it was about judging the conditions you were playing in, making the necessary adjustments. Aggressive stroke play, but technique too. Tight when playing forward, nice bat and pad.'

The people of Antigua had saved up to send these young cricketers to England because they thought they had great promise. No one from the island had played Test cricket for the West Indies. Many hoped that Roberts or Richards would be the first. Such was the expectation that three years previously Richards had caused a crowd invasion during his first game for Antigua. It was against

St Kitts in the Leeward Islands tournament. Batting at the Antigua Recreation Ground in St John's, he was given out first ball, caught off his glove. Richards's recollection is that the umpire from Montserrat almost joined in with the bowler's appeal. The *Antigua Star* reported that he 'immediately demonstrated where the ball struck him (on his thigh), showed some disgust at the decision and left the field.'

The batsman's indignation had an immediate effect on parts of the crowd of several thousand, who had been there since the morning but had not seen any play until after lunch because of a damp pitch. 'Simultaneously, spectators from the ringside swarmed onto the field, brushed aside policemen and began to shout in protest. St Kitts players, apparently alarmed at seeing the hundreds of men converging onto the field, ran to the haven of the Players' Pavilion.'

'Indeed, I saw it all happen,' says Tapley Lewis. He is pointing to the stadium behind him as he sits waiting for a fare in his taxi in St John's. 'I guess Vivi was still a kid, something like that. I was 19 years old, a mechanic in those days, and we wanted to see some cricket. Vivi, you see, we knew was a good player. We knew he was capable of good play and we wanted to *see* good play. He was like a little king to us, but that day he was gone for nothing. That's why there was a rush on the ground.'

According to the *Star* newspaper, the officials weren't as sprightly as the fielders. 'Both umpires were slower in leaving the field, and despite police protection the crowd closed in around George Edwards and cuffed him several times while threatening him.' There was a 50-minute delay and placards with NO VIVI, NO MATCH were held high outside the pavilion. 'In other parts of the field several crowds gathered and heatedly discussed the whole matter.' Telephone calls were placed to St Kitts by Antiguan officials, who ruled between them that, if the St Kitts captain had no objection, Richards should be allowed to bat again.

The cuffed umpire, George Edwards, was replaced by the former Test bowler Bunny Butler. In the dressing room Richards's main fear after naively agreeing to go back out and bat to calm the crowd down, was that his father – a senior warder in the prison next to the ground – would realise that his own son was the cause of the commotion. Malcolm Richards had been a talented cricketer himself but was determined that his son would not take up the sport for a living. He had beaten Vivian and his brother when they were younger for pretending to be ill so that they could take part in a game rather than attend church on Sunday. 'By the mercy of God,' Malcolm would later recall, 'I forgot my hymn book and I returned. When I came home, I met them properly dressed, playing cricket. I was a disciplinarian who brought the discipline of the jail home.'

The riot set off by Richards wasn't the last of the trouble. The following week the final of the tournament between Antigua and Nevis was abandoned after a Nevis batsman refused to walk. The team was chased back to their hotel. Their manager gave a live description on Radio ZIZ of what happened next. 'Bus loads and car loads of people besieged the hotel threatening to shoot some members of the team. Some of them broke bottles,' he said. The locals were apparently hunting for the competition trophy, which Nevis were claiming to have retained. The team had to be driven under police escort to the airport and immediately caught a specially chartered aircraft home, where according to the *Workers' Voice* newspaper up to 4,000 delighted people were there to greet them when they touched down.

The two disturbances are fine illustrations of how seriously cricket was viewed in the Caribbean. It could quickly provoke discontent.

Bitterness could erupt between the territories. Cricket in the West Indies had *never* been a game without consequence played by smiling, carefree islanders.

On top of whatever punishment Vivian Richards received from his father, he was banned from playing for Antigua for two years for causing the upheaval at the game. And those Antiguans who thought Richards had let them down by getting banned and therefore weakening their side shouted abuse as they passed his house. He was ostracised by some, but still supported by many. One ally was a local businessman who believed Richards deserved rehabilitation. He didn't mention the riot when he wrote on Richards's behalf to Church and Oswaldtwistle Cricket Club – who played in the English Lancashire League – in March 1973.

'I would like to draw to your attention', he began, 'a young cricketer by the name of Vivian Richards who would like to play for your cricket club in the league as a professional . . . Vivian Richards is the type of batsman that crowds will walk miles to see', read the typed airmail letter. 'He is sound and polished and full of strokes and he hits the ball very hard. He is a good off-spinner and a very good fields man. He is rated in the same class with Clive Lloyd in the covers (world class).' The sponsor was even willing to pay the young man's airfare, adding that he was a very quiet lad who loved his cricket very much. 'Richards is all set to come now', the letter concluded.

Church and Oswaldtwistle didn't reply. That season they signed Ken Arthur, a Barbadian who would go on to play one 2nd XI championship game for Glamorgan. Vivian Richards had missed out on the Lancashire League, but six months after his winter in Wandsworth his skills were recognised elsewhere in England. Richards agreed to play for a small club called Lansdown in Somerset. For the 1973 season he was paid one pound a day as assistant groundsman, to push the roller and score as many runs as he could while he qualified to play for Somerset.

'He held his bat like a Stradivarius fiddle,' said Len Creed. 'He was superb. His right hand could have been tied behind his back.' Creed was a West Country farmer and betting-shop owner who had connections with Lansdown and Somerset. He had flown to Antigua on holiday with a touring team called the Mendip Acorns, had heard of Richards and, keen for a young overseas player to come to Somerset, persuaded him to fly to England.

When Richards scored 81 not out in his first game for Somerset at the start of the 1974 season Len Creed wept as his discovery was clapped off the field. The county captain, Brian Close, led the applause. It was a fine start. A week later Richards had to face Mike Procter, a fearsome South African all-rounder who would be bowling fast for Somerset's great rivals Gloucestershire. Would Richards cope? In Procter's first over Richards hit him for two fours and a clanging six, sending the ball straight into the old organ works on the east side of Somerset's ground in Taunton.

'You could hear it rattling round the machinery in there, never to be seen again,' said the Somerset coach Tom Cartwright. 'It was a magical few minutes . . . one of the most electrifying moments in cricket that I've ever witnessed.'

By the beginning of the English summer of 1976 Vivian Richards had scored centuries for Somerset and for the West Indies. He was sending newspaper clippings of his success home to his father. Just as the 1973 airmail letter to Church and Oswaldtwistle had predicted, Richards was all set.

* * *

Being from Guyana, Clive Lloyd was used to rain. Storms could last for several days, and in Georgetown, a coastal city built below the level of the high tide, flooding was not unusual. When that happened parts of the outfield at Georgetown Cricket Club, the Bourda, would be underwater. Such a flood occurred during a storm at the beginning of April 1976 when the West Indies were in the middle of a Test series against India. It was a downpour that helped to shape how the West Indies would play their cricket for the next 20 years.

They were to play 12 Test matches in 1976. Five of them would come during the summer series in England. Three had already been lost to Australia. The four Test matches against India at home mattered greatly for Clive Lloyd's future and that of the side.

The West Indies won the first Test in Barbados and were fortunate to draw the second in Trinidad. Two fast bowlers, two spinners and a seam bowler were chosen for both matches. Then it rained in Guyana, and the third Test couldn't be played at the Bourda, so it was decided to use the Queen's Park Oval in Port of Spain again. There was a popular view (which Lloyd would later say was 'mythical thinking') that the Trinidad pitch was good for spinners. The West Indies included three: Imtiaz Ali, Albert Padmore and Raphick Jumadeen. Between them they bowled leg breaks, off spin and slow left arm.

When the West Indies declared their second innings on the fourth day they were well in front. India would have to bat last and needed 403 runs to win. Only one team in the history of Test cricket – Australia against England in 1948 – had scored that many in a fourth innings to win a game. That evening India still needed nearly 300 runs and the match seemed safe. It was a suitable time for Lloyd to be told by the West Indies Cricket Board of Control that he would continue as captain for the tour of England.

On the final morning, Trinidadians who supported India had been to temples and offered prayers for a win. (By the 1970s, nearly 40 per cent of people on the island were of Indian descent. They had been settling in Trinidad since the late 1830s, when workers were brought in to replace freed black slaves on the sugar plantations.) They brought sweets blessed by the priests to the ground. They sang a calypso about their batsman Sunil Gavaskar and in return he scored a hopeful hundred. By the afternoon, with India still batting comfortably, the target had shrunk further and portions of the crowd began to intone Hindu devotional songs. It did the trick. The West Indian spin bowling was now feeble. With seven overs of the day's play to spare, India won.

The West Indies had somehow lost a match in which their spinners had bowled 107 overs in the fourth innings. Just three wickets fell on the last day, and two of those were run-outs. In almost a hundred years of international cricket only five other Test captains had declared their second innings and seen the total passed. This was a West Indian humiliation. From New Delhi, the Indian Prime Minister Indira Gandhi sent a telegram to her side congratulating them on their 'exciting and well-earned victory'. In the West Indies dressing room the captain asked his bowlers to estimate how many runs they thought they could have defended.

Wayne Daniel was listening. He was a 20-year-old fast bowler from St Philip parish in Barbados. He had been selected in the squad, but not the final XI. 'It was a very sombre, solemn dressing room. Lloydy wasn't very happy at all. He was fuming. He felt that the bowlers had let him down. And rightly so. It wasn't his style to pick on people but he was cross.'

'I wasn't put off spinners for life by the experience,' says Clive Lloyd. 'It's just that the ones we had weren't winning games for us. It was a low moment.' What the embarrassment clarified in his mind – combined with the team's experience in Australia – was that he needed bowlers who could be relied upon, match after match, to take 20 opposition wickets. 'I didn't simply crave a pace attack. What I wanted was a formidable attack.' But Lloyd and those who advised him now knew that attack would have to be based on pace. Lance Gibbs no longer played, and if the best West Indian slow bowlers couldn't do it on a Trinidad turner, they wouldn't do it anywhere.

Without the rain in Georgetown, the West Indians' spin humiliation at the Queen's Park Oval would not have happened and the need for a new bowling strategy would have seemed less urgent. Weather had influenced cricket history. In July 1788 a violent hailstorm, with huge stones that were said to have killed hares and partridges, had accelerated the French Revolution by ruining crops, increasing food shortages and further upsetting the urban poor. The Georgetown storm of 1976 brought forward a revolution in West Indian cricket.

'We used to select our teams in the standard way,' explains Deryck Murray.

Two opening batsmen, three middle order, an all-rounder, a wicketkeeper, two fast bowlers, two spin bowlers. That's a balanced team, but we needed to think now in terms of what our strengths were. If, like the Australians, we had four or six fast bowlers, then so be it. We pick four and we put the opposition batsmen under the same sort of pressure that we had known. After the two quicks, who are our next two best bowlers? Ali or Jumadeen may be good spin bowlers but they were not as likely to win a Test match for us as fast bowlers. This was a major change in the thinking of West Indies cricketers. We felt that we could withstand any given situation and we could adapt to it.

After Queen's Park, India and the West Indies had won a Test each and there was one left to play. Only one spin bowler was chosen for the final Test at Sabina Park in Jamaica, and Wayne Daniel was added to the team. If the West Indies were going to win the match and the series, they would do it with speed on a hard shiny pitch.

'Man, it was quick,' says Michael Holding. 'The sun got into it, and that old Sabina gloss showed up.'

India batted first and did well, if slowly, on the first day. The problems came before lunch on the second. The pitch had recently been relaid, and a ridge appeared at the northern end, possibly created by an underground drainage channel. Holding began bowling from around the wicket, which made it much harder for the Indian batsmen – who had scored nearly 200 and lost only one wicket – to avoid the trajectory of the short ball. It was also an act of aggression. The *Guardian* reported that 'the innings was wrecked by a fiery spell from Holding on a pitch which suddenly came to life. Gaekwad caught a vicious bouncer on the left ear and was taken to hospital. Gundappa Vishwanath was caught off his gloves from another bouncer which dislocated and broke the middle finger of his right hand and Brijesh Patel joined the casualty list when Holder found the ridge and sent him to hospital for stitches to a gashed face.'

'It was rearing, rising and flying. I don't think I have ever seen a wicket-keeper stand as far back as Deryck Murray did in that game,' says Wayne Daniel. 'There were times when he would leap into the air, right hand, left hand, and the ball would go over him and bounce into the sight screen. He was a long way back. And yes, even Vanburn Holder bowled a couple of fast deliveries. Show me a bowler who wouldn't exploit the pitch he had been given to bowl on.'

The India captain, Bishan Bedi, declared 'in disgust' at 306 for 6 with two men retired hurt. Later he said it was for 'self-preservation.

Suppose we had got hit on the head.' He was referring to himself and his fellow non-batting spinner, Bhagwath Chandrasekhar. 'Who would have done the bowling?' The manager of the India side told reporters that what had happened was not in the spirit of the sport. 'It was almost like war,' said Polly Umrigar, 'and the whole charm of the game is being lost.'

Nearly 40 years later, Michael Holding now admits that he was not comfortable with the way he was asked to bowl. There may or may not have been a ridge at one end, he says, but 'in truth we bowled an awful lot of short balls'. The tactics were born out of 'sheer desperation' to succeed caused by the pressure of defeat in Australia and the need to go to England as winners, not losers. A more experienced team, reckons Holding, with a more experienced captain would have had the self-confidence to win the game another way.

Bedi's extraordinary declaration changed the direction of the Test. When the West Indies batted, they scored 85 more runs than India, who had several men absent hurt. All 17 members of the India squad fielded at some point, and there was a further hospital visit for one who needed an emergency operation for appendicitis. Because of all the injuries, when it came to the Indians' turn to bat again Bedi closed the second innings after five wickets had fallen and the lead over the West Indies was just 12 runs. He had given the game away. The Indians insisted they had no more fit batsmen. The end came quickly. The Indian seamer Madan Lal pointedly bowled five bouncers in a row in the first over of the West Indies' innings. The West Indians needed less than another over to win.

The victory meant that the West Indies had taken the series by two Tests to one, but the debate over the manner of the win stretched from Kingston to London. On Jamaican television the West Indian journalist Tony Cozier told viewers that when India were in the field 'we had cricket for the connoisseur', but that when the West Indies bowled they had seen 'cricket for the sadist'.

Would the West Indies soon be doing this sort of thing in England? From his office at the House of Lords in Westminster, Lord Brockway – who by coincidence had spent his adult life campaigning against organised violence – wrote to the British press asking if 'the Caribbeans', as he called Clive Lloyd's team, had besmirched cricket, a sport which was 'the symbol of good conduct'? To save the game, he decided, there must be a rule 'outlawing a leg ball which would hit a man above waist level. Is it cricket to aim at a man's head rather than the wicket?'

The fury of Sunil Gavaskar lasted for at least several years. 'That was not great captaincy,' he later wrote of the West Indian tactics, 'it was barbarism.' The local crowd, he said, should be called a mob. 'The way they shrieked and howled every time Holding bowled was positively horrible. They encouraged him with shouts of "Kill him, maaan!" "Hit him, maan!" "Knock his head off, Mike!" All this proved beyond a shadow of a doubt that these people still belong to the jungles and forests instead of a civilised country.'

Wayne Daniel fielded in front of that crowd. He has a different memory.

Now you see I don't remember them shouting, 'Kill him!' It wasn't like that. In those days the crowd were excited and they liked the fact that you were able to make the batsman flinch or run. It was the same in Barbados. It was a thrill to see the fear of God put into the batsman. The crowds went to Kensington or Sabina to see fast bowling. They went to see the ball fly, they went to see bouncers. They wanted to see aggressive fast bowling. And that is what fast bowling is all about. Just like the crowd in Australia were excited by and enjoyed Lillee and Thomson.

Clive Lloyd wasn't greatly upset by the Indians' reaction. His view was that those who couldn't play pace shouldn't play international cricket. 'We had quick bowlers and their batsmen simply couldn't cope.' He was annoyed by the way the game ended. 'The Indian tactics were not exactly a show of guts. If you're brave enough, you'll make runs.' Bishan Bedi's main complaint seemed to be the very particular suffering of modern international captains whose bowlers didn't go above 75 miles per hour: 'it's plain and simple. The West Indies knew we couldn't retaliate.'

The Indians left the Caribbean. Some still wore their bandages as they walked to the aeroplane which would fly them home via England. The 12 players who went on to Bombay were grateful to be shunned by most local cricket lovers. 'They apparently feared that, as on a previous occasion, they might be beaten up by fans disappointed by their play,' wrote one correspondent. 'Bishan Singh Bedi wisely decided to stay on in London.'

The West Indians were soon following Bedi there.

'We'd won the series and we were going off to England,' says Daniel. 'Especially for the guys who had come back from Australia, it was a great moment. Vanburn Holder had told me of the gloom, the heavy silences in the dressing room in Australia. Guys weren't speaking to one another, the blame game was on – "You did this, you should have done that" – all that sort of thing. There was no camaraderie. So this win brought the smiles back. And you know West Indians like to be bouncy and upbeat.'

*   *   *

The England captain Tony Greig had something wrong with his mouth. His county side were playing the West Indies at Hove at the end of May 1976, but Greig had to leave the ground to go and see his dentist. He had gum trouble and instead of joining his Sussex teammates when he returned, he climbed up to the pavilion roof for a television interview with the BBC. The first Test was in two days' time.

Greig soon became impatient. He thought the reporter was writing his side off before the series had begun. He had been in Australia to see the West Indies lose and reckoned they lacked discipline and staying power.

I'm not really quite sure they're as good as everyone thinks they are. I think people tend to forget that it wasn't long ago that they were beaten five–one by the Australians; they struggled very much to handle them and they only just managed to keep their heads above water against the Indians just a short while ago as well. Sure, they've got a couple of fast bowlers, but really I don't think we're going to run into anything any more sensational than Thomson and Lillee and so really I'm not all that worried about them.

Greig was then asked about how he had picked his team. England were short of experienced batsmen, but was the selection of the Somerset captain Brian Close – who was 45 – 'a panic measure'?

'One of the things which obviously must be done,' replied Greig 'is that we've got to handle these fast bowlers. It's been the one thing that we've fallen down on in the past and we're trying to protect against that. Brian Close is a very strong man, a very brave man, and we think he's the best man for the job right now. I've got someone who can stand up and let them hit him all day and he won't worry about it.'

The England captain then came out with the two sentences that would transform the cricketing summer.

'I think you must remember that the West Indians, these guys, if they get on top, they are magnificent cricketers, but if they're down, they grovel. And I intend, with the help of Closey and a few others, to make them grovel.'

To grovel: 'to lie or crawl abjectly on the ground with one's face downwards' or 'to act obsequiously in order to obtain forgiveness or favour'.

'My dad didn't even like cricket, and he got excited about it,' recalls Martin Adrien. 'On Sunday there was no TV at home, but we were allowed to read the newspapers, and I remember him leading a passionate discussion about the word grovel. He kept saying, "This is about more than cricket." I hadn't been overtly Afro-centric at that time, but something about it hit home with me and my friends. It became a big talking point.'

Greig's comments, which were broadcast on the *Sportsnight* programme along with speedway highlights and a British light-wel-terweight championship fight at the Royal Albert Hall, also became a talking point within the West Indies team. It was a Wednesday evening and they were at their hotel in Nottingham preparing for the first Test. They reacted in different ways.

Gordon Greenidge remembers it as a 'serious moment' which

triggered off a feeling of contempt around the team. It felt as if it was a deliberate comment to degrade us. I think the whole team felt very hurt. It was now combat, it was now a battle where there was no way England could have won. That comment alone was sufficient to set the tone for the whole series. No one let up in any way at all because it hurt. Whether he meant it to or not, it hurt, and of course that drove the guys to perform even better, greater than perhaps they thought they could.

Deryck Murray's description is of a 'motivational speech with racial overtones'. What irritated him and several other players was the context of the remarks, given Greig's background. Even though he was playing for England, Greig had been born and brought up in white South Africa, where profound discrimination against black people was an official policy of the apartheid government.

Michael Holding's recollection is that those West Indian players who had lived in England and had played county cricket were more disturbed by 'grovel' than he was. 'It wasn't as if we were all sitting in a room and watched it together. When I heard the word I didn't know exactly what "grovel" meant. I knew to a fair degree what he was talking about but I didn't know of any ulterior motives or connotations behind the word. Eventually you hear people start to say that word is used in South Africa.'

'We were supposed to have gone to a team meeting,' says Vivian Richards, 'and all of sudden there's this clip. The television was on, and we saw Tony Greig saying his stuff. The appetite was there immediately. I remember Clive Lloyd said, "Guys, we don't need to say much – the man on the television has just said it all for us." We knew what we had to do . . . We took that seriously. Very, very seriously.'

Wayne Daniel heard about it later. 'We had the team meeting early that evening. I don't remember anything being discussed there. It was the next day in the dressing room that we talked about it. Deryck and Andy Roberts were saying, "What? He's going to make us grovel?"'

Clyde Walcott was the manager of the West Indies side for the tour. The next day he said that the England captain's interview had been 'just another of those psychological moves . . . that are made before a big match'. Later he would add, 'To say that about West Indians, some of whose countries had only recently become independent of Britain, whose ancestors were slaves taken to the Caribbean from Africa, was an incredible gaffe.'

'It was a slight against all black people, not just black cricketers,' says Martin Adrien. '"Grovel" made people think about the colonial past and slavery. And from a South African cricketer, with all that was going on at the time, it made it worse. It is a very disturbing term coming from that man about a black team. He was saying, "I am up here, you are down there; I have my foot on your throat and I'm going to squeeze." Yeah. It drew an instinctive reaction from me.'

Tony Greig hadn't used the word as a calculated racial taunt, but it was an almighty blunder. In the days that followed he sought to explain himself on local black radio shows. He had been thoughtless and crass, and was not helped by his intense competitiveness. 'On the cricket field', wrote his England teammate Mike Brearley, 'he bears all the marks of one who would compete with his grandmother for the last nut on Christmas Day.'

'Let me see if I can say something on behalf of the sinner!' suggests Ronald Austin. Ronald is from Georgetown in Guyana, a man who has followed the West Indies cricket team closely since he was a boy. In 1976 he was visiting London.

Greig had been in the West Indies in 1974, bowling off spin against a team that included Garry Sobers, Rohan Kanhai, Kallicharran and Lloyd. He succeeded in putting pressure on them. He was adept at containing these batsmen and then purchasing wickets. He scored runs himself and, as I recall, was brilliant in the field. Any charitable human being would be forgiven for thinking that in the circumstances the England captain would again fancy his chances against these Caribbean opponents. Yet overconfidence and carelessness impaired his judgement. Using the word 'grovel' was bad enough. His greater error was to underestimate the improvement in West Indian batting and bowling.

Greig had sharpened the desire of the West Indies to beat England. His ineptitude helped to unify the West Indian team and gave them a specific sense of purpose and a focus for their enmity. 'Tony Greig was the inspiration,' says Andy Roberts. 'Not because of his colour, not because he was from South Africa but because of the word 'grovel'. That is what motivated us. It had nothing to do with anything else.'

The players on the 1976 tour had a simple plan which they repeated to each other often: to do everything as well as they could. Do everything you can to win. Play your best cricket at all times. Never be complacent. 'Because we felt all of those things,' says Wayne Daniel,

we thought we would get our game right. So we didn't let that comment make it personal. We stayed calm. Then, if at the end of the series we had won, had torn England apart, then we could say, 'Who's grovelling now?' So the senior players told us, 'He said what he said, so let's catch well, let's bowl fast, let's get in and stay in. Play your best cricket and we will prevail.' That is what Greig's comment inspired us to do – that was our thought – much more so than, 'Hey, here's a white fellow talking crap and we're going to knock his head off.'

Thirty years after the series ended, Tony Greig reflected on his *Sportsnight* appearance and confessed that he didn't regret his comments because of the effect they had; he regretted them because 'with hindsight, I cringe when I see them. Because it was very inappropriate. I've got no axe to grind with how the West Indians reacted. I would have done the same thing. There are times in your life when you get things wrong and you make mistakes, and that was one of mine.'

As Vivian Richards put it, it was a 'stupid remark'.

*　*　*

Even before the 'grovel' interview, England's players, selectors and cricket journalists knew that it was likely to be a difficult summer. Only Tony Greig, Alan Knott and possibly Derek Underwood had the talent to match that of any of the West Indies players. There had been a Test trial which solved nothing, as the England XI had bowled out The Rest for 48. Selection was further complicated by the fact that two of England's best batsmen – Dennis Amiss and Graham Roope – had both played poorly for a Marylebone Cricket Club XI against the West Indies days earlier. Amiss had ducked into a short ball and left the pitch with a bleeding head. Roope had made 18 and 3.

Neither was picked for the first Test at Trent Bridge; the side chosen was one that could keep a game safe and possibly had the 'tenacity' wrote John Arlott in the *Guardian*, 'to worry a finer but less purposeful team into error and defeat'. Arlott's colleague at the *Observer*, Tony Pawson, predicted, 'We have to rely on John Edrich, David Steele and Bob Woolmer to wear down the West Indian pace and hope that their more exciting stroke play may again get them in trouble from time to time.' This was a team picked to hang on. Winning was a possibility; entertaining was unlikely.

There was also a realisation that this West Indies side was different from the sort of team that had toured England so pleasantly in the past. After watching Vivian Richards make a hundred against Hampshire, the *Guardian* noted, 'There looks to be a greater meanness nowadays about the West Indies' batsmen. They are not the jolly Caribbean beans of old.'

At the team's first news conference Clive Lloyd was asked how many bouncers his bowlers would send down in an over. 'Fast bowling is not all about bouncers,' he replied.

The way the team had recently bowled against India made some

British journalists prickle: 'The West Indies have packed their side with fast bowlers for this summer's tour of England and it is clear that there will be plenty of short stuff,' stated Henry Blofeld. 'Will the English umpires . . . do what their opposite numbers abroad have failed to do? And if they do [warn players about intimidatory bowling], will it be to loud cries of "discrimination" or even "racialism"?'

There came an even more distressing warning from the traditionally sober authority on the game, the *Wisden Cricketers' Almanack*. In 'Notes by the Editor' there was a paragraph about the risk of serious injury from being hit by a cricket ball. The editor quoted a medical doctor and former chairman of the Cricket Society called R.W. Cockshut. Dr Cockshut had well-known opinions on several other subjects: one was the Victorian novelist Anthony Trollope, another was the belief that all young boys should be circumcised to promote chastity and lessen the temptation of masturbation in their teenage years. Dr Cockshut was clearly no stranger to hopelessly unrealistic theories.

As for cricket, he had published research which predicted that in 1976 alone there could be 'up to ten deaths and 40 irreversible brain injuries caused by the impact of cricket ball on skull'. The weekly carnage would be prevented by awarding the batting side ten runs every time a player was hit above the hips. 'Bumpers would disappear overnight,' was *Wisden*'s conclusion. Dr Cockshut's fears were never realised. The West Indies killed no one in 1976. The doctor's desire to outlaw both short balls and foreskins came to nothing.

*　*　*

If Tony Greig wondered how the West Indians might respond to what he had said on television, he probably got his answer when he came in to bat on the fourth morning of the first Test at Nottingham.

He arrived at the crease at 11.49 and was back in the dressing room by noon. Seven balls was all it took. The end came after Andy Roberts bowled two sharp deliveries which bounced and cut back into his body – 20 runs awarded to England in the world of Dr Cockshut – then a fuller ball, one of the fastest of the day, knocked back the England captain's off stump. Tony Greig had made nought. Vivian Richards made 232. This meant he'd now scored more than 1,000 Test runs in 1976 alone. It was not enough to win the game though. The first Test of the summer ended in a draw.

Richards missed the second Test at Lord's in London because he was ill. But Martin Adrien made it. 'That's right. Me and a couple of friends – we weren't sitting where our tickets said we should because we soon realised where the fun part of the ground was.'

They made their way to the Nursery End opposite the famous Lord's pavilion, to join hundreds of other people supporting the West Indies.

'It was the first time I'd seen so many people from the West Indies in one place, and from different islands,' he says. 'At home my father mostly socialised with other Dominicans living in London; the cliques stuck together. There was lots of banter about which was the best island, which had the best players; the Jamaicans were believing that they *were* the West Indies, the Barbadians saying that without three or four of their own the West Indies were no good. "Where the hell *is* Dominica?" somebody shouted.'

Martin Adrien and his friends had brought nothing to eat, but it didn't matter.

'Other people were unpacking fried fish and offering it around, chicken, rice, salad, plenty of rum. It was a complete surprise to be included. It was an eye-opener to see all these different Caribbean people and how we watched cricket.'

It wasn't all peace, love and boiled dumplings at the Nursery End in 1976 though. Just before five o'clock in the afternoon on the first day Tony Greig came to the wicket. There were shouts of 'This ain't no cricket match no more; it's all-out warfare. War, war! Grovel, grovel!' Later on a fistfight between two West Indies supporters started about whether or not their former captain, Rohan Kanhai, should have been selected for the tour. 'Age doesn't come into it,' said the bloody-nosed victor. 'Send for Rohan – ask the great E. W. Swanton!'

Not everyone took the cricket so seriously. The lunch box could be more important than the soapbox. Cricket was a West Indian social occasion.

'Take my mother,' says the cricket writer, Colin Babb.

She does not even like cricket. But she always wanted the West Indies to win because of what the team represented to her as a migrant in this country. It was crucial because it showed that collectively we could beat the English. So people like her were fans of participating in the day. They came and brought food and everything else because it was a day out with the family. For some folks it was more exciting that they were going to meet their cousin from Birmingham rather than anything Viv might do. It was about having a good day out.

By 1976 West Indians living in Britain had been enjoying a day out at the most famous cricket ground in the world for more than a quarter of a century. Lord's – the headquarters of the game – was a special place for their cricketers; it was on this ground in 1950 that the side won a Test match in England for the first time.

'Yes, sir, I was there,' says Sam King, speaking at his house in Brixton, south London. 'I was there in my uniform with my buttons polished.' In 1950 he was Corporal King, a 24-year-old technician in the Royal Air Force who had timed his leave to coincide with the Test match. He had always enjoyed the game and in England had played for RAF sides as a batsman and wicket-keeper. 'In emergencies,' he confides, 'I could bowl some medium. I had signed up for the RAF in 1944 from Jamaica. My mother had said to me, "Go and help. The mother country is at war. If you live, it will be a good thing." I worked on Lancasters and Spitfires at bases across the United Kingdom but my favourite was the American Dakota. I was good with those old propeller aircraft. If it break down, you call me up, even today, and we'll get it going.'

For the five days of the 1950 Test Sam King left his friend's house in Mitcham in south London every morning and took a train to Lord's. West Indies sides had been to England four times since 1928 to play Test matches but had always been beaten. One of the players he saw was Sonny Ramadhin, a slight 21-year-old spinner who had never played first-class cricket, never mind Test cricket, until earlier that year. No one from an Indo-Caribbean racial background had been picked to play Test cricket for the West Indies before.

Ramadhin's grandparents were labourers who had come to Trinidad from India to cut sugar cane in the nineteenth century. Sonny, who was orphaned by the time he was three, had learned to bowl in cleared patches of cane stubble. When he was a teenager, it became clear that he had a particular gift. He was a slow bowler who turned the ball sharply towards a right-handed batsman off the pitch. But with no obvious change to his bowling action, he could also spin the ball the opposite way.

Sixty-five years after he first came to England, Sonny Ramadhin is still here. He lives in a village on the edge of the Peak District, a few hundred yards from one of the pubs he managed after he retired from playing. His son-in-law Willie Hogg and his grandson Kyle Hogg both played county cricket for Lancashire.

'My local club in Trinidad was called Leaseholds Limited,' recalls Ramadhin.

Leaseholds were the oil people on the San Fernando side of the island. In 1950 I had a job driving a tractor, cutting the fairways on their golf course. Leaseholds had two golf courses – not for all the employees of course, just the whites. We weren't allowed to play on it. Anyhow, my hobby was fishing, not golf. As for the cricket, my bowling was something natural. I used to bowl to the older men in the practice net and they were amazed that I could turn the ball both ways. But I didn't know that people couldn't read me until I came to England. All I knew was that I bowled an off break and a leg break.

The official souvenir programme for the 1950 tour of England does little to clear up the mystery of Ramadhin's talent. 'The nature of his spin has not been exactly specified but it is known that he bowled round the wicket in at least one match, which suggests a break from the off. But it is also said that he spins more with the finger than with the wrist and that although he does not bowl the googly he is able to disguise his off break – which indicates a preponderance of leg-spin. We must wait and learn.'

By the last day of the 1950 Lord's Test match England were still learning. Sam King had seen Ramadhin take 11 England wickets. Among others, he had dismissed Cyril Washbrook, Bill Edrich and Godfrey Evans. 'I was surprised to get all these English people out. I didn't know which one was which or who was the next batsman coming in. I just bowled against whoever walked out.'

Ramadhin's room-mate on tour, Alf Valentine of Jamaica, took seven more wickets with his slow left-arm spin. No runs were scored from 75 of the overs he bowled in the game. Like Ramadhin, he had never played Test cricket before he went to England.

'There were hardly any West Indies supporters in the ground to see it at all,' remembers Sam King. 'Certainly no more than 50, probably nearer 20. On several of the days I sat on my own. But don't forget, there were not many of us in the whole country. After the war I returned to England in 1948 – I was one of those Jamaicans who arrived on the *Empire Windrush*. I remember walking once from the Union Jack club in Waterloo to Woolworth's in Brixton to buy some razor blades and I didn't see a single black man or woman on the whole journey.'

Between 1948 and 1950 well under 1,000 immigrants came to Britain from the West Indies. In 1951 the figure was around 1,000 and in 1952 and 1953 it was about 2,000 each year.

Despite their small numbers, the fans from the Caribbean watching the last day's play at Lord's in 1950 were noisy and enthusiastic. 'As each wicket had fallen this morning,' reported the *Guardian*, 'they had leaped from their seats, embraced each other in an ecstasy and danced and sung to the accompaniment of their guitars until they felt Goddard [the white captain of the West Indies] needed their advice once more on exactly how he should dismiss the next batsman.'

The last England wicket fell soon after lunch. The West Indies had won a Test match in England for the first time – by 326 runs. Some of the supporters ran across the field to congratulate the players, although Ramadhin – who often played that summer wearing his pyjamas under his cricket whites because he was cold – sprinted for the pavilion. *The Times* reporter witnessed a rush of people, 'one armed with an instrument of the guitar family singing with a delight that rightfully belonged to them'.

'I was actually on the pitch because I wanted to take a look at the wicket,' Sam says. 'It seemed like a good one, but a little damp. Anyhow, I was thinking about getting the train back to Mitcham and someone says to me, "Kitchener is making a song, man. Come on." So we went up to his side and there were about 20 of us there.'

Kitchener was Lord Kitchener, a musician and calypsonian who had been a fellow passenger of Sam's on the *Windrush*.

'We sat down and Kitch was writing a celebration song, and somebody shouted, "Put Valentine and Ramadhin in". The next time I heard the song it was on the wireless – they played it all the time – even on the news.'

> Cricket lovely cricket, at Lord's where I saw it;
> Yardley tried his best – Goddard won the Test.
> They gave the crowd plenty fun; the second Test and
>   West Indies won.
> With those little pals of mine – Ramadhin and Valentine.

These words are from the version called 'Victory Test Match' recorded soon after by another calypsonian who was at the ground, Lord Beginner. This recording and Kitchener's tunes strummed and sung in London that day were almost certainly the first cricket calypsos heard in Britain.

'I didn't learn of the song until weeks and weeks after,' says Sonny Ramadhin. 'I heard people singing it, and I also heard it on the radio before one of the later Test matches. It was great to hear people singing your own name – it was as if they were worshipping you! When the team got back home after that tour it was the only calypso they played – the steel bands, everyone. People were given a day off work – Ramadhin and Valentine Day they called it. It was like a bank holiday.'

That win at Lord's meant more to the region than most people in Britain could realise. For C. L. R. James, its significance was such that he was certain Caribbean self-identity could not begin to be fully realised until the inventors of cricket had been beaten in England by the West Indies. In *The Development of West Indies Cricket: The Age of Nationalism* the Barbadian academic and cricket writer Hilary McD. Beckles described how the win affected the father of a friend: the man, an immigrant bus driver in the West Midlands, had a formal picture taken of himself in evening dress, gloves, hat and cane the day after the Lord's win. The hire of the outfit came to two pounds and ten shillings, and when his wife found out the cost, she left him for a week. He wore the suit and its trimmings all day in celebration as he drove his bus along its route around Birmingham. He told his son why – despite the trouble it caused him – it had been the most fulfilling day of his life: 'Winning the series three–one. The first time we beat them *wasn't* the big thing. It was Lord's, son – going into their own backyard and taking their chickens out of the coop and frying them on the front lawn. For me, son, the empire collapsed right there. Not Churchill or Wellington could bring it back. Shackles were gone and we were free at last because the chickens were out of the coop.'

'We all knew that England ruled us as a colony,' says Sam King, 'but our attitude was that if we could beat them at Lord's, we could beat them at anything. In the days afterwards we were all a little bolder. At my RAF station it meant that I could stand up a bit taller.'

That determination to beat England, the desire for some sort of change to the way things had been, went completely over the heads of the English cricket establishment. Sir Pelham Warner, who had grown up in Trinidad and captained England, wrote this welcome to the 1950 tourists: 'The West Indies are among the oldest of our possessions, and the Caribbean Sea resounds to the exploits of the British Navy. Nowhere in the world is there a greater loyalty to, love of, and admiration for England.'

'This one cricket match had a great effect. We showed we could do something well,' concludes Sam King. 'After that day employers here began to realise that if you took a West Indian and trained him as a machinist or a car sprayer or whatever it was, he could do it. He could work, he could achieve. And when the English saw that, they asked us to get our Caribbean friends to come to England and work for them too.'

By 1963, when Frank Worrell brought his side to Lord's, there were many more West Indian supporters to watch. And the talk was not just of the cricket. As well as opinionated running comment-aries on the players' abilities, there were arguments about the poli-tics of the Caribbean and the experience of a decade of living in England. The Trinidadian-born writer V. S. Naipaul published a feature article in *Queen* magazine after spending five days sitting with, and listening to, West Indians during the engrossing Lord's Test that summer.

'You know what's wrong with our West Indians? No damned disci-pline. Look at this business this morning [Wes Hall and the England bowler Fred Trueman had been clowning with each other on the pitch]. Kya-kya, very funny. But that is not the way the Aussies win Tests. I tell you what we need is conscription. Put every one of the idlers in the army. Give them discipline.'

'Which one is Solomon? They look like twins.'

'Solomon have the cap. And Kanhai a lil fatter.'

'But how a man could get fat, eh, playing all this cricket?'

'Not *getting* fat. Just putting on a lil weight.'

'O Christ! He out! Kanhai!'

'... And boy, I had to leave Grenada because politics were making it too hot for me.'

'What, they have politics in Grenada?'

Laughter.

'You are lucky to be seeing me here today, let me tell you. The only thing in which I remain West Indian is cricket. Only thing.'

'... You hear the latest from British Guiana?'

'What, the strike still on?'

'Things really bad out there.'

'Man, go away, eh. We facing defeat and you want to talk politics.'

With one ball left in the 1963 Lord's match, all four results were still possible. The England batsman Colin Cowdrey, who'd earlier had his arm fractured by a delivery from Wes Hall, had returned at the fall of the ninth England wicket.

'Cowdrey comes in,' wrote Naipaul, 'his injured left arm bandaged. And this is the ridiculous public school heroism of cricket: a man with a bandaged arm saving his side, yet without having to face a ball. It is the peculiar *style* of cricket, and its improbable appreciation that links these dissimilar people – English and West Indian.'

The game ended in a dramatic draw. The Lord's Test of 1976 was drawn with much less excitement. The third game of the series was in Manchester.

* * *

Cedric Rhoades was a proud host. He was chairman of Lancashire County Cricket Club and was pleased with how the wicket for the Old Trafford Test had turned out. There had been no rain in Manchester for three weeks, but the pitch had been inspected and approved by officials.

'We have got a pitch fit for any Test,' said Rhoades. 'It is hard and fast and will play true. It should give every cause for satisfaction, and both batsmen and bowlers will get a fair crack out in the middle.'

He was certainly right about a fair crack out in the middle. It was almost an inch wide and ran towards the stumps at the Stretford End of the ground. The shorn grass on the wicket grew only in clumps and was encircled by bare patches of dry earth. The ball could rise sharply from a fast bowler's good length or keep trickily low. If it hit the edges of the long crack its movement couldn't be predicted.

Who'd want to open the batting on this pitch?

After he checked into the team hotel, Brian Close was soon found by his captain. 'He said, "Come and have a cup of tea up in my room with me,"' recalls Close.

So I dumped my bags and went to Greigy's room. There he was, lying on the bed. He turned round and said, 'The selectors and I have been thinking, and we want you to open the innings with John Edrich in this Test match.' I said, 'Nay, Tony. I haven't opened the batting for quite a number of years now. And anyway, what's Bob Woolmer in the side for? He's an opening batsman, isn't he?' Greigy said, 'Yes, but the selectors and I have been thinking, and we reckon he's got a lot of Test years left in him and we don't want him killed off.' Those were the exact words. So I said, 'Oh. So it's all right to sacrifice me then.' And that's how I came to open the innings at Manchester.

But it would be the West Indies, not England, who had to bat first. And they struggled. On the first morning they were 26 for 4 and later in the day 211 all out. Only Gordon Greenidge, with a hundred in the best innings of his career so far, kept the West Indies from what may have been a losing first-innings total. England's problem was that they were then bowled out for 71. Wayne

Daniel knocked Tony Greig's stumps out for 9 runs. By the Test's third evening England were batting to save the match after Greenidge and Vivian Richards made second-innings hundreds. England would have to score 552 to win.

Brian Close and John Edrich were the England openers. When Close had batted in his first Test match in 1949, only five men in this West Indies side had been born. Now he was 45, almost bald and had a sticking plaster on his left elbow. John Edrich was 39. When their counties had played the West Indies earlier in the 1976 season, both Close and Edrich had done pretty well. Newspapers reported that the West Indies had been 'powerless to stop' Edrich when he made a hundred for Surrey at the Oval, while Close had 'time to spare' against Roberts and Daniel, scoring 88 for Somerset at the end of May.

It was to be a little different on this muggy evening in June.

There have been many accounts of the aggressive bowling and desperate defensive batting seen during this passage of play. Some versions contradict others. One of the least subjective is likely to be the statistical record compiled by Bill Frindall, who was the BBC radio scorer for the *Test Match Special* programme. He noted each ball with particular symbols he had devised and made additional comments on that evening's play as it took place.

The session lasted for an hour and twenty minutes, beginning at ten past five and ending at half past six. Seventeen overs were bowled: four by Andy Roberts, seven by Michael Holding, three by Wayne Daniel and three by the spinner Albert Padmore. Including one wide and nine no balls, the batsmen faced 112 deliveries – Close 57 and Edrich 55.

Saturday had been very warm with a breeze in the morning but by late afternoon it was just hot and sticky. Noisy too. The England bowler Mike Selvey was playing in his first Test match. 'It was a very strange day. It was humid, building up as the play went on, getting very oppressive. The weather seemed to reflect the nature of the crowd. Among the West Indian fans – and there were a lot of them – there had been this cacophony, a tympanic noise from the drinks cans all day, banging out a rhythm. Building up, building up.'

After four balls from Andy Roberts, Brian Close stepped away because he was put off by the racket and movement in the crowd. At the end of the next over Clive Lloyd walked towards the West Indies supporters to ask them to be less of a distraction. If there's too much noise, he told them, how will the umpires be able to hear our snicks from the bat edge?

According to Frindall, the West Indians bowled 16 bouncers at the two English batsmen that evening. Each bouncer was marked in his scorebook with an upward-pointing arrow. There was also one downward-pointing arrow to signify a ball that kept low; by now this was a pitch of inconsistent bounce. Holding and Daniel bowled six bouncers each and Roberts bowled four. Brian Close was first hit on the chest by Holding from the last ball of the sixth over – not by a bouncer, but by a short-length ball that leaped up.

This was the point when the intent of the West Indies bowling seemed to change. Roberts was replaced by Daniel, who bowled six bouncers at Edrich in his first two overs. In between, Holding bowled a further two at Close.

'I remember bowling a couple of short balls to John Edrich,' confirms Daniel. 'I didn't get to bowl at Close much because he was marooned at the other end. The pitch was a lively one that evening. My main memory is fielding at leg gully and thinking that if the ball came off the bat edge to me, how am I going to catch it? It was fast and hostile.'

By six o'clock, after 50 minutes of batting, Close and Edrich had not crossed or scored a run from the last seven overs. Close had faced all of Holding's last 25 deliveries. Roberts came back on for

Daniel, and Edrich managed to hit him for four through backward point. They were England's first runs – other than extras – for 39 minutes.

Then, at four minutes past six, Holding began his fifth consecutive over to Brian Close from the Warwick Road End. It would be one of the more infamous overs of modern Test cricket. Three slips, a gully, a leg gully and a short leg were waiting for a deflection. Close played at and missed the first ball. The second was a 90-miles-per-hour bouncer which would have hit him straight in the face had he not snapped his neck away from the ball. The third was another bouncer which scorched across Close's nipples. The next ball, also short, caught Close more towards the leg side, and slammed into his ribcage. This was the blow that made him buckle and grimace as if he had been punched very hard. He staggered, stayed up, and for a pace or two the Yorkshireman's bat became a walking stick.

'And that's hurt him,' said the television commentator Jim Laker. 'That's somewhere I think round about the mark where earlier he let one bounce off him. And although he will never show any trace of emotion whatsoever, or give anybody the impression at any time in his cricket life he's ever been hurt, that really must have stung him.'

Vivian Richards was fielding close by at short leg. Yes, he was playing for his country, but this was his county captain in pain. 'I went up to him. "Are you OK, skipper?" Closey eventually gathered himself together and bellowed, "Fuck off." What a man.'

Holding ran in again for the fifth ball. Again it was fast and short, and Close jerked back as if avoiding a jab to the chin. Behind the wicket Deryck Murray caught the ball, fingers pointing up, in front of his own face. And that was enough for the umpire Bill Alley. It was to be the last bouncer, but not the last short-pitched ball, that Close and Edrich would see that evening.

Alley walked towards Holding and, raising his finger as if giving him out, warned him officially that – according to the laws of cricket – he was guilty of 'persistent bowling of fast short-pitched balls . . . constituting a systematic attempt at intimidation'. He could receive one more warning but a third offence would mean Clive Lloyd would have to stop him bowling.

On the edge of the pitch a policeman went into the crowd. 'Scuffles along boundary,' noted Bill Frindall in his scorebook.

Holding's last ball was not short but it hit Close again, this time in the groin.

'Brian Close is going to be a mass of bruises when he eventually gets back into the haven of the pavilion,' Laker told BBC viewers. In fact Close was hit on the body three times, once in Holding's third over and twice in the sixth, Frindall marking each occasion with a navy-blue dot. So Close probably had three bruises on his body. There is a famous photo of him bare-chested in the dressing room with six or seven weals on his torso. But that was actually taken in 1963 after Close's innings against the West Indies' bowlers Wes Hall and Charlie Griffith at Lord's.

'As a fast bowler,' reflects Michael Holding, 'you know that you can do damage, but you still have to go and do what you think is necessary to get people out. If that means bowling a bouncer, if it means bowling directly at someone's body, you have to do it. It is up to the batsman to have enough skill to hit the ball and defend himself to see he doesn't get hurt.'

'The key to it was the poor pitch, it really was,' says Mike Selvey.

They didn't bowl in a way that you'd describe as dangerous. They targeted the torso, that's where most of it went, at rib height. But of course there was this crack at the Stretford End which ran longitudinally down the pitch. Now for a right-hander facing a right-arm bowler, it was irrelevant because it was too straight, but for left-handed batsmen, as Edrich and Close both were, it was lethal. The crack was quite wide by Saturday, and the pitch was just nasty – up and down – and of course it was all exacerbated by their pace as compared to the speed at which Mike Hendrick and I were bowling.

'The umpire was there to regulate the game,' says Wayne Daniel. 'I was just trying to bowl as fast and aggressive as I could, but to intimidate never came into my mind.'

'Fast bowling does intimidate batsmen,' reckons Brian Close. 'The faster you bowl, the more intimidating it is. It's part of the job, and if you're a batsman you've got to cope with it. You just go out and do your job of protecting your wicket and building an innings and scoring runs, that's what a batsman's job is. And whatever the difficulties are – whether it's bounce, pace, swing, movement, spin – you've got to cope with it. You're there to make runs.'

Tony Cozier was covering the series and saw every ball of the evening session. 'A lot was made of Daniel and Holding bowling like they did, but what do you do?' he asks. 'These men out there batting were 39 and 45. You don't blame the bowlers, you blame the England selectors. How can you take a 45-year-old man and make him go out in front of that sort of attack? It was crazy. Absolutely crazy.'

'Brian Close was a brave man,' says Clive Lloyd, 'but at that age should you really be sticking your chest out when the ball is coming at 90 miles per hour? He should have been watching the game from the bar, enjoying a drink. These men were past it. The pitch was not good enough. There was no instruction from me to bowl an intimidatory line. As it was – tactically – the length wasn't right. We should have bowled fuller, and they'd have probably lost four wickets that evening.'

Tony Greig was very clear that Brian Close and John Edrich had been chosen to face the West Indies for a reason: 'We always knew we were going to get into trouble. That's why I picked these two blokes because they could be discarded. There was no real point in putting a youngster in there because I knew what we were in for. It was very dangerous. The truth is that we had to pick a team for a Test match where we knew we were going to be jumping around all over the place.'

Neither did Greig blame the West Indies for the way they bowled. 'Boy, if I had been Clive Lloyd that day and I'd been dishing it out, you better believe I would have let those bowlers go until such time as we were pulled into line. It was not up to Clive Lloyd to say to his bowlers, "Look, be nice to two of the toughest opening batsmen in the history of the game."'

Albert Padmore bowled the last over of the day. It contained two full tosses, but Close was so unused to playing attacking shots, it was still a maiden. He and Edrich headed for the pavilion. In the England dressing room the players who hadn't batted gawped at the pair that had. Somehow they had survived without being seriously hurt. Mike Selvey remembers the scene.

Brian sat opposite me on the other side of the room, almost certainly with a broken rib, saying, 'I'll be all right, I'll be all right. Cup o' tea, just get us a cup o' tea.' And on my left was Edrich. He was sitting with his pads still on and he was leaning forwards on his bat, and his cap was pushed right back on his head. And he slowly started giggling to himself, not manic, but noticeable. And someone said, 'What is it, Eedee?' and through his chuckling, John went, 'Have you seen the scoreboard, Closey? Have a look through the window. You've got one run. All that, and you've got just one run.'

In the *Sunday Times* the former Sussex player Robin Marlar noted the bravery of the England openers and wrote, 'The number of balls pitched at a length on a line to hit the stumps were so few they could have been counted. The rest were, by inference, directed at the batsman's body or to induce a fending-off catch. Intimidation? Of course it was. And umpire Alley finally warned Holding. Some like steak tartare, but this cricket was too raw for my stomach.'

The West Indies would win the match by a huge margin. On the last afternoon Tony Greig, who was barracked on sight by the many West Indian supporters in the ground, was clean-bowled once more, this time for three.

'"Grovel" is an emotive word', wrote John Arlott, 'and it has stuck in more craws than he can possibly have anticipated when he used it.'

Neither Brian Close nor John Edrich played for England again. 'The silly buggers sacked us both,' says Close.

* * *

For two days before the fourth Test in Leeds the International Cricket Conference held its annual meeting at Lord's. In its concluding statement it condemned intimidatory bowling and 'earnestly emphasised the need to bring the spinner into the game'. The same day the West Indies picked four fast bowlers to play in the next Test match. If they won at Headingley, they would win the series.

Gordon Greenidge, who had batted so poorly in Australia, made his third century in as many innings against England. His runs helped his side to a lead, just as Andy Roberts's six wickets helped the West Indies to a win by 55 runs on the fifth day. He was bowling at least as fast as he had in Australia. Standing at second slip, Greenidge decided that he needed to wear a box when Roberts was bowling.

This West Indies side had beaten England in England. Clive Lloyd now shared this feat of captaincy with only four other West Indians – Goddard, Worrell, Sobers and Kanhai. His team led the series two–nil and there was still a Test left to play. Lloyd was in charge of men who were playing entertaining, even dramatic cricket. 'Intense fast bowling, spectacular fielding and aggressive batting' was how John Arlott described it. The day after the Headingley victory he wrote that 'the West Indians' joy at their win revealed how much success matters to them; but no other team of modern times has remotely suggested that they felt the manner of winning equally important'.

On the balcony at Headingley the players who had rushed from the pitch jumped into the arms of those who had watched. Deryck Murray embraced his father, who had been looking on from the dressing room. A long time after the match was over the group was still being serenaded from the outfield by West Indians gathered below. 'I was looking at the faces of the people crowding around and you could *feel* their pride,' says Wayne Daniel.

You could *feel* their happiness standing there looking up at us. You could feel their expectation, their hope. I thought, *I can't let these people turn away feeling bad*. I had to represent the West Indies for these people. What that meant was that we couldn't lapse and have fun. We had to be on top of it all the time. The senior guys repeated this time and again. Andy Roberts, Roy Fredericks, Deryck Murray – they were tough, hard men. I remember bowling a half-volley at Leeds, and the look I got from Andy Roberts at mid-off I'll never forget. He said nothing but his face told me, *What the hell are you doing? You can't be bowling half-volleys for the West Indies*. I had never seen such competitive discipline before. I certainly learned what Test cricket meant in 1976. You could never be off, you always had to be on – and that lesson came to me straight from those guys.

*   *   *

'I was there with my dad, my PE teacher and my maths teacher. They were all cricket nuts. I was 11.' Trevor Nelson is a DJ and broadcaster whose parents came to London from St Lucia. The first time he saw the West Indies play was at the Oval in 1976. It was the last Test of the summer.

> It was like a carnival. Everyone had tin cans; there was a sense of freedom, freedom of expression. I was a kid, but now I can remember that day and understand why there was such a noise. From day to day people like my dad had been wandering around in this society knowing they were the underdog and kind of feeling they shouldn't be there sometimes. There was no sense that these black people could stick their chests out proudly. They were second-class citizens. But in the ground it was the first time I saw black guys boasting, shouting stuff, getting excitable. It was confusing because the county cricket me and Dad watched on TV on a Sunday seemed very quiet, respectful. But here people were selling fried fish and other food. My dad brought a massive hamper, chicken, sandwiches, stuff to share. He was joking with his friends. I'm almost certain I witnessed someone cooking in the ground.

The Oval is very near the London suburbs of Brixton and Lambeth, places where lots of people who had come from the West Indies lived. By the beginning of the 1970s just under half of all the black people in Britain lived in London. For the final Test several thousand West Indies supporters gathered in the stands on the first morning in the northern part of the ground near the Vauxhall End with their backs to the gasworks. There were men in three-piece suits with their wives who had left Trinidad 25 years ago, youths in flared trousers with tight-fitting shirts whose parents had been born in Barbados, bearded teenagers with braids and leather caps who had Jamaican grandparents. There were banners and signs, rum and beer, horns and hand bells. All tickets had been sold for the first three days, and the English cricket authorities had asked Clive Lloyd to appeal to the fans not to make too much noise during play. Their concern was that the din might go beyond exuberance and become intimidatory. But any hope for peace and quiet was a forlorn one. The din would last for as long as the Test match.

Martin Adrien spent two days there with his friends. 'The Oval was a celebration Test. It was an event. You were going somewhere. So for a day at the cricket you could well wear a suit. It was like your Sunday best, and at the time for a fair number of those people cricket would have been second only to church.'

Vivian Richards was the chief celebrant and batted masterfully again. His first Test innings in England that season had been 232 at Nottingham. In this final one he scored 291.

'I was the right age to be impressed by Viv,' recalls Martin.

He was the first man I remember who had a bit of arrogance. His walk was slow, I remember that. 'I'm coming, but you've got to wait for me.' Looking back, I suppose what I was struck by was here was a man representing the region. His success was the region's success. He was scoring runs for the Caribbean. I think for the first time I had seen at close hand a successful West Indian. He was proud. In 1976 that was dynamic and a little bit disturbing.

'You see to me, growing up in London, this wasn't how black people should look,' adds Trevor Nelson.

On TV it was always the white people who were in charge and the black people were always chasing them, but on the cricket field that wasn't the case. My dad and his friends were proud. I had an inner glow that we could beat England at this posh game and we weren't posh. All black people I knew were working class. White people who play cricket were upper class, or so it seemed, but we battered them. We didn't have the equipment they had, the system, the coaches, the pitches – but, yeah, look at that. We're good!

The West Indies made 687. They had never scored so many runs against England in a single innings. As he took it all in, Trevor Nelson was intrigued by how the cricketers affected his father's behaviour.

England seemed to me to look quite old – I don't know, maybe it was David Steele's silver hair. They looked like blokes who worked during the week and played at the weekend. But the West Indies looked like warriors. They looked as if they'd come to steal something, to rob you, take the spoils. And my dad was revelling in the way England were getting beaten. He was so pro-West-Indian, it was unbelievable. It was a side of him I hadn't seen before. I always saw him as a reasonably impartial, reserved man until we got to that ground. Then he became like just a mad West Indian fan taking the living piss out of the English. I mean all of them were. Every time there was a boundary they were just dancing, screaming, singing, rubbing it in. Massively. I actually think there was a bit of payback going on there. There was a *lot* of payback going on there. And I realised that West Indians could be good at something. Cricket. Cricket was it.

When the West Indies declared their second innings late on the fourth afternoon their lead was huge. As he led his sweaty, dusty and downtrodden side from the field, Tony Greig knew England had no hope of winning. In view of all of the West Indian spectators, he sank to his knees and crawled a few yards on all fours. He had grovelled. The crowd howled in delight. And now he had to bat.

*   *   *

Michael Holding walked towards the white disc on the ground that marked the start of his run-up. For now he held the ball in his left hand. Putting some spittle on the index finger of his right hand, he used it to polish the side of the ball. As he reached his mark, he turned towards the batsman knowing he was 21 strides away from bowling his next delivery. Seven months ago he had cried on the pitch at Sydney. Now he had already taken eleven wickets in the match, and would go on to take another three.

The cricket ball in his hand was nearing the end of its life. The royal warrant insignia of a lion and a unicorn stamped on one side in gold leaf had flaked away. The dyed red leather outer case, which had been especially chosen from the hides of Scottish cattle unblemished by the nicks of barbed wire, was scuffed, cracked and swollen. Parts of the Northern Irish linen thread which made up the seam had frayed and loosened. The ball, which had been shaped and baked and stitched and polished by hand in a small Kent village called Chiddingstone Causeway, would soon be discarded into a box or a basket somewhere in a shed or a cupboard at the Oval.

Holding accelerated towards the batsman, each stride longer than the last. Halfway through his run-up he transferred the ball from his left hand to his right without even knowing he was doing it. Two seconds later, running almost as fast as he could, he jumped and let the ball go at 90 miles per hour with a full circle of his arm. Some fast bowlers were ugly to watch and others were beautiful. Holding was beautiful.

Tony Greig saw the ball coming of course. He knew what he had to do to stop it hitting his stumps, but the ball came too fast. It curved in towards him in the air and with a dipping trajectory tore past his feet. Greig, off balance and falling to his right, knew he had been beaten. The ball struck the bottom of the middle of the three stumps, knocking it sideways. The leg stump shot completely out of the ground. A ricochet caused the off stump to lean in the opposite direction.

Michael Holding had clean-bowled the England captain again.

The noise of celebration was intense. It whipped around the Oval stands and could be heard on the pavement outside the ground, where, at a homemade stall, West Indian supporters looked up and added their own cheers. The stall was doing good business selling shots of rum, lengths of sugar cane and a vinyl single called 'Who's Grovelling Now?'

> Who's grovelling now?
> Who's grovelling now?
> Greig, you're a loser somehow.
> If you had your way, you would never let us play,
> So tell me – who's grovelling now?
>
> Lloydy, you're a champion
> You never, never lose your cool.
> Though the bigots try to put you down
> You never, never wear a frown.
> You play the game like a gentleman
> You lick the ball like calypsonian
> You put your men them at ease –
> You're the king from the West Indies.

* * *

In time Michael Holding's 14 wickets at the Oval and Vivian Richards's double century would be seen as jewels in the crown of

West Indian cricket. Big moments in the renewal of a cricket nation. When these young men had been small boys in the early 1960s, the West Indies had risen to the highest level of the international game under the captaincy of Frank Worrell and then Garry Sobers. But by the end of the decade the foundations of that success – the wins against Australia, England and India – had collapsed. The best players were stale after years of cricket and had not been replaced. That weakness caused division, and the qualities necessary for leadership – playing skill, example, authority, insight, cussedness and luck – had evaporated. The period of rebuilding after 1965 had been fitful and incomplete; for nearly seven years, the West Indies didn't win a series. From December '68 until July '73, they didn't win a Test match. And there was no assurance that this latest West Indies would bring lasting success.

'We shouldn't forget,' reflects Ronald Austin,

that the teams Lloyd took to Australia and then to England carried with them no guarantees. Many people back in the West Indies expected little. These men were potentially good young cricketers, but Richards, Greenidge, Roberts and Holding had excelled only in a few regional games between the islands and in a small number of Test matches. Nor had the leadership of the West Indies side – a uniquely important role – been solved by Lloyd's appointment. I think he'd led Guyana in just a few matches in the regional competition. The decision to make him captain of the West Indies was not a unanimous one, and Lloyd has said since that of the selectors who chose him, only Clyde Walcott truly believed in his qualities.

The historical, geographical, racial and political complications of West Indies cricket meant that some in the Caribbean had actually been pleased at the failure of Lloyd and his team in Australia. There were others who suggested that after his catastrophic spinal injury in 1971, Lloyd would always be psychologically feeble. He had lain in hospital for weeks not knowing if he'd walk again, never mind play cricket, after diving for a catch while fielding for the Rest of the World at Adelaide.

A commander will always be more confident of success if he knows that he has protection and support in his rear, and Lloyd did not have that.

Neither had the West Indies ever enjoyed the experience of being a 'professional' team. They didn't play enough regional or Test cricket for that. In 1963, when Frank Worrell's side won in England, Jamaica had not played in Trinidad for 13 years. Barbados had hosted Trinidad – its nearest big cricket neighbour – just six times since 1949. In contrast, during those years the two best county sides in England – Yorkshire and Surrey – played against each other 26 times. West Indian cricketers had to cross the gap between club cricket and the international game almost in one step. This is why in his book *Summer Spectacular* about the 1963 tour of England J. S. Barker wrote that, despite their talent, it was no surprise that the West Indies now and again 'tobogganed into a scarcely credible abyss of ineptitude'.

So as the players drank beer and champagne on the Oval dressing-room balcony, celebrating a three–nil series win against England, all of these things were swirling around the balcony with them. All of these impediments and uncertainties from years gone by, as well as the recent past, were somewhere in Clive Lloyd's mind. But the summer of 1976 had ameliorated West Indian cricket. The professionalisation of the West Indies began in England under Lloyd's captaincy.

The fire in Babylon had been lit.

3

'Regret No Coloureds'

Athneal Ollivierre was an old man. He died in a small room in his house next to the sea. It was 4 July 2000. Several thousand miles away the West Indies had had a game against a New Zealand A side abandoned at Bristol because of bad weather. Two days after Athneal died the West Indies would lose by six wickets to Zimbabwe at the same ground. The old man had known nothing of the one-day NatWest Bank series; the West Indian team knew nothing of the old man's death. There was though a thread of connection between them that stretched back for a century.

Ollivierre had been a renowned athlete. He wasn't a cricketer, but a whaler. One of the very last. In the waters around the small island of Bequia – a fleck in the Caribbean Sea – Ollivierre had handled a cinnamon-wood harpoon shaft with the dexterity and certainty of a javelin thrower. He would fling the 40-pound weapon three feet into a humpback's blubber before jumping on the whale's back to drive his lance towards its vital organs. Once, to the astonishment of his crewmates and his neighbours, he had killed a whale with a single blow to its huge heart.

'Who made the human being?' he would ask if visitors challenged his profession. 'God!' he would answer for himself. 'And who made the whale? God! And he say man shall rule.' Athneal Ollivierre was a man of courage who looked out to sea for adventure and sustenance. His distant cousin Charles had done the same.

On 4 July 1900, a hundred years to the day before Athneal would die, Charles Ollivierre was playing cricket in Leicestershire. The county were about to lose to the first West Indian side to tour England. Ollivierre would stay in England after the tour to make his living with Derbyshire and become the first black man from the West Indies to play county cricket.

Ollivierre had sailed to England on the RMS *Trent* with Aucher Warner's West Indies side. Warner, as captain, was of course a white man. He was a descendant of Sir Thomas Warner, a bodyguard of James I and later a seventeenth-century Caribbean slave owner and colonial politician. Charles Ollivierre – one of five black players in the touring team – had been born in St Vincent, the larger island to the north of Bequia, in 1876. His family were whalers. They had learned the craft from the Yankee crews of New England which had sailed south to the Grenadines to hunt in the middle of the nineteenth century. Alongside the 'estate owners', 'government officials' and 'doctors' listed on the *Trent*'s handwritten manifest, Mr C. A. Ollivierre was described as a 'traveller', aged 47 and married. In fact he was 23 and a single man. He would never return to the West Indies.

Charles Ollivierre and Aucher Warner had met on the cricket field before. After living in Bequia and St Vincent, Ollivierre had gone to Trinidad. Aged 19, he played for the island against the first English side to play in the Caribbean, and Warner was his captain. Before George Headley, experienced cricket watchers in the West Indies thought Ollivierre was the finest batsman they had. He was strong, could cut the ball late and hard as well as loft it over the heads of the off-side fielders for four. At school he had thrown a cricket ball 126 yards and had once played a one-handed cut shot for six. During the 1900 West Indies tour a newspaper would describe Ollivierre as having a 'certain allusive nuance, suggestive of a far-away glamour which no English player possesses'.

When the white batsman Malcolm Kerr returned to Jamaica after the 1900 tour ended, he told people who the team's most valuable player had been. 'The best man was undoubtedly Ollivierre, the black man from St Vincent. There was nobody like him. He's a unique bat. I need hardly say that the blacks were the favourite of the British public. I think most of them suspected us all to be black. The people we met had queer ideas about the West Indies and used to ask us very quaint questions sometimes.' Despite Ollivierre's powers, the West Indies team were weak and not a lot was expected from them. At a lunch in Bridgetown before they left Barbados, the Solicitor General Gerald Goodman gave them a less-than-encouraging pep talk; he told them that they knew very little about cricket and would be lucky to win a single game.

Soon after the side arrived in England, a newspaper cartoon showed infantilised black men grovelling around the towering England batsman W. G. Grace and crying, 'We have come to learn Sah!' Most of the games were lost. At the Grand Hotel in Charing Cross at the end of the tour they were given a dinner by the West Indian Club. At this event Ollivierre and his teammates listened to Lord Harris – politician, cricket grandee, former governor of Bombay, son of a governor of Trinidad – who hoped that the visit to the mother country had been a pleasant one and that 'during their stay in England they had learned something, not only as to cricket but as to the advantage of Empire'. One of the toasts proposed that evening was 'The Colonial Office'.

But Charles Ollivierre had scored nearly 900 runs on the tour, and Derbyshire liked the look of him. They took a very unusual decision. Money was found for him to stay in England so that he could qualify through residence to play for the county. He was soon lodging in Talbot Street in Glossop with a family of six, working as a 'writing clerk'. That year Glossop Cricket Club, two minutes' walk from Talbot Street, won the Central Lancashire League for the first time – with Ollivierre's help.

Ollivierre's funding came from Samuel Hill Wood, who had inherited family money made from local cotton mills. Hill Wood enjoyed football and cricket, or at least was shrewd enough to recognise that sport connected him to voters who would put him on local councils and eventually into Parliament. Between the wars he would turn away from Glossop, sell up and leave for London, where he became chairman of Arsenal Football Club, but at the beginning of the century he spent a lot on Glossop North End FC and played for them on the wing. He also played at the cricket club and was captain of Derbyshire. The allowance he gave Ollivierre meant the West Indian had a private income and could play cricket as an amateur. This gave him a higher status than a 'professional' cricketer, who was paid a club wage for his services.

The *Derby Daily Telegraph* thought Ollivierre took risks that his regular batting partner, 'the Midland amateur, Mr L. G. Wright, declined'. Neither was he free from 'dubious strokes. Still, those blemishes are so hopelessly outnumbered by the general beauty and grace of his hitting that they may well be overlooked.' The Leicestershire professional Albert Knight believed Ollivierre to be 'the Bernard Shaw of the cricket world' because 'the plain common tack is beneath him. When you see Mr Ollivierre play a fine innings, you see a batsman unexcelled save by Ranjitsinhji.' In the six years Ollivierre played for Derbyshire as a batting all-rounder, his best-known innings came in 1904 when Essex scored 597 in their first innings at Chesterfield – and lost. Ollivierre made 229 then 92 not out to help Derbyshire win by 9 wickets.

Ollivierre was a cricket pioneer – the first West Indian to be rewarded for his talent in England. Over the next 80 years, others would follow – George Headley, Learie Constantine, Frank Worrell, Sonny Ramadhin, Garry Sobers, Clive Lloyd, Vivian Richards, Joel Garner, Malcolm Marshall – all hired by the leagues or counties to fill their grounds. Ollivierre, though, was not by any means the first black sportsman in Britain. By the time he arrived, black athletes had been known of for at least a hundred years. One – a former slave called Tom Molineaux – boxed 39 rounds against the all-England champion at Copthorne Common in Sussex in 1810. He lost but became famous. 'The Black stripped, and appeared of a giant-like strength,' wrote one correspondent on the day of the fight, 'large in bone, large in muscle and with arms a cruel length.' This description is an important one, according to the academic Ellis Cashmore. It was one of the first instances of sports journalism in which whites associated blacks with 'natural, instinctive ability rather than learned competence. The trope continued.'

Nor was Ollivierre an oddity, even though he was almost certainly in an ethnic minority of one when he walked along Spire Hollin from Talbot Street heading for Glossop Cricket Club. Black men had been stationed in Cumbria in the third century, guarding Hadrian's Wall on behalf of the Roman empire. Twice in five years Queen Elizabeth I ordered that the black urban poor of London be transported out of England: 'there are divers[e] Blackamoors brought into this realm, of which kinde of people there are already here too manie . . . Her majesty's pleasure is that those kinde of people should be sent forth of the land.'

These attempted expulsions failed; black people – probably between 15,000 and 20,000 in her day – were already too embedded in English society to be removed. So the chambermaids and domestic servants, the musicians, labourers and prostitutes remained – to the distaste of some. In 1788 the author Philip Thicknesse decided that, 'London abounds with an incredible number of these black men . . . and every country town, nay in almost every village are to be seen a little race of mullatoes, mischievous as monkeys and infinitely more dangerous.' By the time of Charles Ollivierre's arrival in 1900, there had been a small continual black presence in Britain for at least 500 years.

. Photographic portraits of the time, paid for by the sitters, show that black people had their pictures taken in Chichester and Tunbridge Wells, Sunderland and Bury. Others lived in Doncaster, Glasgow or Canterbury. Ollivierre's was another black face in the headquarters of an empire that had never been so powerful or as ideologically endowed. In 1897 the diamond jubilee of Queen Victoria's reign had been a celebration of empire. Watching the procession of colonial troops in London on the anniversary, the *Daily Mail* recorded, 'We send out a boy here and a boy there, and a boy takes hold of the savages of the part he comes to, and teaches them to march and shoot as he tells them to obey him and believe in him and die for him and the Queen.'

The sport that Ollivierre played so well was one which was woven into the empire – and the empire was blended inseparably with the idea of racial superiority. 'What is Empire but the predominance of race?' wondered the former Liberal prime minister Lord Rosebery in 1910. 'In the late Victorian period . . . cricket was taken to encapsulate the essence of England and had a key role in how the English, particularly the economically privileged, imagined their national identity . . . cricket and imperialism became mutually supporting ideologies,' wrote Jack Williams, the author of *Cricket and Race*. By playing cricket a man had to accept a set of binding values – fair play, sportsmanship, decency, acquiescence to the will of the leader. He had to accept that behaviour was governed by certain laws.

As a cricketer, Ollivierre would have absorbed these realities quickly enough. And although his status as an amateur sportsman would have given him some advantages, he was still 'this coal-black batsman', an immigrant trying to earn a living in a country defined absolutely by class and colour. As one Victorian essayist put it, 'The English poor man or child is always expected to remember the condition in which God has placed him, exactly as the negro is expected to remember the skin that God has given him. The relation in both instances is that of perpetual superior to perpetual inferior, of chief to dependant, and no amount of kindness or goodness is suffered to alter this relation.'

More pertinently for Ollivierre, this view existed within the Derbyshire dressing room. One of his teammates was the England professional Bill Storer. According to the author and Essex batsman E. H. D. Sewell, Storer 'believed in England for the English and was not enamoured of importations, especially of the ebony hue'. There seems to be little evidence, though, of such enmity outside the dressing room. Newspaper reports of Ollivierre batting for Derbyshire often record the warmth of the crowd when recognising his skills. On the cricket field he was forgiven his colour because of his talent. But away from the field he was less protected. The British practice of stopping young black men is not a recent policing innovation. Ollivierre was once pulled over and fined five shillings by the Bakewell Bench for riding his bicycle on the pavement as he made his way through the Derbyshire town of Baslow.

Charles Ollivierre played cricket in a country where racial discrimination was not a casual accident of empire, but a central characteristic of imperial Britishness. Racial superiority was as important to the philosophy of empire as coal was to its industrial furnaces. This was an arrangement that some black contemporaries of the sportsman wanted to change. In July 1900, while Ollivierre was playing for the West Indies against Staffordshire in Stoke-on-

Trent, the first Pan-African Congress was being held in London. It was organised by a lawyer from Trinidad called Henry Sylvester Williams. He wanted the meeting to be the 'first occasion upon which black men would assemble in England to speak for themselves and to endeavour to influence public opinion in their favour'.

The delegates, including the black American intellectual William Dubois, demanded improvements to the social, political and economic lives of descendants of Africans dispersed through slavery to America and the Caribbean. They discussed the legacy of slavery and European imperialism and the significance of Africa in world history. In his closing address 'to the nations of the world' Dubois predicted that the issue of the twentieth century would be 'the problem of the colour line [racial discrimination]. The question of how far differences of race – which show themselves chiefly in the colour of skin and the texture of the hair – will be made the basis of denying to over half the world the right of sharing to utmost ability the opportunities and privileges of modern civilisation.'

*　　*　　*

Like Charles Ollivierre, Lebrun Constantine tried to make the most of those limited opportunities. In 1895 he had been the first black man allowed to play cricket for Trinidad, and in 1900 he was on the England tour with Ollivierre. When Lebrun couldn't afford to travel to England again for the 1906 tour, a white Trinidad businessman was so aggravated that he bought the player a chest of clothes and provisions, hired a fast launch and put the cricketer on board to catch the liner which had already sailed for England with the West Indies side.

Lebrun's grandfather had been a slave and his own family name was almost certainly that of a French slave owner. Lebrun knew all about the wickedness of the plantation system. The family told the story of Lebrun's son being hustled back inside as a white estate owner on horseback, who 'would happily have ridden over any nigger children if they had got anywhere near his path', galloped along the street.

That child was Learie Constantine, who was to become even more important a black figure in Britain than Ollivierre. Because he was a better cricketer and more people noticed him, he was able to alter some British perceptions of race through his own achievements, patience and intellect in a way that Ollivierre could not. His biographer Peter Mason wrote that in Constantine were mirrored 'many of the struggles, tensions and aspirations that the West Indians experienced during the twentieth century. His life story was a reflection of the initial rejection, gradual acceptance and, in some areas, final acclaim, that was the lot of immigrants in Britain during the period.' C. L. R. James believed that Constantine belonged to that distinguished company of men who, through cricket, influenced the history of their time.

Learie Constantine had proved his all-round skill on two cricket tours of England with West Indies sides in 1923 and 1928. In 1929 he rebelled, in the words of James, 'against the revolting contrast between his first-class status as a cricketer and a third-class status as a man'. Constantine was determined not to be, as his father was, famous but poor. He moved from Trinidad to Lancashire.

Constantine was contracted to play for Nelson Cricket Club in the Lancashire League, proving again the curious British axiom that the pursuit of sporting success could temporarily at least make people colour-blind. Nelson wanted Constantine's talent and were prepared to pay for it. Within a few seasons he was one of the wealthiest professional sportsmen in the country.

Nelson had been in debt when Constantine joined them, but the gate money their West Indian brought in soon made them rich. Sometimes there were 14,000 spectators at their ground. The league had 14 clubs, but Nelson brought in 75 per cent of its total match receipts. In 1934, when a different league tried to sign Constantine, the other Lancashire League clubs tipped in money to help Nelson keep him where he was. They did so because Constantine's play was a brilliant money-making spectacle. His fielding was extraordinary. He once took ten wickets for ten runs. He once scored a century in just over half an hour. He once made 192 – an inconceivably large score in Saturday-afternoon league cricket. For Lancashire League spectators, Constantine was an exotic circus act. These were 'the impulses not common to the psychology of the over-civilised places of the earth. His cricket is racial,' is how Neville Cardus put it. 'His movements are almost primitive in their pouncing veracity and unconscious beauty . . . a genius!'

The trope continued. Cardus was an admirer but attributed the black man's success to an instinctive, visceral sorcery rather than the combining of intellect, athleticism and strategy. However, the writer was perspicacious enough to recognise the effect of Constantine's skill on those from the West Indies who saw him play. He could have been writing about Vivian Richards in 1976: 'While Constantine played a wonderful innings, a number of his compatriots wept for joy and shook hands in brotherly union. Con was their prophet; they saw in his vivid activity some power belonging to their own blood, a power ageless, never to be put down, free and splendid.'

But even for a superstar such as Constantine, there were limits to his acceptance in British society. After the local paper described his fast bowling during a match in 1933 Constantine received a letter. 'Dear Nigger,' it began. Constantine was then warned not to bowl aggressively against Colne the coming weekend. 'Well, Nigger, if you start bumping them on Saturday you will get bumped, not half, so try to play the game – and remember you are playing against white men and not niggers.'

The following season there was a suggestion that Constantine, who had by now lived in the county for long enough, might play for Lancashire in the first-class game. Years later in the *Manchester Evening News* one of the Lancashire players – Len Hopwood – revealed the tension that the idea had caused.

He was the most exciting and electrifying cricketer of his era . . . rumour grew that Lancashire wanted that attraction. In those days the thought of a black chap playing for Lancashire was ludicrous. We were clannish in those less enlightened times. All hell was let loose when it was heard that negotiations were going on. In the dressing room we wanted none of Constantine. We would refuse to play. Constantine never did become a Lancashire player. We had nothing against him personally. He was, in fact, very popular with us. But the thought of a black man taking the place of a white in our side was an anathema. It was as simple as that.

Nelson – eventually – grew very proud of its most famous citizen. After Constantine retired from cricket and qualified as a lawyer in London, the headline in Nelson's newspaper was LOCAL BOY MAKES GOOD. When he became Britain's first black peer in 1969, Constantine made sure his title included the town. He and his wife enjoyed living in England, but there were frequent episodes of racism about which he would not remain quiet. Many were included in *Colour Bar*, the book he wrote in 1954 after he had left the game. It was an intelligent and reflective memoir based on his experiences as a black immigrant sportsman.

Even though he had made innumerable white friends since 1929, Constantine's considered view was that the United Kingdom of the 1950s was only a little less intolerant than South Africa or segregated

America. He thought most British people were 'quite unwilling' for a black man to enter their homes, nor would they wish to work with one as a colleague, nor to stand shoulder to shoulder with one at a factory bench. 'Hardly any Englishwomen and not more than a small proportion of Englishmen would sit at a restaurant table with a coloured man or woman, and inter-racial marriage is considered almost universally to be out of the question.' Constantine also criticised the Queen and the Commonwealth for what he reckoned was a false portrayal of unity. 'However misled the people of Britain may be over Commonwealth matters and however they are made to think that the Christmas broadcast is an unbiased picture of a completely happy empire, the rest of the world is under no such delusions.'

These were not the remarks of a sour, worn-out failure. Constantine was not just one of the best cricketers of the first half of the twentieth century, he was a well loved public figure. During the Second World War the government had asked him to be the civil servant responsible for the welfare of the tens of thousands of West Indians who came to Britain to assist the war effort. He was also a radio broadcaster, a journalist and a barrister, and after independence in 1962 a government minister in Trinidad and the country's first high commissioner in London. He would sit in the House of Lords as Baron Constantine of Maraval in Trinidad and Nelson in the County Palatine of Lancaster. Yet 54 years after his father had watched Charles Ollivierre bat in Stoke-on-Trent and the first Pan-African Congress began in London, Constantine asked his English readers,

How would it seem to you if we applied the lessons you have taught us? If we shut you into reservations, kept you in slum ghettoes in towns, taught our children to shout at white houseboys, kicked your white rulers off their thrones for asking questions? It is hard to make it understood by white people how much we resent – and fear – this perpetual undercurrent of jeering, this ingrained belief in the white mind that the coloured man, woman or child is a matter for mirth or – at the very best – a kind of devoted loyal dog to a white all-powerful master?

Colour Bar was published in 1954. That same year about 24,000 people from the West Indies emigrated to Britain. Similar numbers followed over the next four years. In 1958, ten years after the *Empire Windrush* had docked at Tilbury carrying Sam King and the Lords Beginner and Kitchener, there were 125,000 Caribbean immigrants in the country. All of them were British citizens. Almost all had been invited by Conservative and Labour governments or other official bodies to fill job vacancies. The historian Peter Fryer noted that 'willing black hands drove tube trains, collected bus fares, emptied hospital patients' bed pans'.

Most headed for Britain expecting the best. The Barbadian novelist George Lamming described the optimism he and his fellow travellers felt as they left the Caribbean. 'Migration was not a word I would have used to describe what I was doing when I sailed with other West Indians to England in 1950. We simply thought we were going to an England that had been painted in our childhood consciousness as a heritage and a place of welcome.' Many were greatly surprised by the sort of welcome they got.

'Dan Jacobson, walking along Finchley Road looking for somewhere to live,' recounts the historian David Kynaston in *Austerity Britain*, 'was struck by how many of the little notices advertising rooms to let included the rubric "No Coloureds" or even, testifying to some obscure convulsion of the English conscience, "Regret No Coloureds".'

The writer and broadcaster Trevor Phillips was born in London in 1953.

On the face of it, my parents came here for the same reasons as everybody else – to find work. Well, actually, the other reason a lot of the people came here was because they were bored. British Guiana in the 1950s was a dull place. My father came because he was a man with a lot of energy – some of which he put to good use, some of which he didn't – but he realised after the war in Guiana that he would spend the rest of his life at best – *at best* – as a clerk on the docks. And he wanted better for himself and his family.

People leaving the West Indies hoped that the mother country would give them something that their homeland could not. The cost of living had almost doubled across the Caribbean after the war; there was high unemployment and almost no social security. 'No one knows how the jobless live,' wrote the journalist Joyce Egginton at the time. 'It is not surprising that thousands have left the West Indies. The surprising thing is that so many have stayed.'

Contrary to popular views in 1950s Britain, the immigrants weren't all labourers without skills. About half the men and a quarter of the women were skilled manual workers, but many had to accept jobs which weren't equal to their abilities and accommodation which didn't fulfil their needs. The houses and flats in which single men had lived together when they first arrived in the early 1950s were not suitable for their wives and their children who now joined them. They were no longer willing to bunk up six to a room in parts of town that no one cared about. Very quickly immigrant families were competing with the settled population for housing.

The parents of the DJ Trevor Nelson arrived in London in the early 1960s.

Dad had been an overseer on a banana plantation in St Lucia, but here he started as a bus conductor. My mum was a child minder. They lived in a room with a lot of other people in Hackney. Freezing cold. There was racism about, it was hard to get a job, hard to get accommodation. A lot of West Indians were very proud and very well brought up. They were clean, well dressed, always liked to wear a suit – they came off those boats looking pretty smart, you know. And they were hard workers. But British people didn't know that.

What many British people did know was that they didn't like so many black people in the country. The tension was soon noticed by the government. Evidence about the effects of immigration was gathered. A Cabinet working party concerned with 'Coloured People Seeking Employment in the UK' which sat from 1952 to 1953 heard from the Metropolitan Police that 'on the whole coloured people are work-shy and content to live on national assistance and immoral earnings. They are poor workmen . . . they are said to be of low mentality and will only work for short periods.'

This description of his parents' generation does not surprise Trevor Phillips.

These people had to swallow the indignities and the ghastliness of the early days. And they did. It was real, but its impact could be overstated. My parents didn't expect too much more. Bear in mind that my father was amazed coming in on the train from Southampton that there were white people sweeping the platforms. There were many humiliations visited on people like my parents, but you had to consider that where they came from their humiliations and indignities at the hands of the colonial power were if anything worse. So they weren't surprised by much of what they encountered in Britain. What they did expect was something better for their children.

The experiences of these Caribbean immigrants to Britain in the 1950s did much to shape their lives – and their children's lives – for at least the next 30 years. The Jamaicans living in Lambeth and Brixton, the Trinidadians and Guianese who settled in Notting Hill, the Dominicans who stayed together in Paddington, and the Vincentians who bought homes in High Wycombe, not to mention those West Indians in Bristol, Leicester and Birmingham: many of them had expected to be in Britain for just a few years. For better or worse, most of them soon realised that they would not be going home. Their future was in a small country which was cold and where it often rained. They soon knew that most of the English people they met wouldn't like them. They had taken a calculated risk.

*　*　*

There were disturbances in Nottingham and the North Kensington area of London in the summer of 1958. These were quickly described as 'race riots' but were as much to do with poverty, inept policing and working-class exclusion as the frustrations felt by poor whites living alongside recently arrived blacks. Trevor Phillips believes the events, though violent and frightening, were not unexpected. In the book *Windrush: The Irresistible Rise of Multi-Racial Britain*, which he wrote with his brother Mike Phillips, North Kensington is described as an area with

transient single men packed into a honeycomb of rooms with communal kitchens, toilets and no bathrooms. It had depressed English families who had lived through the war years then watched the rush to the suburbs pass them by while they were trapped in low income jobs and rotten housing. It had a raft of dodgy pubs and poor street lighting. It had gang fighting, illegal drinking clubs, gambling and prostitution. It had a large proportion of frightened and resentful residents.

In riots over several weekends, petrol bombs were thrown from rooftops, black men were chased and beaten (as were a good number of white youths who came from other parts of London to take part in or watch the disorder), but no one was killed. It was not until nine months later, in May 1959, that there was a racist murder in Notting Hill. Kelso Cochrane was a 32-year-old carpenter from Antigua who had broken his thumb at work. Late on a Saturday evening he was returning to his girlfriend's flat off the Golborne Road, having visited Paddington General Hospital, when six men attacked him. One of them stabbed him to death.

More than 1,200 people walked up Ladbroke Grove from his funeral service to his burial in Kensal Green Cemetery. Politicians took an interest in the murder and the circumstances surrounding it. The housing minister toured the area to see how the slum clearances were going. The Duke of Edinburgh visited nearby youth clubs. The murderer was never found. Kelso Cochrane was buried on 6 June 1959. Nine years earlier to the day Alf Valentine had been bowling out Lancashire before the first Test at Old Trafford. The decade which had begun for West Indians in Britain with the novel joy of Sonny Ramadhin sprinting from the Lord's outfield with his pyjamas beneath his cricket flannels was ending far more darkly.

*   *   *

Until the late 1960s or early 1970s it was easy enough for white people, even in Britain's cities, to be largely unaware of the presence of black people unless they were living next door. But this changed when the immigrants had children who went to school. Black families were now visible in the playground and at the school gate in a way that they never had been before.

'This was phase one,' says Trevor Phillips.

Fast-forward a few more years and then those children are in their mid-teens and are visible on the city street. Some of them hanging about, cheeking people. A few may be stealing and getting into rucks with the police. Of course black families had the same concerns as most other people – how to get a job, where to live – but what was unique was this whole generation of children coming past puberty, confronting the world and being confrontational themselves.

As Andy Roberts and Vivian Richards sat on a London bus heading for batting and bowling lessons in the winter of 1972, they were travelling through a city where relations between immigrants and the authorities were bad and getting worse. The previous year the police had been given greater powers to arrest suspected illegal immigrants. Black welfare organisations in London were getting more complaints about encounters with the police, particularly with small groups within the Metropolitan force – the Special Patrol Group and the Immigration Intelligence Unit – which they accused of racism and violence. When the home secretary proposed altering the Police Code to contain a sentence that would make it an offence to discriminate against black immigrants, the officers' union replied that it was a 'gross insult even to suggest it'.

Black immigration was now widely perceived as a problem, while a small number of MPs such as the Conservative Duncan Sandys believed it their duty to express their fears about topics such as inter-racial marriage. 'The breeding of millions of half-caste children would merely produce a generation of misfits and create increased tensions,' he said. Nearly 200 years after the complaints of Philip Thicknesse, some were still afraid that in every English village there would been seen a little race of mullatoes.

The government was sufficiently concerned by the poor relations between the police and black people to appoint a select committee of MPs to consider the issue. In 1972 it concluded that while there was some racial prejudice within the force, most of the issues were caused by cultural misunderstandings. Young West Indians in particular were a problem, their behaviour often intended to make police officers 'lose their cool'.

The stereotype that black youngsters were more likely to break the law than white teenagers was complemented by another – that they were less intelligent. Educational theories about black capability went back many years. In 1947 an anthropology student from Cambridge was dispatched on a field trip to Cardiff with calipers and a tape measure to record the size of black children's heads. By the late 1960s many black parents were certain their children were being discriminated against at school. In west London and the West Midlands immigrant pupils were bussed to overflow schools because white parents had complained that there were too many in each class. The initiative had the blessing of the minister of education.

More seriously, a disproportionately high number of immigrant children were being sent to 'educationally subnormal' schools. Black parents knew this was happening, but there were no official figures to confirm it. Then in 1970 a PhD student called Bernard Coard who taught at one of these schools was handed a leaked Inner London Education Authority document that comprehensively confirmed their fears. In at least six London boroughs, while the immigrant school-age population was about 17 per cent, the figure for black children at ESN schools was twice that. Three quarters of immigrants at ESN schools were West Indian. In such an environment the pupils had little hope and no role models.

They expected to be failures, and their teachers expected them to be failures. Once in this type of school, it was almost impossible to return to a better one. 'It was a racist scandal,' wrote Bernard Coard. 'The system was using these schools as a convenient dumping ground for black children who were anything but educationally subnormal.'

These issues – education, housing, rough policing, discrimination at work – may have been an irrelevance for some in the crowds who came to support the West Indies at Test matches in Leeds, Manchester, London or Birmingham in 1969, 1973 or 1976, but for many others applauding Sobers, Kanhai or Lloyd they most certainly were not. In 1974 Horace Ové directed the first black British feature film. *Pressure* was shot in Ladbroke Grove in west London and examined the tensions of growing up in urban Britain. The central character was Tony, a school leaver born in England yet unable to convince himself that he is either English or part of an oppressed black minority. After being picked up by the police he has a furious row with his ashamed mother.

'Ma, you don't have to do anything to be arrested by the police when you're black.'

'Anthony, me and your father live in this country for years. And we never had anything with the police. Never! We work hard and we mind we own business. All we must respect the white people's laws. They know best. They own the place. They is the lord and masters. We have to work hard and hope they leave we alone. Oh God! Why is the Lord punishing me?'

'To hell with the bleeding respect! Where has that got us?' [He tears the wig from his mother's head.] 'Look! This is what they do to us. They make us feel inferior. Look how you have to cover up your own hair with this piece of shit just to be like them.'

'I wasn't being picked up every week by the cops,' reflects Trevor Phillips, 'but for people like me there was this constant sensation, the everyday experience of being black – the regular, grating humiliations you suffered – and certainly much of what happened took place at our schools and on the street.'

'I went to a grammar school and didn't have much contact with the police but I was still confused,' adds Trevor Nelson. 'I was English, but black. In Hackney there were lots of us – as well as Turks, Cypriots, Irish people – but I never saw anybody like me on the telly. I didn't really know what the West Indies stood for. Nothing to hang my hat on.'

On 24 May 1976, as Michael Holding and Andy Roberts were bowling out MCC at Lord's, the MP Enoch Powell was on his feet four miles away in the House of Commons. He wanted a halt to immigration. Assaults on the police happened every day, he claimed. 'There are cities and areas in this country where in daylight, let alone after dark, ordinary citizens are unwilling and afraid to go,' he told the chamber. The people who lived in these places had seen their environment 'transformed beyond all recognition, from their own homes and their own country to places where it is a terror to be obliged to live'. Mr Powell predicted that tomorrow or next year or in five years there would be terrible violence. 'Nothing can prevent the injection of explosives and firearms with the escalating and self-augmenting consequences which we know perfectly well from experience in other parts of the United Kingdom and the world.' Compared to these areas, he concluded, Belfast in Northern Ireland would seem an enviable place.

The author Colin Babb grew up in south London in the 1970s. 'I didn't feel British at all,' he says.

I wasn't comfortable with my Britishness until I was much older. At home in Streatham I was West Indian. I ate Caribbean food; I listened to Caribbean music. Everything was geared to 'back home', and it was constantly talked about. I had an English friend called Nick. At his house for tea we had toad-in-the-hole. When I told my family, no one knew what it was that I'd eaten, and they'd been in Britain for ten years. My family thought that English people were strange. 'English people do that' or 'That's an English thing' were phrases I'd hear. They drank too much – too much alcohol and too much tea – and they couldn't dance. When *Top of the Pops* was on the TV, my mother would say, 'The rhythm is over here and the English people are dancing over there.' But more than anything else, we wanted to beat them at anything we could.

Cricket offered that opportunity. 'People don't realise it was very strange for us being brought up in a blanket-white world,' says Trevor Nelson, 'despite your immediate environment being full of black and Asian kids. That's why cricket was such a big deal to people like my dad. I remember him talking about Sobers, Worrell, Valentine, Everton Weekes. We had *Wisden* in the house. So I knew that history in cricket was very important. The history of the game seemed as significant as what was going on at the time.'

In 1976 Clive Lloyd's side was what was going on. They were being watched by a new crowd. Every time the West Indies had come to England since 1950, more and more West Indians had come out to see them play. But that summer was the first time that large numbers of second-generation fans – British West Indians – had been able to connect the success of the team with what was happening in their own lives. This point wasn't lost on Trevor Phillips.

This was different. These guys were taking to the field, and not only were they in charge, they behaved as though they had the right to be in charge. On the cricket pitch they were anybody's equal, and I suppose for young people it was quite simple: these guys didn't take any shit from anybody. And I think there would have been a perception – an unfair one by the way – that our parents had taken shit for all their lives, and suddenly along come these athletes who just couldn't imagine that anybody would treat them in an inferior way. For me there was a sense that if you disrespected Holding or Roberts or looked at them in the wrong way, they could take your head off, and that was exhilarating for a young person.

*   *   *

On the Saturday of the first Test at Trent Bridge in 1976 those spectators who had brought a copy of *The Times* with them to the ground may have glanced at the letters page while Bernard Julien was bowling to David Steele or Bob Woolmer was facing Wayne Daniel. One correspondent warned that London was going the same way as New York, which was now a 'ruined city'. The principle cause was West Indians, who had 'an appalling reputation for mugging, illiteracy, juvenile delinquency, trafficking in drugs and vice, etc'. The solution in London – because 'ordinary marriage and the typical nuclear family' were largely unknown among the immigrants – was to 'repatriate as many of these unmarried or unsupported West Indian mothers with their children as soon as possible, with the lubricating help of generous grants'.

'I know that our spectators in England struggled more than those anywhere else in the world,' says Andy Roberts. 'They said to us, "You don't know how we feel when we lose and have to go back to the assembly lines and the factories. When we win, we can go back and hold up our heads high." Some of my best bowling was against England.'

4

'My tradition is all cricket, no pay'

Shortly after the West Indies arrived in Australia in October 1975 two reports appeared side by side on the sports pages of the *Sydney Morning Herald*. Unintentionally they exemplified the wretched financial arrangements of modern international cricket. The first story announced that there would be a rematch of the World Cup final, to be played in Adelaide five days before Christmas. The original game at Lord's had been one of the most exciting days of limited-overs international cricket, played by the world's two best teams and watched by millions on television.

'Picturesque Adelaide Oval is certain to be packed for the one-day fixture which will be sponsored by Benson and Hedges and Gillette,' predicted the *Herald*. The winning team would receive 1,800 Australian dollars, or about $150 per man.

In the next column was a short story about a new men's tennis tournament to be held in Hawaii in 1976, sponsored by the Avis car rental company. The players would be competing for a prize of $249,600. Arthur Ashe would get to the final of that competition. A year later the American was a guest at the centenary Test match between Australia and England in Melbourne. Looking around at the crowd of more than 60,000 he said to one of the Australian players, 'You'll be enjoying the gate money from this.'

'No, mate,' was the reply. 'We're all getting 200 bucks each.'

'Athletes from other sports were being paid properly, and cricketers were playing for the love of it,' says Clive Lloyd. 'We played 24 Tests in my first two and a half seasons as captain. We were playing attractive cricket. People would come to see us, and not only were all the seats sold out, but they'd run out of food too. So someone was making a few quid. It just wasn't us. Don't call me a legend, an icon, a superstar, then pay me nothing.'

* * *

A year before the centenary Test nobody who played cricket knew Kerry Packer or was aware that he had recently taken over his father's publishing business. Even Packer himself hadn't expected that. He was the second son of a millionaire, and until the early 1970s had merely had responsibility for some of his father's magazines. The boy whose childhood nickname had been Boofhead because of his apparent dim-wittedness wasn't supposed to inherit the company. That only happened because his elder brother fell out with their father.

Frank Packer was a better businessman than he was a parent. Kerry had been sent to boarding school when he was five, even though it was only half a mile from the family mansion. 'He used the polo whip very well,' Kerry Packer once revealed in a television interview, 'but I never got a belting from him I didn't deserve.'

'Kerry had a sort of Stockholm Syndrome relationship with Frank,' one of his friends would later remark.

When Frank Packer died in 1974 and Kerry took over Australian Consolidated Press, he was determined to show investors – and probably his dead father – that he could make the business into a bigger, richer company. He was looking for opportunities.

Packer liked most sports and he liked television; the company owned a couple of TV stations. Packer thought sport and television suited each other and could make him money. Cricket had particular potential. It had never been more popular in Australia, and a day's play was long enough for a rewarding number of commercial breaks.

However, Packer's plan to show lots of cricket in order to make lots of money was thwarted by the men who controlled the first-class game. The Australian Cricket Board had a long-standing arrangement with the national public broadcaster, the ABC. Packer offered the board much more money for the contract. In June 1976, at a converted carpet showroom in Melbourne which was the headquarters of the Victorian Cricket Association, he famously propositioned the ACB chairman and treasurer: 'Come on, gentlemen; we're all whores. What's your price?'

The board didn't recognise itself in Packer's collective description. There would be no deal. But within a year the consequences of this meeting would have a permanent effect on international cricket, particularly for the West Indies. Packer decided that if he couldn't buy the cricket, he would buy the cricketers instead and broadcast the matches on his TV channels. His plan was extraordinarily bold, if inchoate. He didn't yet know who would play in those matches or where they would take place. To succeed he would need the world's best cricketers. Fortunately for Packer, they would not need much persuading.

'I was playing for Middlesex – the money was nothing really,' remembers Wayne Daniel. 'I toured with the West Indies – the money was nothing. In '76 we were playing to packed houses but we weren't getting anything for it. Then when we saw what Packer was offering, we said, "You can really be paid this to play cricket?" We knew we could not pass this up. We knew it would not happen again in our lifetime.'

'We were a winning team, and when we looked at our pay and what other people were getting, we were at the bottom of the heap,'

'It sounded like a bloody gun going off.'

Ian Chappell considers walking after edging the ball to Deryck Murray – but thinks better of it. This moment in the Sydney Test in 1976 changed the way the West Indies would play their cricket forever.

'If this was Test cricket, you could forget it.'

Michael Holding completing his over through his tears at Sydney.

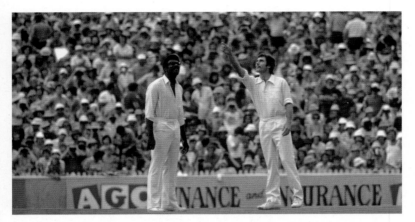

Clive Lloyd tossing up with Greg Chappell before the Sydney Test at the start of 1976. 'Australia had just been rescued by its captain,' wrote the cricket reporter John Woodcock at the time, 'the West Indies not led by its.'

Some of the MCG spectators celebrate an Australian boundary during the third Test. 'In the crowd there was a different tempo when it came to this race stuff. There were a few rotten apples in the sack,' remembers Vivian Richards.

'The gloom, the heavy silences... guys weren't speaking to one another. The blame game was on.'

Another defeat in Australia – this time at Melbourne at the end of the third Test.

'He should have been watching the game from the bar, enjoying a drink. These men were past it.'

John Edrich (39) looks on as Brian Close (45) avoids a short ball on that Saturday evening at Old Trafford in 1976. Neither would play for England again.

A shirtless Roy Fredericks had forearms like 10-pound trout, observed *The Times* – 'and wild ones at that'.

Here he shares a moment of joy in the Headingley dressing room with Vivian Richards after the fourth Test of 1976. The series was won.

Vivian Richards drives square off the back foot at the Oval in 1976, adding more runs to his record total of 1,710 for the year. Alan Knott is the wicket-keeper.

The Test and County Cricket Board had asked Clive Lloyd to appeal to supporters before the match to make less noise. He did, they didn't.

Michael Holding turning England to dust at the Oval in 1976. He took 14 wickets.

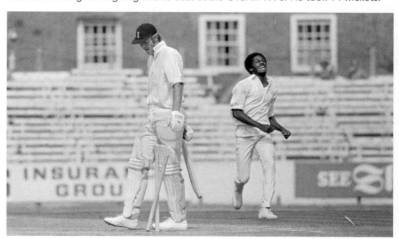

Tony Greig has his stumps knocked over for the fifth and final time against the West Indies in 1976. Who's grovelling now?

Greig's wicket at the Oval is a delight for the players – and a spectator.

From Bequia to Buxton. Charles Ollivierre in the Derbyshire XI at the turn of the 20th century.

Charles Ollivierre batting in the nets for Derbyshire during the 1905 season. He was the Neil Armstrong of Caribbean cricket, but his achievements have never been widely acclaimed.

'Cricket is the most obvious and apparent, some would say glaring, example of the black man being kept in his place,' said Learie Constantine.

Learie Constantine was a brilliant West Indian all-rounder, highly-paid league cricketer, politician and diplomat.

The Times reported a rush of people, 'one armed with an instrument of the guitar family singing with a delight that rightfully belonged to them.' Lord Kitchener and his backing band on the Lord's outfield in 1950.

'The nature of his spin has not been exactly specified… we must wait and learn.'

Sonny Ramadhin, aged 20 in England in 1950.

The body of Kelso Cochrane is driven up Ladbroke Grove in June 1959. More than 1,000 people were at the funeral service but his murderer was never found.

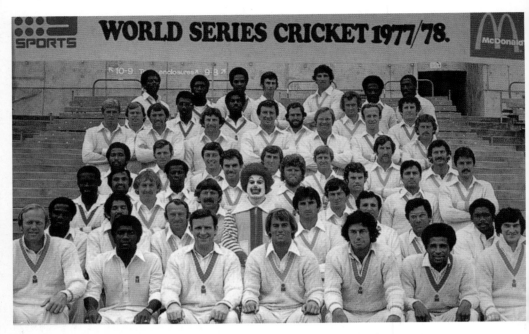

WORLD SERIES CRICKET 1977/78.

'We were crossing from one world to the next,' recalls Clive Lloyd. He wasn't wrong. World Series Cricket in 1977. R. McDonald, centre, second row.

'It was a colour that is, should we say, less than manly in the Caribbean parts.' Wayne Daniel does his best to look butch in Packer Pink during the second season of World Series Cricket in 1979.

says Deryck Murray. 'I'll give you an example. When we were in England in 1973 it was a short tour, just three Tests. At the end of the first one the English authorities announced that they had covered all their expenses, including the entire West Indies' fee! And we were saying. "Hang on! Who negotiated this? Why has our own board sold us so short?" Even our own board members didn't respect us.'

Packer did respect the players – up to a point. If they were prepared to turn their backs on traditional cricket, he would pay them more than they thought they could ever earn from the game and he would stick up for them in the almighty row that would surely follow. Many Australian cricketers were ready to rebel. They were no longer motivated just by the honour of playing for their country, as the authorities thought they ought to be. Ian Chappell – even though he was no longer captain – met Packer, was sworn to secrecy and was told to raise an Australia side for a competition that would be known as World Series Cricket (WSC).

Tony Greig was also recruited. It would cost him the captaincy of England, but he would lead a World XI to play the Australians. He needed the best West Indians in his side. In April 1977 he flew with a WSC lawyer to Trinidad, where the West Indies were playing Pakistan in a Test series. Also on the plane was Austin Robertson, a director of WSC and one of Kerry Packer's most senior officers. He had been a brilliant Australian Rules footballer in the late 1960s before getting involved in journalism, marketing and promotion. Over several years he spent days next to Packer, planning and executing this extraordinary cricket project. He has never spoken in detail about his experiences before now.

The first thing people ask me about Kerry is, 'Was he frightening?' Well yes, he could be – he did shout, but he was a very funny man too. And he could be thoughtful. There were many times when we sat in his office in companionable silence. He would take hours deliberating over what would go in the hamper that each member of staff received at Christmas. 'Should we have the Scottish short-bread or the spiced hazelnuts?' he'd ask. 'Aw, put 'em both in.' He'd anguish about what would go in the hamper, then he'd go downstairs the next afternoon and sack three people.

Robertson had already been on the phone to Clive Lloyd from London, and he came to Trinidad hoping to finalise a deal.

'I'd told him we wanted to sign him, Viv, Michael and Andy. I also wanted to sign four Pakistanis while I was there. So we met. Michael wasn't there because he was injured in Jamaica. We talked it through and they had a few questions but were fairly quiet. At the finish Tony Greig said, 'What do you think?' Clive nodded, Vivi just laughed and said yes and then Andy said, 'I am saying yes, but I am not saying finally yes until tomorrow.' Clive asked him what the hell he meant, and Andy just repeated the sentence. Anyway, Clive and Viv signed that night. And at nine o'clock the next morning there was a knock on my hotel room door. It was Andy. He signed his contract with hardly a word.'

The offer made to the West Indies captain in the Hilton Hotel in Port-of-Spain left him staggered. Lloyd accepted around AUS $90,000 plus expenses for a three-season contract. This was three times as much *per year* as he had got from the West Indies Cricket Board of Control in England in 1976. It was the sort of money that could give a man financial security for life. Robertson paid him a third before he left Trinidad.

These West Indian cricketers were temperamentally suited to

such an experiment. (In fact the code name among the West Indian recruits for the Packer tournament was The Experiment.) For seven decades cricketers from the Caribbean had been used to leaving the region to earn money. Would Charles Ollivierre have signed for a Victorian Packer? Almost certainly. Lloyd, Richards and Roberts were from the same tradition. There was a long-established willingness within West Indies cricket to make money from the game off the usual paths. Lloyd had always told his team that they would only improve their salaries if they won Test matches, and part of his job as captain had been to negotiate pay and bonuses for his players with the WICBC before every series.

But deciding to play for Packer could well mean never playing for the West Indies Test team again. Money aside, the decision imperilled a goal that these West Indians had striven for since they were boys. Colonial black and Indo-Caribbean teenagers knew that being a cricketer and hearing their names on the radio improved a man's life in a land where skin colour permanently limited prospects.

'It was all about playing for the country,' says Lloyd. 'Being a household name, being somebody. In the 1950s and 1960s in the Caribbean, cricket brought you social status. The guys who walked through the gates at Bourda in their maroon blazers on the morning of a Test match were elite people – that was the perception. You were no longer some little kid from Guiana, but a man whom people from different colours and classes held in awe.'

One of the first phone calls that Lloyd made after he signed was to Michael Holding's parents. Their son was living at home, having won a government scholarship to study computer science at the University of the West Indies in Jamaica. He didn't expect to be playing cricket for much longer. His shoulder injury wasn't going away, and despite the success in England in 1976 he disliked touring. Sussex had offered him £10,000, a car and a house to play for them in 1977, but he wasn't interested. He was mindful of his mother's insistence that he had to have letters after his name, some sort of diploma 'because you have got to earn a living later on'.

Clive called from Trinidad and he said, 'Mikey, there are a couple of gentlemen coming to see you. They want to talk about some cricket that is going to be played in Australia by a private enterprise.' I said, 'Exactly what do you mean by that?' 'They will explain everything,' he replied. I said, 'Who are they?' When he told me that one of them was Tony Greig, I said, 'Tony Greig?!' I still remembered what had happened with him in England. 'Why should I be wanting to talk to Tony Greig?' Clive said, 'No, just listen to what they have to say.'

In Sydney Kerry Packer was impatiently wondering how his Caribbean shopping spree was going. In Trinidad Austin Robertson was in bed.

The phone went at three in the morning. I picked it up and the voice said, 'Packer.' That was his way of saying hello. 'Oh yes. Hello, Mr Packer.' 'Have you signed them yet?' was his next sentence. 'Well, we've got everyone except Michael Holding . . . ' 'Why haven't you got him?' 'He's in Jamaica, Mr Packer, but we're heading there first thing in the morning. I'm sure it'll all be right.' 'Call me when you've got him.' And he hung up. He was a man on a mission.

At the Sheraton hotel in New Kingston, Robertson and Greig got out the contract. The England captain also pulled out of his briefcase a brochure which had been designed to convince clients of Packer's bona fides. Greig was anxious for Holding to read it. Laughingly, the young bowler pushed it aside. 'If Clive says it's OK, it's OK,' he said.

They showed Holding the contract. Twenty-five thousand Australian dollars a year for three years – about US $27,600. Holding was used to earning US $200 per Test match. It was 'an incredible package'. But there was a problem. Packer's competition planned to bring together players from throughout the cricket world, including from South Africa. The first plans for WSC included the possibility of playing matches in the apartheid republic. For many black West Indians entering racist South Africa was inconceivable, and even those for whom it wasn't knew their lives would be made very tough once they returned to the Caribbean. Holding was concerned that five white South African cricketers had also been offered WSC contracts.

Three of them – Mike Procter, Eddie Barlow and Barry Richards – played county cricket in England and had regular contact with black players from the Caribbean; Richards opened the batting for Hampshire with Gordon Greenidge. Governments in the West Indies, as well as the WICBC, had reluctantly come to terms with this situation. To prevent black players from playing English county cricket was to stop them from earning salaries that could never be matched at home. However, two more South Africans – Graeme Pollock and Denys Hobson – were also wanted by Packer, and they lived and played in South Africa. By the simple logic of this crick-eting arrangement, they represented the regime.

Holding told Greig and Robertson that he would sign his Packer contract only if the prime minister of Jamaica, Michael Manley, gave him permission. Packer needed the West Indians but he also wanted the South Africans, particularly Pollock, who had proved before South Africa were isolated from international cricket at the beginning of the decade that he was one of the game's best batsmen. So in August 1977 Packer and Clive Lloyd flew to Jamaica to meet the prime minister.

Manley the socialist liked Packer the capitalist. At their meeting in Jamaica House he judged him to be an 'amiable pirate', a risk-taker who was shrewd enough to withdraw before risk-taking became recklessness. Their discussions were frank and humorous, but Manley made it clear that he held the anti-apartheid struggle to be a 'sacred responsibility'. By the end of the meeting Packer had agreed that players would not be brought into the World XI directly from South Africa. He had yielded. It was an unusual sensation for Packer, so back in Australia he thought he would have another go.

He made a long-distance call to Kingston for a further discussion with Manley. He got put through to the prime minister's special adviser. Look, said Packer, Graeme Pollock is no supporter of apartheid – he once walked off the ground with Procter and Barry Richards during a protest against black players being excluded from the South Africa side. The reply from Jamaica was that this was not about one man's decency; it was about using any opportunity to exert pressure on the South African government. The answer was still no.

Graeme Pollock had signed a three-year WSC contract. Kerry Packer paid him a full year's salary and bought him a plane ticket back to South Africa from Australia. He didn't play a single game.

The way was clear for West Indians to be Packer players, and Michael Holding's prospects were about to change. When he checked at his bank that the WSC advance had arrived, it was the first time he had seen a comma in his account book. No wonder cricketers signed for Packer. As Clive Lloyd says, 'We were crossing from one world into the next.' Pay for Test cricketers had risen noticeably throughout the decade, but had started from a such a low base that it was still comparatively poor. Graham Marsh, a professional golfer and the brother of Rodney Marsh, earned more than the entire Australia Test side put together. Vivian Richards recalls county players paying more attention to their petrol expenses than their batting averages. John Snow, the England fast bowler who would also sign for WSC, put it like this: 'If I'd have been outside Lord's on St John's Wood Road emptying the dustbins instead of inside playing cricket, I would have been earning more money in the course of the week and been finished at midday.'

'They were being paid fish-and-chip money,' says Austin Robertson.

Michael Holding has few pleasant memories of life on tour as an international cricketer before WSC.

We were staying in hotels in the Caribbean and in England that would be considered one star, or one and a half stars. You didn't even have a TV set in your room. If you wanted to watch TV you would have to sit in the lobby to watch the communal television. Some of the hotels where we stayed, you went into your room, you and your room-mate, and you had your cricket bag and your suit-case. When you put them on the floor there was no room to walk. You had to be stepping over everything. You'd be dying to get to the ground just so you could leave your cricket bag there.

The West Indies were stronger than they had been for a decade and wanted recognition for it. The 1976-77 series against Pakistan would be won with two new young fast bowlers called Colin Croft and Joel Garner taking 58 wickets between them. As their captain points out, 'we played some damn good cricket far from home and, to be honest, stayed in some pretty crappy places.' They were first-class sportsmen travelling in economy. Some of them couldn't get their legs into the space behind the aircraft seats. It was the old way.

*   *   *

By the early weeks of May 1977, the plans for World Series Cricket had been made public. In England, after the touring Australian Test side had been at his house for a barbecue, Tony Greig told the press, 'There is a massive cricket project involving most of the world's top players due to commence in Australia this winter. I am part of it along with a number of English players. Full details and implications of the scheme will be officially announced in Australia later this week.'

The extent of Packer's ambition left the cricket establishment aghast. Thirty-five cricketers had signed deals to play each other in a series of five-day 'Super Tests' and one-day games. The winners of the competition would share AUS $100,000 in addition to their salaries. The scheme was immediately condemned by the authorities and some newspapers: it was a 'circus' and those who had got involved were 'pirates'. In the weeks that followed there were talks between the International Cricket Conference and Packer. These came to nothing. The high priest of establishment cricket journalism, E. W. Swanton, wrote in *The Cricketer* of the game's 'sinister upheaval'. He said that the ICC – which administered the world game – had responded reasonably to try 'to legitimise the bastard child' of Kerry Packer 'despite the sordid circumstances of its conception'.

Speaking outside Lord's after one failed meeting in June 1977, Packer told reporters that his tournament was expanding. He had signed up 16 players from the West Indies, which meant WSC would now have three teams: an Australia XI, a World XI and a West Indian side. 'I will now take no steps at all to help anyone. It's every man for himself and the devil take the hindmost.'

The cricket boards of control in England and Australia were outraged by Packer's plan. They had been humiliated by its secrecy, outflanked by its ambition and were ill prepared for its arrival. They felt betrayed by the defection of so many cricketers. Public opinion in the two countries broadly matched the boards' emotions.

It was different in the West Indies. There was no great feeling that their players had been disloyal by signing for Packer. Those from the lower classes who did well for themselves usually got a slap on the back, not one in the face. 'Indeed,' wrote Michael Manley, 'empathy between player and public was automatic, fashioned in the crucible of the common historical forces.' The WICBC knew it could not confront its rebel players in the way that the England and Australia boards had confronted theirs, by trying to ban them from playing 'official' cricket. It realised quickly that the West Indians involved had the support of the people. The board had little choice but to recognise – for the time being at least – that its Test team would also be a Packer team.

'The board didn't like it at all. Not at all,' says Wayne Daniel. 'I've no doubt their true feeling was that we were traitors who had abandoned West Indies cricket and we were going to be cut loose. But the West Indian public wanted to see the best men play for the West Indies. It was very much driven by the public, and that made it very difficult for the board to strong-arm us. We were the West Indies' team.'

The board was further weakened because it had little money. The distances between Caribbean territories and the small cricket grounds meant that the board couldn't make cash from touring teams. There was no full-time professional cricket played in the region and little meaningful sponsorship. Knowing all this, in the privacy of their meeting room the WICBC had disagreed with the ICC's decision to exile Packer players from Test cricket. Yet publicly it voted to support the ICC.

In November 1977, Packer supported the High Court challenge to an ICC ruling that three of his cricketers be banned from playing

Test matches. The judge in London agreed with the cricketers that they had been subject to an unreasonable restraint of trade. The decision was received joyfully in the Caribbean. Crowds in the Antiguan capital, St John's, celebrated because their two local heroes, Roberts and Richards, would be allowed to continue to play for the West Indies. The *Daily Gleaner* in Jamaica said the ruling was a triumph for human rights. 'The International Cricket Conference had sought to impose limitations on how professional cricketers should earn a living, a right as basic to the everyday tradesman as to the sportsman who plays for pay.'

When the £200,000 legal bill for the High Court failure came through, the ICC decided it was to be shared equally by all members, despite the clear position of the West Indies board. The WICBC president, Jeffrey Stollmeyer, thought it a 'morally indefensible' decision. In order to avoid bankruptcy, the board was forced to ask for donations. The WICBC may have been weak but it had no ideological empathy for its own players. Historically it came from a different place. As in almost every other area of colonial life, West Indies cricket administration was closely linked to the elite white culture of the plantations. The board had existed since 1927 but there would not be a black president of the organisation until the 1980s.

In 1977 the captain and the president were not close, and they never would be. 'Jeffrey and I never really clicked,' says Lloyd.

We had something in common, of course, because we both captained the West Indies. But there was little else. We were from different eras. I remember, later in my career, I had led the side for a long time and we were in Trinidad, and a friend of mine said to me, 'Are you coming to Jeff's for dinner tonight?' And I said, 'A dinner at Jeffrey's? I hadn't heard there was one. I've been skipper for seven years now and he hasn't ever invited me in for a bite; I don't expect he's going to start now.' It was as if it was still the days of the elite. Now, I'm not saying there was a colour issue going on between us, but let's say we never quite gelled.

*   *   *

Seven months after the secrecy, revelations, bitterness and court cases came the cricket. The first Super Test began on 2 December 1977. Clive Lloyd tossed up with Ian Chappell in the middle of a stadium that had seats for 80,000 spectators. Fewer than 500 had people sitting on them. 'Scattered round like confetti in a graveyard' was how John Thicknesse of the *Evening Standard* described those watching.

The Australian Cricket Board had made certain that Packer's players were not allowed inside the main cricket grounds so the venue was VFL Park, an Australian Rules football field half an hour outside Melbourne on the Mulgrave Freeway. The wicket for the match had been grown in a greenhouse on two huge concrete trays before being moved to the ground to be left to settle while an armed guard patrolled nearby. After plans to manoeuvre the trays by hovercraft failed, they were carefully taken into the middle of the pitch on trailers and lowered by crane. The curator was John Maley, the man who had succeeded the impulsive and unpredictable Clem Jones in Brisbane. He was young and clever and had managed to make good wickets at the Gabba without resorting to mud and grass clippings.

'Look mate,' explains Austin Robertson,

if you don't have a pitch, you can't play. Without John Maley's foresight, WSC wouldn't have happened. He had a staff of four plus himself to create wickets in four stadiums. At the showground in Sydney he started from scratch and made a Super Test wicket in less than four months. All sorts of new ideas – chicken wire in the soil to hold it together, a tent with lights in to kid the grass that the sun was shining at night. Richie Benaud said it was one of the best cricket pitches he had ever seen – true, lightning fast, wonderful. Maley was a magician.

A thousand miles away from Melbourne in Brisbane, the 'real' Australia Test side was beginning a series against India in front of a larger crowd of 9,000. Clumsily, a Packer press officer would claim that WSC was more entertaining because the boundary count was higher in Melbourne. The propaganda continued in the *Sun-Herald* on the Sunday of the first match with a full-page advert. It promised, 'Australian lawns won't be cut today' because Packer's 'top pro' cricket on Channel 9 would 'separate the men from the boys'.

When the Test and the Super Test ended (both were exciting games of cricket) there was only one winner when it came to numbers. More than 30,000 tickets had been sold to watch the loyalists; only about 13,000 were bought for the Packer game. A WSC executive tells a story from the time of standing next to Kerry Packer on the street outside the ground, saying, '"Look, this car's coming in." But it would drive by.' The numbers of spectators were an embarrassment to WSC, but for the viewer who tuned in at home it was a new television experience. There were eight not four cameras at the ground, and for the first time play was filmed from both ends of the ground, which ended the frustration of watching alternate overs from behind the batsman. Zoom lenses brought close-ups of the cricketers' faces while they played.

'Before Kerry Packer, there was no way of seeing someone really grimacing when they got hit – no way of seeing the strain on a fast bowler's face when he was running in,' says Michael Holding. 'Packer made people at home recognise exactly what was taking place on a cricket field. You couldn't hear when the ball hit the bat in years gone by. With stump microphones you heard the impact. The ball hits someone's body and now you could hear a slight thud. You heard everything. If someone said something, you heard it. So it was a completely different world. It was no longer a distant thing. All the nuances were brought into your living room.'

Very few large crowds went to see World Series Cricket in its first season of 1977–78. The one-day games were more popular than the Super Tests, and the innovation of playing at night under floodlights was a success. A white ball was used and there were black sightscreens. Players, spectators and commentators all agreed that it was easier to see a white ball at night than a red ball during the day. The only difficulty was for the umpires. Giving LBW decisions when a white ball hit a white pad tested their judgement. It may be that the crick-eters would have to wear a different colour. Yet among all the uncertainties of WSC's first year, the players knew one thing for sure. This was the highest standard of cricket they had played.

'Each day we were against the best,' says Andy Roberts. 'Every team had genuine fast bowlers, world-class fast bowlers, every team. And every morning you wake you know that your cricket is going to be harder than the day before.'

Wayne Daniel had never played tougher cricket.

Oh yeah, it was hard. So competitive. The opposition were hard and mean. There was no friendship on the pitch. The verbals – especially from the Australians – would just fly. But we had been given these contracts and we had to perform. We had been given this money and we had to prove that we were good enough to earn it. Out there it was a fight – no sense at all that this was just a game of cricket. And to handle it you had to be in the elite bracket.

'The competition between them was pretty bloody fierce,' says Austin Robertson, 'but off the field it was like a travelling family, a big multicultural family. They got on well but, gee whizz, there was not much quarter given or asked for on the field. It was bloody serious.'

'Serious cricket,' echoes Michael Holding. 'Every match you played in WSC was a serious match. You never went to play against, say, a state team that had perhaps two outstanding cricketers and a lot of others making up the numbers. Whether you were playing in Toowoomba or Melbourne, you were playing against the best cricketers in the world.'

'You had Viv Richards facing Dennis Lillee. You had the Chappells facing Colin Croft, and David Hookes facing Andy Roberts. Zaheer Abbas facing maybe Wayne Daniel. It was gladiatorial. Gladiators fighting against each other. Not unlike ancient Rome,' suggests Colin Croft.

Not quite. Still, Croft was right that playing WSC – like entering the Colosseum – came with some personal risk. The world's fastest bowlers were letting the ball go on pitches that were not used to cricket. Some of the drop-in wickets were good, others were dead, and some were dangerously fast. The crowds had been told they would get drama and excitement, and that included the chance of injury. WSC had amended a convention of the game to allow bouncers to be bowled at anyone in the opposition, not just the most able batsmen, and for the first time players began to wear protective headgear.

The first batch looked like what they were – white motorcycle helmets with visors. Dennis Amiss, who was playing for the World XI, didn't mind; the company that made his said it could withstand a shotgun blast from ten yards. That was fine, but if anyone had fired a gun at Amiss's head he probably wouldn't have heard it go off. His hard hat completely covered his ears and he couldn't hear his batting partner calling to him. It was modified after a series of run-outs.

David Hookes didn't have a helmet. Against the West Indies in the second Super Test at Sydney in December 1977 the young Australian batted like he didn't need one. Wearing his bright-yellow Australia WSC felt cap, he smashed Joel Garner for 17 in one over followed by 22 off Michael Holding. Then he faced a spell from Andy Roberts.

Roberts was not a demonstrative man, and his silence could perturb those who didn't know him. He was most content listening to music on his boombox in his room: the Commodores, the Manhattans, Teddy Pendergrass. Only rarely would he come to the hotel bar. 'Me and Bernard Julien, Collis King, Albert Padmore, we would be down there or at a party, but not Andy or Mikey Holding,' says Wayne Daniel. 'Paddy and I might be out at the disco shaking it a bit, but the two bowlers roomed together and kept themselves together.'

Roberts needed little save his boombox and a cricket ball.

'I remember him bowling for the Combined Islands against Barbados – must have been '75 or so,' says Daniel,

and he was lightning. Bowling at the speed of light. And the only person who would take him on was Collis King. No one else would come out. They all had diarrhoea, twisted ankles, broken arms, hiding in the cupboard. It was fear, naked fear. He got six wickets or something, Andy came out of the ground that evening and people went berserk. There was utter adulation – crowds on this side, crowds on that side, and they were calling him, shouting out, 'Fruity! Fruity, man!' – that was his nickname – 'Fruity, you so quick, man. You so fast, Fruity.' They loved it. Well, Andy walked straight on – not a smile, didn't look right, didn't look left, still sweating, face solemn – straight on the bus. Not a word. That was Andy. He didn't need that connection with people. The only person he spoke to a lot was Holding.

If Roberts didn't give much away to friends, he certainly wouldn't pass the time of day with batsmen. Vivian Richards remembers the confrontation with Hookes. 'David got a bit cheeky and he was signalling these sixes himself, you know. He didn't leave that up to the umpire. We all knew Andy, and Andy did set him up.' One of Roberts's skills as a fast bowler was to bowl two bouncers in a row. The first would be slow, which he hoped the batsman would hook for four. The second, which the batsman thought would be more of the same, was a yard and a half quicker. 'Oh yeah, Andy was one of these guys who could set you up easily. He knew how to catch a fish,' says Richards. 'He gave Hookes the bait first time and bang! He took it. And the next one had the ingredients on it and just hit him.'

Roberts doesn't recall much about the ball that struck Hookes, but he does remember how he used to take on attacking batsmen.

I would make all my adjustments at the top of the run and not when I get to the crease. All the adjustments I need for that ball are calculated in my mind. If I'm going to bowl a bouncer then I watch for the movement of the batsman. If his first movement is forward I know I have to bowl the bouncer a little bit shorter than the length I would like to bowl. If he moves back then I have to bowl a little bit fuller than the length I would like to bowl.

Sometimes you watch the demeanour of a batsman. Any time I look in his eyes and he looks away then I know yes, I have him. Because the minute he can't look at you then you know there is something wrong. I don't have to sledge. My eyes and the ball do all the sledging for me. I never said a word to a batsman. I didn't have to. Basically, I never show any emotion.

Hookes moved back and across in his crease as he saw the second bouncer coming, but he was fooled by its speed. Even though he had scored 81 runs, he was nowhere near in position. The ball shattered his jaw. His yellow felt cap fell to the ground, and he had to be helped away. In *The Cricket War* by Gideon Haigh the author recounts how in the dressing room Hookes spat out blood mixed with tiny slivers of bone.

Kerry Packer drove him to hospital in his own car, and the batsman stayed there for two days. Five weeks later he was playing and made a pair of 50s on his return. His jaw had healed, but the recollection of the accident remained. As his career went on, Hookes had flashbacks about the ball that hit him. It didn't matter who was bowling – even slow bowlers brought back the memory. More often than not, after such an episode he would get out.

'We didn't want to see that,' recalls Richards, 'but at the time David was behaving in this cocky sort of fashion, Andy just got one in the right spot, and that was it. And that just changed the whole career for David Hookes – he was never the same player after that.'

The West Indies won the second Super Test easily, as they had the first. They had now taken AUS \$36,000 of Packer's prize money to the Australians' AUS \$3,900. 'We are much better now than in 1975–76,' said Clive Lloyd at a news conference. 'Our pace attack is much more penetrative.' Dennis Amiss's wife landed in Australia on the same day that Hookes spent his first night in hospital. She had four new helmets in her luggage. Two were sent straight to Sydney. WSC officials immediately ordered another half-dozen.

*   *   *

As the first season of World Series Cricket continued, the animosity between traditionalists and modernists deepened, and a stand-off between the West Indies board and the team became inevitable.

The pragmatism of the WICBC only went so far, while its traditions and ideology seemed more irrelevant with every day's play of a Packer match. A confrontation had been deferred largely because there had not yet been a calendar clash between WSC games and the official West Indies Test itinerary.

The tensions that had already fractured cricket in Australia and England came to the Caribbean when a weakened Australian Test side played in the West Indies in March 1978. The West Indies – with a team that had completed its first WSC season – won the first two of five matches. Clive Lloyd went into the selection meeting for the third Test in Guyana expecting it to last ten minutes or so. Instead it went on for six hours. By early the next morning Lloyd was no longer captain.

At the Pegasus Hotel in Georgetown two simmering arguments provided the context for what followed. First, the board had insisted that the WSC West Indians declare their availability for selection to tour India later that year, a series that would coincide with the second Packer season. Second, the board had been piqued by the decision of three young players – Colin Croft, Desmond Haynes and Richard Austin – to accept deals from Packer rather than offers put to them first by the WICBC.

Lloyd was handed a team sheet that didn't include Haynes, Austin or Deryck Murray. Murray was the players' shop steward and had been negotiating with the board over the team's welfare. Lloyd was furious.

They wanted to get rid of guys who had just helped us win a Test match. It made me mad that the selectors were bowing to pressure from the board. They were saying stupid things in that room like, 'Are you telling us we can never drop anyone now?' but these weren't cricketing decisions. It was simple malice. After the meeting I left the hotel and it was the early hours – two, three o'clock. I spoke on the phone to Joey Carew, who was one of the selectors, and I told him I was going to resign because I couldn't put my name to such a side. He said, 'Oh, you'll feel different in the morning,' and I said something like, 'Look at your watch, Joey – it is the morning.' And that was that.

So the Test side needed a new leader. Within hours the team also needed two new batsmen, three bowlers and a wicket-keeper. Gordon Greenidge and Vivian Richards said that they no longer wanted to be considered for the Test side, as did Andy Roberts, Joel Garner and Colin Croft.

By an apparently extraordinary coincidence, and despite a regional airline strike, half a dozen new West Indies players happened to be in Guyana and were selected for the third Test. The WICBC had prepared for this moment. The WSC players who had been dropped even found the luggage of the new players in their hotel rooms. Alvin Kallicharran – who had returned his AUS $600 advance cheque to Packer uncashed – was promptly appointed the new Test captain.

Had there been any doubt about whether the WSC players should be loyal to the West Indies board or an Australian businessman, they were resolved by the selection row in Georgetown. The team had no choice but to stick together because Packer and his brand of cricket was all they had. At a news conference held by the WICBC in Guyana, Jeffrey Stollmeyer had called Packer 'a parasite on cricket'.

The estrangement of the board and the players changed the character of West Indian cricket permanently and gave the players a new independence. Lloyd, Murray and Fredericks were now not only the senior members of the side, they were also its administrators and disciplinarians. They, not a tour manager working for the WICBC, had to tell the players when to practise and when to be back at the hotel in the evening. If a bowler swore at an umpire or if a batsman stayed out late, they would punish him. Only a faint connection remained with the cricket authorities in the Caribbean: Deryck Murray's father was a member of the board. Should they need one, there was still a discreet avenue of communication between Australia and home.

*   *   *

When the first season of WSC came to an end in February 1978 Kerry Packer claimed, 'We are still amateurs, but we are more professional than we were, and we will become even more professional.' The West Indian team had won the one-day competition and two of the three Super Tests they played against Australia. The verdict of traditional cricket was that the season had fallen well short of the sensation that Packer had predicted. The editor of *The Cricketer* magazine, David Frith, believed that as a greater number spectators had enjoyed seeing a shadow Australia XI play India, the success of the coming winter's Ashes series – England against the same Australia side – was practically guaranteed. 'There is a strongly held expectation,' he wrote, 'that World Series Cricket will chase its tail and end up devouring itself.'

The Cricketer got it wrong. By the end of the next WSC season the Australian Cricket Board had capitulated almost entirely to Packer's wishes. The loyal but weak Australia Test side was thrashed so easily by England that crowds lost interest before the series ended. Its star player, Jeff Thomson, would finally succumb to a Packer contract. 'How did we get him?' Tony Greig was once asked. 'Oh, probably by parking a new speedboat in his front yard.'

One match illustrated the success of World Series Cricket in that second season. It was held on the night of 28 November 1978. Packer had won the legal fight for his teams to play at the Sydney Cricket Ground. Australia versus the West Indies. Six huge lighting towers had been built around the grand old stadium with the political assistance of the Labor premier of New South Wales, Neville Wran. Packer had hoped for a crowd of 20,000. More than twice as many had arrived by the early evening when the police asked him if they could relieve pressure on the gates by allowing thousands more people inside. Packer agreed and let them in for nothing.

He was watching from the stands when the floodlights powered on to wash the ground with white light. *World of Cricket* recorded that the 'buzz of excitement never left the game throughout the Australians' innings as the players stood out like white porcelain statues on the light green field'. A new era in Australian sport had begun. Richard Cashman noted in *'Ave a Go, Yer Mug!* – his history of cricket crowds – that from this night floodlit cricket 'became as much an integral part of a Sydney summer as the annual expansion of the city's cockroach population'. The *National Times* reporter Adrian McGregor wrote that Packer had 'achieved the proletarian-isation of cricket'.

A quarter of a million tins of beer were drunk. There was free car parking. Old-age pensioners and the unemployed were allowed in for 50 cents. In between innings the crowd was let onto the field – usually an offence. A fruit fight at the front of the Noble Stand was allowed to continue without interruption. The event, reflected John Woodcock in *The Times*, was 'an awesome display of modern manners'. To compare it to the Australia versus England Test match taking place in Brisbane was impossible, he said. The two had as much in common as a pop concert and Trooping the Colour. The match was as much a layman's picnic as a bigot's nightmare. The revolution was superficial, he concluded, but had gained so much strength that it would cause some serious heart-searching among the establishment of the game. 'The first round of 1978–9 had gone to Mr Packer'.

'I remember it like it was last night,' says Colin Croft, 'because it was one of the most exciting nights I've had in my life. You just saw people coming into the cricket ground. They threw the doors open and they had a wonderful time. The intensity of the crowd, the expectation, the novelty, the difference – all of that made Kerry Packer's WSC what it was. It was an anomaly, it was something unique.'

The uniforms that the players wore later in that second season were unique too: yellow for the Australians, sky blue for the World team – and pink for the West Indies. The organisers claimed the colour was 'coral' but coming as they did from a region that had rigidly conservative views on manliness, it was a great embarrassment for the players. The West Indies was a place with strict limits on brotherly love. As Wes Hall once said in a speech to honour Garry Sobers, 'Garry, we love you as much as a man can love another man – and still be a man.'

'We had a modelling session with just the players,' recalls Austin Robertson. 'Greig came out first in his sky-blue World uniform, then Ian Chappell in the yellow, and then – it wasn't Clive, it was Viv – came out in the pink. And you know that swagger he has? Well it was no use, the whole bloody room was in uproar.'

Complaints to Kerry Packer were gruffly rejected. 'If you don't stop moaning, I'll buy you matching bloody handbags as well.'

'It was a colour that is, should we say, less than manly in the Caribbean parts,' says Colin Croft. 'A wonderful colour for ties and shirts but certainly not for an outfit to be playing in for the West Indies, and a lot of the guys were upset. But we couldn't change it, so we decided that the only way to use that pink to our advantage was to make sure we didn't lose.'

Other things were upsetting the West Indies. Some in the squad were complaining about the busy schedule, which included late finishes and early starts, last-minute flights and rearranged trips to rural towns to play in the Country Cup competition. The pay was good but the itinerary was cruel. Dissatisfaction leaked from the dressing room onto the pitch. 'We were feeling very sorry for ourselves,' admits Deryck Murray. 'We felt the bus was leaving too early in the morning and the games were too far away. All the things you see when you're not in form and not winning.'

The captain decided that some in his side liked the money but not the graft. There needed to be an intervention, and he spoke to Packer. It came after Lloyd's side had been bowled out for a gutless 66 by Australia at the SCG. Six of the team were out for nought and only two made double figures.

In the stand Packer was unimpressed. 'He got up abruptly and stormed towards the door,' remembers Austin Robertson. 'I thought, *Fuck. Something's going to go on.* So I followed him. The West Indies dressing room was always as I remember it – the music was on and no one seemed too worried about anything. And Kerry said, "I've got a few things to say." When it was all over, there wasn't a bloody whisper.'

'He certainly wasn't using language fit for the dinner table,' remembers Colin Croft. '"Gentlemen, you are wasting my time. Most of you are walking around Australia with your appendage in your hand. I could get rid of you immediately. Qantas 001 leaves here every afternoon and some of you could be on it."'

'There were a few Fs, Bs and Cs flying around,' says Clive Lloyd.

'He said, "You're the most exciting cricketers in the world, but I'm not seeing it,"' remembers Wayne Daniel. '"It's not good enough. You're just here playing with your dicks. But I didn't bring you down here for that. I won't have it, and that will be the end of you." It was the quietest moment I've known in a full dressing room. Viv,

Lloydy, Gordon – all silent. It was a real dressing-down. Like talking to schoolboys.'

What struck Michael Holding was that a proud Australian was berating a side that had been beaten by Australians. 'It was the way we had lost the game that made him mad. This was a man who had put up millions of dollars trying to build something, to project something: "This is going to be great, the best cricketers in the world, the greatest cricket that you will ever see." We had been trounced, but he was not interested in that; he was interested in the product, and we let him down. We were well paid and he expected better.'

The threat of having their livelihood taken away had an effect on the WSC West Indies. They began to improve. The change coincided with the arrival of a new member of the team.

Dennis Waight was an Australian rugby league trainer who had grown up surfing on the northern beaches in the suburbs of Sydney. He liked boxing, beer and footie but didn't have much time for cricket. Kerry Packer wanted each of his three sides to have a physiotherapist, and Waight was assigned to the World team but decided he could get more out of the West Indies. But the relationship didn't begin well.

When Waight first met the players, he had been drinking late into the evening with Jeff Thomson, Rod Marsh and Len Pascoe at a hotel bar in Perth. 'We'd been giving it quite a serve,' says the trainer. Clive Lloyd appeared in the lobby with his tired team, straight off a flight. Thomson drawled to Waight, 'Aw, your new mates are here.' Red-faced and beery, Waight wobbled over to introduce himself. He returned to his drinking pals a few minutes later having promised the underwhelmed West Indians that he would meet them at 0600 out the front for an inaugural team run.

I carried on drinking for an hour and then said to the receptionist, 'Ring me at 0430. Keep ringing, and if that doesn't work, knock the bloody door down.' Anyway I got up and felt terrible and had a 20-minute cold shower. But in those days I was pretty fit and went for a good long run. I arrived back in the foyer to hear Clive say, 'I told you he wouldn't turn up.' I tapped him on the shoulder and said, 'Where have you been? I've been waiting outside!'

He led the players on a run – and kept running with them for the next 22 years.

Fitness programmes for cricket teams were unusual in 1978; players were left to get themselves ready for matches. Some were lazier than others. Waight introduced the West Indies to lots of running, some weight training and regular stretching. 'At first they weren't interested when I took them to the local park,' he says. 'I told the skipper what my plans were and that they weren't putting any effort in. He said, "You'll have a rebellion on your hands here, but I'll back you up."'

Slowly the players accepted Waight's methods. They had fewer injuries and discovered that their new endurance and flexibility helped them.

'They thought it was funny that a cranky, red-faced little guy who liked a drink was pushing them all so hard. I mixed with the players up to a point. I've always taken people as they are, and if a bastard's a bastard, he's a bastard. I tried to treat them all fair. I didn't want to be one of the boys because I had to yell at them every day. And that's why it worked for so many years.'

Despite the yelling, the players took Waight to be their totem; they even insisted on giving him a cut of the prize money. They knew that he had become an important part of their success. He brought them a discipline that Caribbean cricket had never previously known. Dennis Waight made them a better team.

The only time he didn't open his hotel-room door was if there was an episode of *The Phil Silvers Show* on TV. Otherwise, bowlers would visit for a muscle rub that turned into a fraternal chat. Often they would leave cheered up by his straightforward wisdom and a mug of wine from the cardboard cask he kept in his kit bag.

*　　*　　*

It had never been Kerry Packer's intention to keep his cricket in Australia. The success of the second season confirmed that the product was robust enough to be exported. WSC headed to the Caribbean, where the WICBC was not in good shape. It had lost its best cricketers to Packer, its Test side was a weak second XI which was losing matches as well as the support of fans. Just a fortnight after the WSC project was made public in May 1977 one of the board's senior members had said, 'The West Indies board is in need of money and if there was a Packer in the West Indies, the board would welcome him.'

WSC officials had done reconnaissance work in the Caribbean as early as April 1978. Meetings were held with a rather nervous Jeffrey Stollmeyer, who desperately needed the money but was anxious not to be seen to be sabotaging ICC unity. Stollmeyer made it plain that he was entering into a rather distasteful relationship. Super Tests did indeed come to the Caribbean in 1979, but Stollmeyer would grant the negotiations and the matches only three sentences in his autobiography: 'The games came and went. There was some good cricket and some bad, but I have no doubt these games, like so many of the other Packer contests, will be quickly forgotten for they form no part of cricket records. I would accept Mr Packer's money for our board's survival, but I could not bring myself to attend any of his matches.'

The series – between the West Indies and Australia – wasn't so quickly forgotten by the players. The cricket was hard, the schedule was relentless and there were crowd disturbances in Barbados and Trinidad. But what happened there was 'as a vicarage tea party is to a bar-room brawl compared with Guyana', wrote the *Observer* columnist Peter Deeley. During the fourth Super Test at Bourda Ian Chappell and his teammates barricaded their dressing-room door with kit bags, put batting helmets on, and were poised with upturned chairs for weapons, expecting the rioting fans outside to attack them.

'Oh shit, yeah, it was pretty fucking serious' is Chappell's particular memory of the 'quickly forgotten' game. Bottles had been thrown onto the pitch, hoardings broken, wire fences mangled and administrative offices trashed by some of the 13,000 spectators after hours of delays blamed on a supposedly damp outfield. Some fans had been in the ground since eight in the morning, their mood not improved by people running onto the field, rolling around and standing up to show that their clothes were dry. However, the umpires believed the bowlers' run-ups were unsafe.

'It's gonna blow, man,' the former fast bowler Wes Hall predicted from the stands. And it did.

'Wes and I ended up hiding behind an overturned table,' says Austin Robertson.

We couldn't get to the dressing room because there were too many bricks and bottles and Christ-knows-what being thrown. How someone wasn't bloody killed that day, I don't know. When they pulled the fence down, there was nothing between us and the mob. Wes and I were stuffed. It was bloody terrible. It only ended because the police turned up with these trucks and turned the water guns on them. It was the most frightening experience of my life.

At the height of the riot the West Indies players wedged their pounded-upon dressing-room door shut with the team's massage table. Bottles and stones crashed through the broken windows. Desmond Haynes, who was hiding in a lavatory, realised how serious the situation was when a police officer dived in to join him. Lawrence Rowe tried to smash an exit through with his bat, but the wooden planks were cemented into the wall.

After a frightening 90 minutes, police saturated the stands with tear gas and baton-charged the rioters, and the players were safe. That evening the West Indians tried to rationalise why their own supporters had attacked them. Joel Garner decided that it was a sign of the general urge to revolt: people were 'symbolically attacking political leaders that they dare not confront in reality'. David Hookes put it slightly differently when interviewed for *The Cricket War*: 'We were told West Indians are "just great cricket lovers" and they are. But they're also very physical, very aggressive and very pissed.' Michael Manley concluded that a cricket match had once again 'revealed the tense indiscipline that lurks beneath the surface of any society still uneasy with itself'.

Several of the players thought that the violence of the Sunday crowd would cause the match to be abandoned. It wasn't, and the Monday spectators were as clement as those the day before had been fractious. Even though large parts of the ground had been ransacked, play began on time. But the weather and the riot meant that there was not enough time for anything but a draw.

The tour ground on: there were still six one-day games and a Super Test to get through. All in all, 37 days of cricket had been planned in less than two months. Most rest days were taken up with travel. Bringing Packer cricket to the Caribbean was in part a goodwill gesture to West Indian supporters who hadn't seen their best cricketers play at home for two seasons. But the schedule was hastily conceived and exhausting for the players. The West Indies could always rely on one of Roberts, Holding, Daniel or Croft to get wickets, but the workload expected of Lillee and Thomson for the Australians had diminished their powers, and they would never really return.

The cricket boards had also been weakened by the two seasons of World Series Cricket. The ACB in particular had been greatly wearied by the struggle. For all the frustrations of the WSC tour of the West Indies, it had been a huge political victory for Packer because the WICBC had cancelled an official visit by New Zealand in order to host it. Packer even paid the board compensation for the lack of Kiwis – a larger sum than it would have got had they arrived. Money and influence had trumped traditional authority. The boards had been bearded.

'The old crowd have taken a lot out of Caribbean cricket but have given little back,' said one of the local WSC organisers during the tour. 'In the old days they got the MBE, and the players finished up on the dole queue. People today want to see their stars but they also want to feel they are properly taken care of. For the first time a West Indies player can stroll into a bar at the Hilton, hold his head up high and order a round of drinks as an equal.'

The calypsonian the Mighty Sparrow put it this way:

Sobers, Worrell and Learie get title
But money, we give them very little.
When they dead write a book say how good they used to play
My tradition is all cricket, no pay

Packer was close to victory. Nearly three years after meeting those ACB officials in a Melbourne carpet showroom, the same two men invited Packer to lunch at the Melbourne Cricket Ground. Once,

Bob Parish and Ray Steele had denounced Packer as a wrecker; now they wanted a way out. Their official Australia side had been thrashed by England, and more people now watched Super Tests than Tests. Profits were down and morale among loyalist players was terrible. Most significantly, the ACB had changed its mind entirely about television rights and had accepted the principle of exclusivity.

At the end of May 1979 the details of the settlement were made public. In effect, the deal gave Packer exclusive rights to Test cricket in Australia for the next ten years. Packer promised not to put on rival games, while the ACB got to select the national side and pledged not to discriminate against WSC cricketers who wanted to play in Test matches. A Packer subsidiary company would control the future marketing of cricket in Australia. For all this, Packer would pay about AUS $1,000,000 a year. The price of the authorities' harlotry had at last been revealed. In *The Cricket War* Gideon Haigh wrote, 'Journalists, photographers and television cameramen jockeyed round the table as Parish read from a statement with customary gravity . . . Melbourne 30 May 1979 is official cricket history's equivalent of Munich 30 September 1938 with Parish as Neville Chamberlain.'

World Series Cricket had changed almost everyone who had taken part in it, but none more so than the West Indians. The money had transformed their personal lives. It was a very long way from 1961, when Frank Worrell had returned as a hero from the tour of Australia only to sell his house in Barbados to survive – and this was a man who had prepared for the future by obtaining a university degree.

'Whether we liked it or not,' says Ronald Austin, 'Australia had again played a role in the development of our cricket. Kerry Packer taught the players to understand that to be paid as professionals they had to perform as professionals. Apart from any of the other transformations, Packer gave West Indians a fair wage so that they could lead comfortable and decent lives.'

The choice between the old cricket pay and the new was, as Joel Garner says, 'a no-brainer. The difference was so vast it was unbelievable.' The players' welfare had also been thought of. Their wives were allowed in their hotel rooms; their families were given vouchers for McDonald's meals and taxi fares; their children were looked after in Kerry Packer crèches. None of this could or would have been matched by the WICBC, whose poverty and strictures had hastened the players' liberation from its stifling authority.

That estrangement brought advantages. In Michael Holding's words, the squad 'became more like a family'. Previous West Indies sides on tour had tended to fragment into island or cultural cliques. 'Yes, you knew them as players and you knew about their cricket, but you didn't know too much about their personal lives. During WSC we found out about what we liked and what we disliked, about the wife or the girlfriend of your room-mate, how many kids were in the family.'

'We were athletic, we were fit, we were big, we were strong,' says Colin Croft. 'That might have been because we were black, but we were also victorious, we were winning and we seemed to be having a good time doing it. Now that is a wonderful combination.'

'It created a bond between these men,' concludes Wayne Daniel. 'We recognised that we had to fight all the time to show the board that we were good enough. That we were too good to be discarded. That was the experience of battle. We were tougher, harder, psychologically stronger. We knew we had to come out of it as winners. We had a meanness that a West Indian team never had before.'

'After Packer it was like a door had shut on the past,' reflects Clive Lloyd. 'We had some power, we had better conditions, we had some money, we had some negotiating muscle. The players, not the administrators, could call the shots a bit more. We weren't there yet, but we were getting there. Above all, the cricket played by these boys from the West Indies had got pretty good too.'

And yet, for all its successes, Packer's enterprise did not bring the players absolute satisfaction. For two years Test cricket had not been the best cricket. Yes, the West Indies wanted to play the most competitive cricket they could, but they also wanted to be – officially – the best Test side in the world. The pull of the maroon blazer was still strong. 'Playing for Kerry Packer, yes. Making a good living, yes. But that is not ultimately what we wanted,' says Holding. 'Despite everything, we felt like outcasts.'

The players wanted to retain what they had learned, and use their new confidence to win Test matches. Not least because they now realised that Australia could be beaten. There had been 43 matches of all types between the two sides since December 1977, and Lloyd's side had 26 victories to Australia's 11. 'We saw for the first time that the Australians had a soft underbelly,' says Lloyd. 'They weren't as tough as they seemed. They had some great cricketers, but we found out that they suffered under pressure. That was a huge discovery.'

The final matches of Kerry Packer's tournament were played in the West Indies. On each side there were eight men who had taken part in the 1975–6 Test series in Australia, but there had been a profound shift in strength since then. This Caribbean round of Super Tests ended one all, but there was no doubt that the West Indies were the better team. It all finished in Antigua in April 1979. Australia batted well in their second innings to draw the game.

In the dressing room afterwards Rod Marsh turned to Ian Chappell and asked him a question of the West Indians that would have been inconceivable three years earlier: 'We made 'em respect us, didn't we?'

5

'No point in planning to take their queen out'

The second cricket World Cup was held in June 1979. The West Indies had come to England as champions to defend the trophy. After the convulsions of the past two years, the tournament appeared to be a sign of restored harmony in the international game.

On the outfield at Lord's the eight teams – Sri Lanka, Pakistan, West Indies, England, Australia, New Zealand, India and Canada – lined up in rows marked out by the ground staff and stared up to the pavilion balcony to have their photograph taken. Most wore a uniform of blazer and slacks, but England and New Zealand allowed their players to choose their own suits; they all looked as if they were between seminars at a secondary-school teachers' conference. The West Indies were in mufti too – Deryck Murray in his ironic post-colonial beige safari suit, Larry Gomes dressed as a best man, Joel Garner in a fawn jacket that if supported by tent poles could have shaded a family of four.

It looked like unity, but it wasn't really. Neither England nor Australia had included players who had taken part in World Series Cricket. The International Cricket Conference had yet to agree to the settlement between Packer and the Australian board. (There would be talks throughout the World Cup in the hope of arriving at an agreeable position.) And in the qualifying tournament the Sri Lankan government had forbidden its team to play against Israel for political reasons.

Alvin Kallicharran was back in the West Indies side, the most senior player to have rejected a WSC contract. Three other men whom he had captained during the schism had been selected too: Faoud Bacchus, Gomes and a young fast bowler from Barbados called Malcolm Marshall. Kerry Packer's demand that his players would not be ostracised once back in their national sides was being tested out in reverse in the West Indies team. Those who had shunned WSC needed to be reintegrated, but reminders of the recent past were evident. Vivian Richards played wearing a white WSC shirt with sticking plaster taped over the logo on his breast.

On the morning of the final, which the West Indies had reached with little trouble, Richards woke up and before even saying good morning to Desmond Haynes in the other bed announced, 'There's going to be a lot of people at Lord's today. It would be a good time to really turn it on.' The opposition would be England. Several young players who had been thought too green to face the West Indies in 1976 were now in the side: David Gower, Ian Botham, Derek Randall and Graham Gooch. They were a useful one-day team, especially in the field, and were led by an intelligent captain, Mike Brearley.

Four years previously Brearley had gathered up his sandals and sprinted barefoot onto the field at Lord's with hundreds of other invading spectators after Deryck Murray ran out Jeff Thomson to win the 1975 World Cup for the West Indies. Now he had to work out how to beat them. How to score enough runs against the bowling of Roberts, Holding, Croft and Garner. How to stop Greenidge, Haynes, Richards, Lloyd and Collis King from smashing his own bowlers.

The lower tier of the Grand Stand and the front of the Mound Stand were filled with West Indies' supporters. One man held a banner saying VIV – SUPERBAT. HOLDING – BIONIC SPEED. But England started well, taking four West Indies wickets for 99 runs. Batting at number six, Collis King left the dressing room wearing Desmond Haynes's boots and went down the back stairs to walk through the Long Room to the pitch. As he put on his gloves in the pavilion, he felt something inside one of them. It was a miniature bottle of brandy, one of the half-dozen or so he kept in his kit bag. Too far from the dressing room to return, he decided that he could do only one thing. In the calm of the pavilion he drank it all in one gulp. As he made his way to the crease his chest burned with the spirit.

'You been drinking rum?' asked Vivian Richards as they met in the middle.

'Brandy.'

Almost at once King was fizzing with Barbadian power. He square-slashed Botham for four down the hill to the Mound Stand. Phil Edmonds went the same way and a pair of innocent seam-up wobblers from Wayne Larkins were clubbed into the crowd for consecutive sixes. England's fastest bowler, Bob Willis, had been injured in the semi-final and his allotment of twelve overs had to be bowled by three stand-ins: Gooch, Boycott and Larkins. Richards warned King to be wary of Boycott; no one in their right mind would want to be tagged with the label of getting out to such ordinary bowling in a World Cup final. King, who had spent two seasons at Nelson – Learie Constantine's club in Lancashire – wasn't worried:

'Smokey,' he said to Richards, 'I ain't gonna let Geoffrey get *this* man. In the league there would be no mercy, so why should this be any different?'

Between them, England's part-time bowlers gave away 86 runs

as King and Richards sped the West Indies towards 200. The usually astute Mike Brearley reflected later that watching the partnership had brought him close to tactical impotence. It was, he said, like attacking tanks with pea-shooters. King made 86 before being caught on the boundary. Richards stayed on. Past a hundred and with the lower order coming and going, he took his team to 286 from their 60 overs. In the last over of the innings Richards twice walked across his stumps to the off side as Mike Hendrick was about to bowl and hit him for six through square leg. He left the field undefeated and the owner of a century in a Lord's final. 'That shot is my invention,' he said to himself.

*   *   *

Batting in a helmet for the first time, Geoffrey Boycott opened the innings for England with his captain. Neither had the flair of Richards or King. Boycott was a remorselessly efficient accumulator of runs but not known for stylish improvisation. Brearley had made a 50 against New Zealand in the semi-final but a pair of noughts against Pakistan and Canada. In fact they both played well against the pace of the West Indies, but their runs came too slowly and Boycott took 17 overs to reach double figures. They preserved their wickets but batted without intent. England had got their tactics wrong. Vivian Richards – who would have been delighted to bat against his own bowling – was allowed to get through 10 overs of off spin for 35 runs.

During the tea interval Mike Brearley was in the England dressing room telling his side he now wanted to get on with it, and increase the scoring rate. But while he drank several glasses of lemon squash, two cups of tea and ate a rock cake, he was talked round by the rest of the side, who valued wickets in hand over quick runs. But scoring seven an over against Garner and Holding, Croft and Roberts and even the fast-medium of Collis King was far too much to ask. In the last session of the day Joel Garner twice took two wickets in two balls as England were forced to hit out. 'The innings disappeared like names rubbed from a blackboard,' wrote John Arlott. Eight wickets fell for eleven runs. England had been routed for 194, and the West Indies had won the cup again. They were – no doubt – the best side in the world.

The West Indies board decided that the captain should be rewarded for the team's historic achievement. It offered Lloyd a £50 bonus. He declined. They came back with an improved offer – £100. 'Can you imagine what would happen to English men who won two World Cups?' asks Lloyd. 'They'd be given the freedom of London and never have to buy a drink again. I got offered £100. It was as if Packer had never happened.'

* * *

After the World Cup, there was travel. At the end of 1979 the West Indies toured Australia again to play Test cricket. Every time since 1930 they had left the country defeated; this though was a new world controlled by Kerry Packer. Australia would face the West Indies, but they would also play England at the same time in a separate Test series. All three sides would also play each other in a one-day tournament designed to mimic the success of WSC. The new arrangements required explanation, so a half-page advertisement appeared in the *Sun-Herald* in early November 1979 to make it all clear. Appropriately, the headline was CRICKET 1979/80 – OR WHO'S PLAYING WHO FOR WHAT.

'For two years the loyalties of players and supporters alike have been divided between the Australian Cricket Board and World Series Cricket,' chirped the advert. 'Now the two bodies have united.' The new economics of the game were heralded, not hushed up. The West Indies and Australia would not only play for the Frank Worrell Trophy, but for prize money of AUS $19,000 in each Test.

At Sydney Airport Clive Lloyd said that this would be his final overseas tour. He was 35 and his knees hurt when he batted. He missed the first Test because he needed an operation, so Kerry Packer found him a surgeon. Lloyd's players expressed their concern by rifling through his kit bag for souvenirs to remember their skipper by. Without him the West Indies drew the match at Brisbane.

But there was to be no repeat of the West Indian capitulation of '75–76. This Australia side was older and frailer. Whereas the fire of WSC had tempered the West Indies, the experience had scorched the Australians. With Lloyd recovered and Gordon Greenidge batting as well as he ever had, the team won the one-day tournament and with it AUS $32,000. Four days later, at the end of January 1980, they began the third and final Test in Adelaide, having won by ten wickets at Melbourne in the second. Eight men in the West Indies side remembered the humiliation of their previous tour. With centuries by the captain in the first innings and Kallicharran in the second, the West Indies won easily by 408 runs. LLOYD TAKES HIS REVENGE FOR 1976 was the headline on the back page of the *Sydney Morning Herald* the next day.

It was impossible to see this victory in isolation. To the West Indies it was so much more than winning a Test series. Never before had they succeeded in Australia. Lloyd's vision – to deliver victory with searing pace and extraordinary batting – had been perfectly realised. Vivian Richards had proved beyond doubt that he was the best batsman on earth. The four great bowlers were Colin Croft, Michael Holding, Andy Roberts and Joel Garner. Malcolm Marshall couldn't get in the side and Wayne Daniel couldn't even get on the plane. The fast bowlers shared the Test wickets equally and almost exclusively. They took 55 of the 56 Australian wickets to fall in the series.

In the Caribbean their supporters delighted in the accomplishment.

'We had always feared in the West Indies that the Australians were too big to be beaten,' says Ronald Austin. 'Mentally and physically too big. I do remember my father and his friends speaking of the physical attributes of the Australians with awe when they first laid eyes on Keith Miller and Ray Lindwall in the 1950s. Now, when Worrell almost defeated these big Australians in '61, something stirred in all of us, but the fiasco in 1968 and the drubbing in 1976 took us back to a kind of mental prison.' This first victory by Clive Lloyd's side achieved two things, he goes on. Not only had West Indians avenged the disgrace of 1975–76, they had also crossed a psychological barrier. 'We now had a team equal to any in the rest of the world. In fact I would go further and say that as we developed this capacity to match Australia, the West Indies also planted the seeds for the victories by India and Pakistan in Australia which were still to come. We had sculpted a model for success. The West Indians had contributed to the change in the order and structure of world cricket.'

Sitting back in a dressing-room chair with a beer at the Adelaide Oval, Lloyd told journalists that his side had finally got rid of the notion that they were only good when they were on top. They had proved that they could fight back when things weren't going well. 'We have learned a lot over the years.' His knees seemed better too. He would be available to lead the side in England in the coming summer and before then on a short tour of New Zealand.

* * *

Jeremy Coney was making plans to bat against the West Indies.

'I did some preparation. I thought about things. One of them was *How do I not get out?*' says the former New Zealand batsman. 'Don Neely had some ideas.' Neely was a New Zealand selector, and like Coney from Wellington. During January 1980 he took the batsman to Kilbirnie Park, where he had cut a practice pitch – not in the middle but at the edge, abutting a large concrete terrace where spectators usually sat. 'Don stood on the third step back and hurled the ball at me,' says Coney. 'We were trying to recreate what might occur when I was facing Joel Garner. So straight away I had to think differently about where the ball would be coming from, what lengths would it be hitting?'

Joel Garner was six feet eight inches tall, and when bowling would release the ball from about ten or eleven feet. At some grounds his arm reached higher than the top of the sightscreen.

Neely's approach was, says Coney, a typically New Zealand way of thinking. 'After all, our cricket in those day was a cottage industry. The national side was run from the secretary's garage. All the sweaters and caps were kept there. But we have a saying in New Zealand – the "number eight piece of wire" mentality. Using what- ever ordinary material you have to hand to improve something. A simple method to solve a complicated problem. That's how we took on the West Indies.'

When they weren't at Kilbirnie Park, Neely and Coney wound the country's only bowling machine up as fast as it would go. *How can I stay in?* was the simple thought that kept returning to Coney as he faced the 90-miles-per-hour plastic balls. He knew that if he could stay in, things usually got better.

Some shots would have to go, of course. There weren't many you could play against Croft, Garner, Roberts and Holding – they were too quick, and the middle of the bat would not arrive soon enough. Unless the pitch was very slow, you gave away the hook. Coney knew there would be a man at fine leg and one behind the square-leg umpire waiting for the half-hit shot. So against the bowling machine he worked on his square cut. Yes, he was prepared to play the cut shot because it was a little easier to control and he could hit it hard, but he also practised how to get out of the way. A lot of the time he just did that.

Swaying, ducking, crouching – watching the ball until the last possible moment, resisting the temptation to scrunch up his shoulders and just close his eyes. *How am I* not *going to play the ball?*

'There is no shot in the coaching manual called the Drive off the Throat,' he says. 'It doesn't appear.'

The other thing he found time to do was to get a chin strap fitted to his helmet. He'd not attached one before and he didn't want to jerk his head out of the way in the middle of a carefully-built innings only to see his hard hat fall on the stumps.

*   *   *

The West Indies arrived in New Zealand on the first day of February 1980. They had finished playing at Adelaide in the final Test against Australia on 30 January. Their next game was against the New Zealand Cricket Council President's XI at Eden Park in Auckland three days later. There was no time for a break.

New Zealand were the world's worst Test side. Many of the teams that came their way flew across the Tasman Sea as an afterthought to a tour of Australia. New Zealand had never won a Test series in their own country and for their first 31 years of Test existence not a single game. And yet in 1980 they had some good players. Richard Hadlee was becoming a genuine Test all-rounder; Geoff Howarth was a fine batsman and an indefatigable young leader. John Wright and Bruce Edgar were at the top of the order and in the middle was Jeremy Coney.

The West Indies, says Geoff Howarth, were probably expecting a few quick wins inside three days. They had flown out of Australia with more than AUS $140,000 in prize money. 'We got carried away thinking we were God's children,' admits Michael Holding. 'We'll walk this.' Instead, one of the most rancorous, ill-disciplined and quarrelsome Test series of all time was about to begin. 'They were supposed to be unbeatable – there was no contest. They had been through a hard trip of Australia; they were a little blasé, a bit homesick. We caught them on the hop,' says Howarth.

'They needed to get used to the New Zealand ways, and they didn't,' says Coney. 'They had to carry their own luggage; they stayed in smaller hotels; the food they expected and the service they expected as top of the pops didn't quite match up. There was no gamesmanship about the arrangements on our part – that was just New Zealand at the end of the '70s. That's how we all lived. The sort of money they'd won in Australia – well for us that was like all our lottery numbers coming up at once.'

The West Indies' first warning came in Christchurch, where they lost the one-day international by a single wicket. But as long as the three-match Test series was won, this wouldn't matter. The first Test was in Dunedin, where the weather was cold and the West Indies didn't like the endless servings of sausages and beans. There was almost no prize money on offer.

After three months in Australia on wickets that usually bounced and on which it was safe to play back, the West Indies batted badly. Vivian Richards was not there – back pain and a hip problem had forced him to return to the Caribbean. The ball kept lower and the batsmen didn't get sufficiently forward. A record number of 12 LBW decisions were awarded by the two home umpires at Dunedin, seven of them against the tourists.

New Zealand did bowl well, but quite soon into the game Lloyd's team felt that the decisions being made by the umpires were not always impartial. By the fifth day the West Indies were bowling to save themselves from defeat. The New Zealanders needed only 104 in the last innings to win. The world's worst Test side were looking like they would beat the world champions.

'Before the series started we honestly didn't think about the result,' says Coney.

We just wanted not to be humiliated. I think the only way we thought we could beat someone so superior was ball by ball. Stay in this ball. Hang in there the next ball. Beat them by a hundred thousand little cuts to bring down the giant. No point in planning to take their queen out – it was much more a case of trying to trap a pawn. We weren't prepared to throw the bat at the ball and give it away. We defended and defended, letting go, letting go. Getting hit, letting go. Not giving them easy wickets.

And the win in the limited-overs match had meant a lot. 'We realised that they panicked a bit in that game as we took it away from them, and we thought, *Wow! They are human. It is possible to see the Plimsoll Line*. We got a lot of confidence from that.'

With New Zealand's score at 28 for two in the fourth innings, Michael Holding was bowling to the number four, John Parker. Paper blew across the outfield in the breeze. Holding, wearing a sweater, came at Parker off his short run. It was a good ball that rose quickly, and Parker had to play at it. The ball touched his glove on the way through to Deryck Murray, who caught it. There were immediate and loud appeals, but umpire John Hastie thrust both hands into his coat pockets. He wasn't going to give Parker out.

'Holding bowled a perfect leg cutter,' remembers Colin Croft. 'Not only did the ball hit his hand, it tore off his glove. I was fielding at mid-off so I couldn't miss it.'

The bowler was so exasperated by the decision that he carried on down the pitch and kicked down two of Parker's stumps. At the crease Parker looked down and fiddled with the fastening on his glove. In the crowd a man sitting on the terrace beyond square leg put his hand to his mouth in shock.

'Michael couldn't believe it,' recalls Coney. 'He let loose this wonderful, flexible, refined drop-goal of a kick. The leg, up over the waist and past the shoulder then the head. Stumps flying. Fantastic. Ballet teachers throughout the world furious with envy and John Parker almost saying, "You can't give that out; it only *just* touched the glove!" Yes, of course it was out, but those were the days when you had your own umpires in your own country. New Zealand umpires umpiring in New Zealand conditions.'

Fred Goodall was the other official. 'I walked in from square leg to remake the wicket,' he recalls. 'I said to Clive Lloyd, "What your fast bowler has just done is unacceptable. Please have a word with him." And from somewhere in the field I heard a player say out loud, "You're nothing but cheats." That was my first inkling of how serious the situation was.'

Parker was soon caught behind again, this time with Garner bowling. He was given out, and other batsmen followed promptly. Three wickets fell with the score on 44, and at tea New Zealand were 95 for 8, needing 9 runs to win. Take away the extraordinary animosity, and you had a terrifically exciting Test match. The post-tea crescendo included a ball from Holding that grazed the stumps but did not remove the bail. Then Lance Cairns was caught. His team still needed four to win but had just one wicket left. The end came with a frantic leg bye run by the last pair at the crease. New Zealand had won a Test match against the West Indies for the first time since 1969.

Lloyd's team were not happy. They were no longer used to losing. They complained that the umpires' decisions had 'aided and abetted' the New Zealand victory. Only Desmond Haynes attended the post-match ceremony, and the team manager, Willie Rodriguez, told the press that he had given Michael Holding a 'talking-to' but not a reprimand. He later told a journalist that it had been 'impossible for us to win' on the last day because of the umpires' ineptitude.

'When Willie Rodriguez said something like "We were set up,"' recalls Coney, 'we felt that went too far. It was slightly insulting because it suggested a collaboration between the administration and the officials. These guys were not professional umpires.'

The West Indies' state of mind had hardly improved by the start of the second Test at Christchurch nine days later. Rodriguez had asked publicly for the umpires to be changed. John Hastie was, but Fred Goodall remained from Dunedin. Goodall was a second-ary-school teacher who had first stood in a Test match in 1965. In 1978 he had spent half a season umpiring in the English county championship.

'It was an awful bloody atmosphere,' recalls the New Zealand cricket journalist Don Cameron. 'By the time of Christchurch and the second Test it was getting worse and worse. A local radio station composed a satirical calypso ridiculing the West Indies.'

'It was a calypso that 30 years ago everyone in New Zealand might have had a giggle at, but it wasn't very nice,' reflects Coney.

'My memory is that it was to the tune of the Simon and Garfunkel song "Cecilia",' says Fred Goodall. He begins to sing:

Mr Goodall, you're breaking our hearts,
You ain't seeing straight, and we're losing.
If you carry on going this way,
We'll pack up our bags and go home. Go on home.

'The players thought it was a joke,' he adds. 'I remember both sides singing it when they walked onto the pitch at Christchurch.'

Again the West Indies didn't bat well; again the New Zealanders did. But present throughout was the visitors' sincere belief that the umpiring was at best incompetent and at worst conniving. On the third day the New Zealand captain, Geoff Howarth, on 68, touched a ball to the keeper. 'I leaned back to a short ball and got a thumb on it,' he confesses. 'Everyone behind knew it was out but not the umpire. I think that was probably the straw that broke the camel's back for the West Indies.'

'I saw nothing and heard nothing,' says Fred Goodall, 'but apparently there was a brush of the glove.'

By tea Howarth was still in and had scored 99. As the break came to an end, Jeremy Coney was getting ready to continue their partnership.

'I was waiting in the little pavilion corridor at Lancaster Park, and the umpires went out but there were no West Indians. We waited two minutes, five minutes, eight minutes. Still no team. Umpires in the middle looking at their watches. Then administrators running past me in the opposite direction and knocking on doors, going into dressing rooms.'

The West Indies were refusing to come back out.

Fred Goodall remembers: 'The other umpire said to me, "I've got news for you and it's all bad. The West Indies aren't coming." They wanted me changed there and then.'

Captain Lloyd had had enough. He was prepared to make the protest alone so that the younger players in the side wouldn't get into trouble, but the dressing-room door stayed shut with everyone inside. 'It was a protest against seeing and hearing some extraordinary things on the tour,' says Lloyd.

Lots of stuff happened on the field and off. When one of my senior players checked into a hotel, he asked for directions to his room and the guy said, 'Why don't you go and sleep in that tree over there?' Then, during the match, the umpires were telling me that we were bowling too fast for them to see what was happening. 'What you really mean,' I replied, 'is that you're unable to umpire at this level.' Players were gloving the ball all over the place; fellows were plumb in front and not being given LBW. 'Our livelihood is on the line here,' I remember saying. 'Why don't we just call this a goodwill tour and forget that these are Test matches?'

The West Indies were 12 minutes overdue when they were persuaded back onto the pitch, but the last part of the day could not be described as Test cricket. The bowling was repetitively short; little effort was made to field or even catch the ball.

'That final session took the game into disrepute,' says Goodall. 'The West Indies let the ball go to the boundary and they dropped catches accidentally on purpose.'

Jeremy Coney experienced the West Indians' ill will very personally. 'Colin Croft bowled the last over of the day to me. Geoff was the non-striker, and I noticed he'd taken his batting gloves off, so he had no intention of coming down my end. Now Colin was a bowler who came from very wide, so his front foot went outside the return crease. The ball came back at quite an acute angle towards you and the stumps, so you always had to arch your back to get out of the way.'

Coney received five short balls in a row from Croft.

I thought, *That's OK – last ball coming.* Colin ran in. Quite quick, 90 miles per hour maybe? Brett Lee pace. Anyhow, I didn't see it. I thought, *He's held on to that one*, and then it hit my helmet. Beamer. Straight at my head. You see, you get used to looking at a certain area of the pitch for the bounce of the ball, but there was none. Just nicked the helmet and I wasn't wearing a visor, so I thought, *Another couple of inches there and I'm hit in the face.* Not a word from Colin. I was a bit riled. It was so close to cleaning me out. I should add the next morning – very quietly as he was walking past me to slip – Clive Lloyd said, 'Sorry about that, Jeremy.' It needed to be said.

Given the events of the day, the journalist Don Cameron was surprised to bump into a smiling Desmond Haynes in the hotel that evening. Haynes was snacking on a piece of fried chicken. 'I went into the players' room and they were all there. "Why the party?" I asked Dessie. "Oh, we're going home," he said. Straight away I phoned Jeff Stollmeyer in the Caribbean and asked him for a comment. "It won't happen," he told me. "The manager will be told that they'll be carrying on."'

Six players in the squad wanted to leave New Zealand immediately – halfway through the Test match, halfway through the tour. They had cleared their kit from the dressing room at the ground and packed. The next day was Sunday, the rest day. It was spent in negotiations between New Zealand officials and the West Indies.

At some point Geoff Howarth spoke to Clive Lloyd. 'I said to Clive, "Look, I'm sorry about the umpires. Can we have a truce? I'll go into your dressing room and say, 'If we nick it we'll walk,' and you do the same in our dressing room."' The negotiations seemed to work. The West Indies had another team discussion and by one account decided to stay in New Zealand by thirteen votes to two. The tour would continue. Very quickly though any goodwill created by the rest-day rapprochement disappeared once the players were back on the field.

In New Zealand's first innings, Geoff Howarth was eventually out for 147 but Coney and Hadlee continued to build the score. Colin Croft was bowling again. Coney was the non-striker when Hadlee tried to hook a short ball. 'Richard was batting and there was a little edge – there *was* an edge – a fine one, and the players knew. And given not out by Goodall,' says Coney.

'By this stage I was having a running battle with Colin Croft,' says the umpire. 'He was bowling very wide of the crease and was being no-balled for his front foot but also for being outside the return crease. "Go back to teaching," he'd say. "You don't know the rules." Hadlee slashed at a bouncer; everyone appealed, and I thought I'd made a good decision giving him not out. Only years later did Hadlee tell me he'd got an edge on it.'

Behind the wicket Deryck Murray had his arms wide open with the ball displayed in his glove. He thought it was out and said so. He threw the ball back to Croft, who walked past Goodall. Something unpleasant was said.

'If we're bowling too quickly for you to be a proper adjudicator then you shouldn't be standing there,' says Colin Croft. 'I don't blame them for their incompetence; I blame the New Zealand cricket board for appointing them. If you have a lousy umpire to operate with the world's best fast bowlers then you get crap umpiring. End of story.'

'Following that loud appeal from the West Indians, Colin Croft was noticeably upset,' the television commentator told viewers. 'He had a word or two to Fred Goodall, and this has prompted Goodall to go down and speak to Clive Lloyd.'

Goodall paused play. Lloyd wasn't moving from slip, so the umpire, now joined by his colleague, walked the 40 yards to where Lloyd and Murray were standing. Both looked like wronged innocents with the constable approaching: arms behind backs, legs relaxed, weight on one hip, looking down, Murray picking at the turf with his boot.

A short discussion took place before the umpires walked back to their positions. Croft bowled again and Goodall shouted, 'No ball,' the bowler's eleventh of the innings. Clearly still fuming, Croft headed for his mark but as he passed Goodall at the stumps deliberately and petulantly flicked both bails off with his fingers. The crowd jeered. Goodall looked about him.

'I said, "I'll get those Mr Umpire," and I bent down and put them back on,' says Jeremy Coney. 'Next ball – and remember Colin usually came in quite wide to get his position at the stumps – he just ran in straight and barged Fred, who went past me at a rate of knots. I think it hurt him a bit.'

It looked as if Croft had deliberately run into the umpire.

'I will maintain until the day I die that he was standing in the wrong place,' says Croft. 'If you studied my approach you would know that I would hit umpires. He was not the only umpire – I've done it in England, I've done it in the Caribbean. The man made a big noise out of it, and I suppose if he was in Hollywood he would have gotten an Oscar. I'm six feet six inches and 230 pounds. If I'd meant to hit him, he wouldn't have got up. It's crap that I barged him deliberately.'

In the dressing room the watching New Zealand captain was less sure.

'Colin Croft should have been banned for life for what he did,' says Geoff Howarth.

He tried to pretend he'd lost his run-up. It was disgraceful. It was nothing to do with cricket; it was the worst session I've ever seen or been involved in. I heard shouts of 'Hit him' from fielders. It was because it was 12,000 miles away in little old New Zealand that the authorities turned a blind eye. Fred was a stick-in-the-mud but he wasn't a cheat, just out of his depth. The West Indies said that many decisions went against them. Well that's a lot of crap. We had rough decisions too. They just behaved like kids.

Yet again Goodall had to take the long walk to Clive Lloyd.

'I said, "I've taken verbal abuse as an umpire but I've never been struck before. You deal with Croft because we mean to in our written report to the New Zealand board."'

Lloyd allowed Croft to continue bowling. He was done listening to the officials. The game had been ruined. It would be drawn as the West Indies gave away easy runs and in their second innings scored some themselves. Haynes, Rowe and King all made hundreds as the Test ran out of time. New Zealand could now not be beaten in the three-match series.

'We were very drained mentally,' explains Alvin Kallicharran. 'It wasn't indiscipline. The tour shouldn't really have gone on. As for the umpiring, oh boy. That messed up the tour more than anything else. I don't blame Colin Croft at all. I don't blame him if it was accidental or intentional.'

As a result of the controversy the *Evening Post* newspaper reported that a local cricket official who had praised the West Indies for being well mannered and enjoyable company had received abusive phone calls at his home. 'What do you think of your black boys now, nigger lover?' one caller had asked him. In an editorial the next day the *Post* made it clear that 'narrow-minded bigots who indulge in racial stereotyping deserve only one reaction from decent people in the community – absolute contempt'.

*   *   *

The final Test in Auckland also finished as a draw. The West Indies, Test and one-day world-beaters, had been defeated in a spiteful, sour series. A journalist dispatched from Australia by *The Age* to investigate the tour wrote, 'It has taken the West Indies only three and a half weeks to obliterate the world champion tag they had earned in the past three and a half years. Three and a half weeks of petulance, bad temper and violent behaviour.'

The West Indies' team manager, Willie Rodriguez told the press that there was no point in having a news conference before his side left for home. 'It would be an insult and a waste of time because none of you listens to anything I say.' However, he was able to slip in that he had many things to report back to the WICBC, mostly about how the game should be improved in New Zealand.

'I don't remember this tour with any real pleasure,' says Jeremy Coney. 'The acrimony increased as it went on, and they just didn't want to be there. However, having captained New Zealand in Pakistan in 1984 – a very difficult experience for a visiting team getting used to local umpiring – I got an inkling of how the West Indies might have felt.'

In the Caribbean the popular view was that the West Indies had been cheated of victory. The *Chronicle* of Guyana believed 'the deliberate design to defraud the West Indies team out of the series was so glaring that not even the Pope captaining a Vatican team would have taken it like a Christian'. In Trinidad, the cricket official Lance Murray, Deryck's father, castigated the West Indies umpiring association, which in a show of international fraternal affection had come out in support of their colleagues in New Zealand. Such a stance, said Mr Murray, was 'bold-faced, out of place and sacrilegious'.

Of course there were consequences. And contrition. Clive Lloyd wrote to the president of the WICBC after the tour ended and accepted some responsibility for what had happened: '. . . under the strain we were responsible for certain acts of protest which were unprofessional and in retrospect I take the blame for not being firm . . . I wish to offer an apology to the WICBC and the New Zealand Cricket Council.'

'They were just bad umpires,' he says now,

but we should not have behaved in that manner. If I had my time over again I'd have handled it differently. I wish those things hadn't happened – no man wants black marks on his record. But it's a lucky man who gets through life without having the odd confrontation. Every boy has had a little fight in the playground at some time, or else you wouldn't know what the other side is like. I was captaining men of character; we'd been through a lot together and we were no longer going to take whatever came our way. I think I'm as fair as the next person and that I played my cricket hard. If I got beaten, then no problem, but I don't like incompetence. At the highest level of sport you cannot have incompetence. Are there bad tennis umpires at Wimbledon? I don't think so. If there were, people wouldn't come back the next day.

'They were angry, and understandably so,' says Jeremy Coney. 'There *was* a sympathy for the West Indies. They'd been away from home for a very long time. They encountered a young team that even though they weren't sophisticated, were going to fight tooth and nail. But the umpiring did go against them when they created a dismissal. So it made them cross. They began to dwell on the unfairness of it all and then in their minds it became bias. Then they started to sulk.'

Before the 1980 tour to England the West Indies players were required by the WICBC to sign a contract that included penalties for bad behaviour. Willie Rodriguez was not asked to continue as manager. As for New Zealand, visiting teams had long complained that the umpiring wasn't of the highest quality. The previous season the Pakistan captain had commented that 'regrettable decisions' had been made while his side were there and that some of the routine work of the two umpires had been inefficient.

Ian Chappell had toured New Zealand as captain of Australia in 1974.

Fred was around then, yeah. I just think he was a very bad umpire, which was par for the course in New Zealand. They were 'not out' men. And as always happens with that sort of umpire, when they do eventually give one, they crack and give a shocker. Fred wasn't a cheat, but I just thought he was a very, very bad umpire. The only umpire I knew who was a cheat was an Australian from Perth, but he didn't umpire Test cricket. There were a couple of South Africans I played under who were dead-set cheats. Well, if they weren't cheats, they were extremely patriotic.

'Fred was regarded as our top umpire,' says Jeremy Coney. 'There is no doubt that he was intractable, and officious if you didn't know him. He was unbending and unyielding. He wasn't frightened to make a decision. But I never felt that he was a cheat. He was, like the other umpires – Hastie, Woodward – out of his depth.'

'I think it was probably true that we were out of our depth,' reflects Fred Goodall 35 years after the series ended.

We weren't used to the quartet of fast bowlers. By the time you watched the front foot land on the popping crease, the ball was in the wicket-keeper's gloves. There were no professional umpires in New Zealand then of course. We all had other jobs. Our training in those days was all about knowing the laws of the game; we weren't ever trained for instance in the body language of batsmen who nicked it and then stood there. There's a heck of a lot more to cricket umpiring than just knowing the rules.

Despite the apologies and the firm purposes of amendment, the rancour between New Zealand and the West Indies did not wither. After the tour finished Fred Goodall made some after-dinner speeches about his experiences at the hands of the West Indies.

According to Don Cameron, those engagements included 'biting and racial criticism of the West Indians'.

'I did say something at an after-dinner speech in 1981,' admits Fred Goodall.

It was a flippant remark that could have been taken the wrong way, and some people decided it was a racist remark. It was a pun that badly misfired back on me. There was a popular confectionery bar in New Zealand at the time called a Coconut Rough. My joke in relation to their cricketers and that series was that I didn't know the main export from the West Indies was the Coconut Rough. It wasn't intended to be racist, but it has rebounded very seriously against me. Which I fully accept. I didn't last long on the public-speaking circuit, for obvious reasons.

When the West Indies next toured New Zealand in 1987, umpire Goodall was introduced to Vivian Richards, the new West Indian captain.

'He wouldn't shake my hand but said, "We've heard about you." I was sent to Coventry by the West Indians and only Richards talked to me. It was very unpleasant. It was hell. H-E-L-L. Personal comments that were cleverly said out of earshot of anyone else. They were gunning for me. One thing Richards did say to me was "We'll teach you to make fun of our people."'

6

'Unless the cricketer had heroic qualities, we did not want to see him'

David Murray had always wanted to play cricket for the West Indies. He had been born very close to the Kensington Oval in Barbados and while he was still a boy his talent was evident. He captained his school team and was chosen for the Barbados youth side, then the West Indies youth XI. Few were surprised by his skill because Murray was the son of a West Indian cricket king.

David's dad was Everton Weekes – the middle batsman of the three Ws. Frank Worrell, Weekes and Clyde Walcott were the brilliant Barbadian triptych in the West Indian side that played such exciting cricket after the Second World War. Weekes, a working-class genius who would one day receive a knighthood for his talents, first scored runs for fun in the Thursday afternoon blue-collar Barbados Cricket League. Then he got to a thousand Test runs faster than Donald Bradman. The Ws had been born within a few-dollars-on-the-meter Bridgetown taxi fare of each other between the middle of 1924 and the end of 1926. They were a holy trinity, three consubstantial persons in one almighty side. Local people, almost without qualification, loved them.

The writer Ramachandra Guha tells the story of Archbishop of

Canterbury Michael Ramsey visiting Bridgetown in 1969 to preach to the Anglican flock gathered in the pews of St Michael's Cathedral. 'He began by saying he had come to talk about the three Ws. A huge cheer went up, to become a collective groan when the prelate continued, "Yes, the three Ws – work, witness and worship!"'

David Murray knew the cathedral's pews, its perfume and its prayers. He had been brought up in the Anglican faith and was a choirboy. He knew the wooden benches of the Kensington Oval just as well and had seen Nari Contractor hit by that infamous Charlie Griffith bouncer in 1962. 'Just a schoolboy, but I still hear the *conk* of the ball on his head.' Murray also knew the sands of Brownes Beach, Brandons Beach and Bayshore Beach.

'I would get up early every morning and train at five o'clock,' he says. 'I knew every scavenger in Barbados at that time when I'm up on the road. I do a lot of road work myself. And beach work. For the team and for yourself as a wicket-keeper you should be fit. We had these fast bowlers coming – there was a whole heap of them at the time.'

Murray – whose famous father was batting at Cardiff Arms Park against Glamorgan when he was born on a Monday in May in 1950 – was touring England himself with the West Indians by the time he was 23. But the keeper's job he wanted was held by another Murray – no relation – the vice-captain, Deryck. David would have to wait. He did not start a Test match until the Packer schism of 1978 offered him a place. Malcolm Marshall once said that David Murray was the best wicket-keeper he ever bowled to. But this Murray would play only 19 Test matches in his life. By the beginning of 1983 he was flying to a forbidden land and towards his final games of cricket.

*   *   *

In the first week of January 1983 a story appeared in the Jamaican newspaper the *Daily Gleaner*. The batsman Lawrence Rowe was denying having signed a contract to play cricket in South Africa. The newspaper's source – thought to be another player – named 14 other West Indian cricketers who would be going. They were, said the source, to be paid at least US $90,000 each and would return for another tour at the end of 1983. In South Africa a club official in Pretoria had let slip that he had been told to make preparations for the arrival of an 'international team'. Would there be more than one side? There could be players from Australia, New Zealand and England too, said the *Star* in Johannesburg.

To most readers of the *Gleaner*, this was extraordinary news. Black players travelling to a country ostracised by much of the world because it practised state-sanctioned racism? But the next day the mystery tour was called off. Cancelled by the South African Cricket Union. Its president, Joe Pamensky, said that the leaking of the story had put pressure on several players – whom he wouldn't name – and they had withdrawn. The tour would now be scrapped because it was no longer of 'true international standard'.

In the Caribbean the WICBC was mightily relieved. At a cricket lunch in Jamaica its president, Allan Rae, praised both Lawrence Rowe and Colin Croft – who were at the table with him – for not going to South Africa. 'I believe the cricketing fraternity of the West Indies ought to say a big thank you,' he told his audience. 'The gentlemen have put temptation behind them.'

Except they hadn't. There still was a tour. It would be made by West Indian players and, secretly, it was going ahead. Within a week, six cricketers from Barbados met at Grantley Adams International Airport heading for Miami. They had gathered at a house near the airport before leaving it as late as they could to check in. Collis King was there, covering his face with a straw hat to hide from a TV news crew that had picked up the story. As he strode past the camera with an Adidas sports bag on his shoulder, he walked into a pillar and the hat fell off.

Reports in South Africa now claimed that the idea of a tour had been conceived in London in the summer of 1982. Ali Bacher, a former South Africa captain and recruiter-in-chief of rebel cricketers, had tried to persuade the West Indian Sylvester Clarke, who was playing for Surrey, to become Vintcent van der Bijl's opening bowling partner for Transvaal. Clarke said no but kept the business card he had been given. He passed it on to the former Barbados bowler Gregory Armstrong, and by October 1982 there was a fully formed plan to take an entire West Indies XI to South Africa. Code names were used for the players and contact between them was apparently maintained via public telephone boxes.

And now, at the beginning of 1983, they were about to depart. With King were Alvin Greenidge (no relation of Gordon), Emmerson Trotman, Ezra Moseley and Sylvester Clarke. Albert Padmore arrived at Adams airport 20 minutes late and caused the flight to be delayed. Derick Parry would fly from Antigua to join them in Miami. Lawrence Rowe was heading there too, from Kingston, but when he was asked why he was flying to Florida, Rowe assured reporters that he was due in Miami on business and would be back in Jamaica the following evening.

He didn't return. He was heading to South Africa to captain a team of black men in a country where black people had few rights. He was heading into the heart of apartheid.

* * *

South Africa hadn't played proper international cricket for 13 years. The last Test side to go to the republic had been Australia in 1970. At Port Elizabeth that March the visitors were beaten for the fourth time in four matches by a brilliantly talented – and entirely white – South African side. There would be no more Test cricket for nearly a quarter of a century. Most sporting nations refused to play South Africa because of apartheid. By law, black and white were forbidden to mix freely. Segregation was everywhere and people who challenged the iniquity were punished. By the mid-1960s those punishments ranged from the pettily bureaucratic to imprisonment, detention without trial, torture and extrajudicial killings.

One of apartheid's chief architects was Hendrik Verwoerd, who was prime minister from 1958 until he was stabbed to death in the House of Assembly in Cape Town on a September afternoon in 1966. He was very concerned that sport must not undermine apartheid. In 1962 Verwoerd's minister of the interior proclaimed, 'The mixing of races in teams taking part in sports meetings in the republic and abroad must be prevented. The government cannot allow teams from the republic to be composed of whites and non-whites. Conversely, foreign teams which are so composed cannot be permitted to enter the republic.'

In 1964 South Africa's invitation to appear at the Olympic games was withdrawn. Later the same year the governing body of international football, Fifa, suspended South Africa. Neither of these decisions was straightforward; there were many within the football and Olympic worlds who had argued it was right and acceptable to include the apartheid republic.

In the years that followed, South Africa's governing National Party tried a little window-dressing to present the republic as a nation of multiracial sport, but nothing meaningful had changed. Black sports unions may have been given some leeway, but rigid racial separation remained. Black, coloured and Indian spectators – if they were allowed in at all – still had to enter sports stadiums by different gates, sit in different seats and use different lavatories. In 1968, when Verwoerd's successor B. J. Vorster refused to allow the England cricket team into the country because one of its players was Basil D'Oliveira – a 'Cape Coloured' batsman who had left South Africa to play for England – the worldwide reaction against the republic helped to accelerate its full sporting isolation.

And so for many nations – not least, independent post-colonial black nations – the idea of their athletes taking their skills to South Africa was all but inconceivable. The anti-apartheid struggle was both principled and visceral, wrote Michael Manley. 'To the members of the black diaspora, the oppression which continues unabated in South Africa has become the symbol of more than a tyranny to be overthrown. Apartheid points like a dagger to the throat of black self-worth in every corner occupied by the descendants of Africa.'

*　*　*

On Wednesday 14 January 1983 Lawrence Rowe and most of his side touched down at Jan Smuts Airport in Johannesburg.

'The last five minutes of that flight,' he would recall,

> I can remember it vividly. There was total silence. I think everybody was more or less thinking the same thing: *We are now getting ready to land in South Africa*. Whoever was thinking about a career for the West Indies again, it is now gone. It hit everybody now that, *Hey, this is it*. This is the moment of truth now. We are here, we're coming down. What are we to expect when we get down there? What would the black people be feeling when we walk off the plane? This was the thinking of most of the guys.

At the airport they were served beer by black waiters with bottle openers and protected by white policeman with guns. Lawrence Rowe told reporters, 'We are professionals. We are here to do a job.

Obviously we are feeling a bit jittery.' A hundred or so people had cheered and clapped as the players arrived. Three black people stood silently holding a poster: FREEDOM FIRST – CRICKET LATER.

Other West Indian team members flew in during the next few days. The South African Cricket Union arranged with the Department of Internal Affairs for their passports not to be stamped to indicate that they had visited South Africa, as it might cause the cricketers problems in later life. A few other players were expected to join the rebels but never arrived. Alvin Kallicharran was already there, playing for Transvaal. He was no longer part of the West Indies Test team. In 1981 he had signed a contract for the provincial side, a decision which ended his international career. Now he would play county cricket for Warwickshire in the English summer and for Transvaal in the English winter.

When all the players eventually gathered, there were the Jamaicans Rowe, Richard Austin, Everton Mattis, Ray Wynter and Herbert Chang. Barbados was best represented – by Alvin Greenidge, Emmerson Trotman, Collis King, Ezra Moseley, David Murray, Franklyn Stephenson and Sylvester Clarke. The manager and his assistant – Albert Padmore and Gregory Armstrong – were from Barbados too. Derick Parry was from Nevis, Bernard Julien from Trinidad. Colin Croft and Kallicharran were Guyanese.

Back in the West Indies the official reaction was forthright. 'They had better not come here,' warned Trinidad's national security minister. 'I wouldn't be able to guarantee their safety if they did.' Michael Manley – now the opposition leader in Jamaica – said the players' decision amounted to 'selling out their patrimony, humiliating their race and country for a mess of pottage'. They should get nothing less than life bans from cricket, he said.

Another Jamaican politician said the players had 'deceived the nation up to the very last moment that they began their blood-money mission to racist South Africa. The dignity of man and in particular the fight of the black man in South Africa for his normal, basic, God-given rights cannot be quantified in terms of money – not even the fortune of Croesus or the gold at Fort Knox.' The minister concluded that Lawrence Rowe and Colin Croft's deception of WICBC president Allan Rae as they sat next to him at the lunch table was 'especially vicious and heinous as they caused Mr Rae to make an embarrassing and premature expression of gratitude'.

Rae later recalled how he had passed Rowe a note before speaking. 'I wrote, "I have to make a speech before this luncheon is finished. Is it true you're going to South Africa?" He wrote at the bottom of the paper, "I'm staying," and I got up and praised him to the highest heavens.'

Secrecy – and in consequence deception – had been critical if the rebels were to make it to South Africa unmolested. In *The Times* some days before the tour's beginning Alvin Kallicharran had let it be known that he was considering legal action because his name was being 'tarnished' in connection with the enterprise. 'How is it possible for me to arrange such a tour when I'm currently playing for Transvaal?' However, eight days later in the same newspaper Joe Pamensky commended the Guyanese batsman for his role in the planning of the trip: 'Alvin Kallicharran has proved to be one of South Africa's greatest ambassadors.'

The Barbadian cricket journalist Tony Cozier wrote at the time that the revelation of the tour was a 'shattering blow to the collective morale of the governments of the region, who in common with other black, third world countries, have waged a steadfast campaign against South Africa'. The barriers that these governments had sought to erect around the republic and had strenuously sought to maintain 'were being trampled over by their own cricketers'. A black team had been lured to a country that despised black people. 'It was a major accomplishment by South Africans both political and cricketing,' he said.

But not everybody condemned the rebels. On Caribbean phone-in radio shows and on the letters pages of the region's newspapers there was regular support for the cricketers. They were praised for trying to better themselves financially. Al Gilkes went on tour with the side to report for the *Nation* newspaper in Barbados, the only black journalist to do so. As the trip went on he formed the belief that 'Rowe and his rebel team had become not the mercenaries they were being labelled outside South Africa but black missionaries converting and baptising thousands and thousands of whites into a religion of black acceptance and respect from Cape Town to Johannesburg, to Durban and right into the throne room of Afrikanerdom itself, Pretoria.'

The WICBC was of course wounded by the deception. It had been betrayed by those it least expected to breach the sanction. But in fact there had been several warnings. In 1982 Clive Lloyd had even submitted a paper to West Indian governments predicting that a tour by a renegade West Indies XI was likely. 'If members of what might be considered the West Indies first and second XIs were to give in to the considerable temptations that could be offered, the implications for both West Indies and world cricket could be grave,' he wrote. 'The problem is a political and economic one and requires a political and economic solution . . . It would be idle to pretend that the Caribbean could hope to match the scale of the South African offers . . . but if an attractive offer of alternative employment is provided, cricketers would then be put on the spot if they were to take up offers to go to South Africa.'

Lloyd's plan – which would have meant a stipend for certain players – wasn't seriously entertained.

* * *

David Murray had made the journey to South Africa by himself. He arrived in Johannesburg from Australia, where he had been playing club cricket for Glenelg in Adelaide. 'I was booked in at the Carlton hotel,' he remembers 'and as soon as I walked in I got a lot of looks: *This man is a black man.* I got to the desk to sign in and they looked at me. I didn't sleep that night. I just wanted to get to the guys. You could feel the segregation between black and white and coloured. It was in the air. It was frightening.'

Murray had left his pregnant Australian wife behind him. Kerry Murray said that her husband was trembling when he made the final decision to go. Within a fortnight she had given birth to their child, a daughter called Ebony. The SACU sent Murray champagne to celebrate, but very quickly he was threatened with never being able to see his daughter in Australia. The Australian Prime Minister Malcolm Fraser let it be known that no West Indians who played in South Africa would be allowed back into the country. The plan would prove politically unworkable, but for a while it unsettled Murray still further. 'It's hard to play cricket with all the stories coming out,' he said at the time. 'Of course I don't support apartheid, but I don't get involved in the political side. I just know how to keep wicket and bat a bit.'

The South African cricket authorities needed this tour to work because previous visits had failed. The West Indies were not the first rebel team to be lured to the republic, but it was hoped they would be the most exciting. An English team captained by Graham Gooch had been easily beaten by South Africa the season before, but not as easily as a pitifully lame Sri Lanka side that hadn't won a single match in late 1982. South African cricket watchers wanted to believe that their side, despite its years of banishment, was still capable of beating a classy opponent. Nothing had been proved by the visits of the English and Sri Lankan mercenaries.

The West Indies' arrival also coincided with substantial changes within South Africa, which were making the white population uneasy. While there was plenty of cash available to turn some black athletes' heads ('We have all the money we need to induce the best cricketers in the world,' boasted the SACU), the country had been experiencing a sharp recession. Many white people were becoming poorer. Moreover, the extraordinarily elaborate bureaucracy set up to administer apartheid had never been more costly. White professionals were leaving South Africa to find work and to escape what was fast becoming the world's number one pariah nation, and notable divisions, previously unthinkable, were opening between working-class and middle-class Afrikaners.

South Africa had never felt so estranged. 'Instead of being at the southern end of a continent controlled by Europeans, in a world dominated by Europeans and North Americans, South Africa had become an isolated anomaly,' wrote Leonard Thompson, a scholar of the republic's history and politics. 'Whereas the structure of Southern African society had been compatible with the structure of the societies in tropical Africa, the Caribbean, much of Asia and the United States before World War II, that was no longer the case. Since 1948, systematic racism had become the bedrock of South Africa's law and practice. The ways had parted between South Africa and the rest of the world.'

Of all the measures taken against South Africa, the sporting boycott appeared to be particularly effective. By the late 1970s white sports administrators were pleading with the government to authorise mixed events in the hope that they might just prove to be the beginning of the republic's reintegration into international sport. Cricket was one of the first games to experiment with mixing, but according to Sam Ramsamy, who ran the South African non-racial Olympic committee, mixed cricket in the apartheid republic was a trick and a failure.

Writing in *The Cricketer* at the time of the rebel West Indian tour, he revealed,

black clubs – on innocently affiliating to the previously all-white provincial leagues – discovered that they could only play in fixtures that were approved by the white government. Blacks were not allowed to join white clubs or vice versa. Blacks discovered that they were not allowed to use shelters where food or drinks were served. Blacks were told that the clubhouses and changing rooms were for whites only. Black players were forced to change in their cars while whites enjoyed the luxury of the clubhouses. During lunch breaks blacks had to leave the ground for their meals while the whites could eat in the clubhouse. Blacks quickly discovered that they were being used to create a showpiece of propaganda for the outside world so that white South Africa could again enjoy international participation.

Joe Pamensky insisted that there had never been any question of conning black cricketers. Naturally, he said, there were some teething problems in bringing about such important changes, 'but these happily were isolated incidents and quickly settled'. There was, he said, no place in the SACU's set-up for clubs that practised racial discrimination.

And so South Africa desperately needed a distracting sporting success – and was prepared to pay for it. Even after Lawrence Rowe's team arrived, the recruitment of black cricketers to add to the West Indian squad continued. Michael Holding, who was playing for the

Australian state of Tasmania, was telephoned in bed by the rebel captain, who offered him US $250,000 to join the gang. 'I made it plain to Lawrence that I wasn't interested. I know it's a lot of money but the principle of the thing is far more important,' said the fast bowler to a newspaper at the time.

Now he can elaborate.

My reaction when I heard about the team that went down to South Africa was that they were traitors. They were selling out the region. I could not understand why anyone would want to play cricket there with the apartheid regime still in force. That was my immediate reaction. Having watched what had taken place in the townships with the killing of the black people there, the way black people were treated. I just could not understand why any West Indian cricketer would want to go down there, and I was disgusted.

Others had been asked too. Their decision to reject the South African money took them a little longer. Several early press reports about which players had decided to take part in the tour named Malcolm Marshall, Desmond Haynes and Hartley Alleyne. Certainly they were tempted, and when the rebels returned for a second tour at the end of the year Alleyne would be with them. Like David Murray, all three had been in Australia at the end of 1982.

Marshall recalled that Ali Bacher had somehow got hold of the number of the flat where he was staying in Melbourne and in the strictest secrecy called to offer him $50,000 to join up. Tickets in his name were ready at the airport. Marshall told Bacher that he was intrigued and flattered by the offer. Bacher told him not to mention it to a soul. Marshall agreed but went straight round to see Haynes and Alleyne to tell them.

The three men discovered that they had all been made similarly secret offers by Bacher but of very different amounts. They were conflicted. Marshall was only 24 but knew that the money would be enough to set up a business in Barbados – if he was allowed to return there. However, he was interested to learn that Colin Croft had signed up for the tour. If Croft was banned from the Test team, it was very likely that Marshall would be his replacement. Like Haynes, he immediately thought about how he would be treated back home if he took apartheid money. 'I was plagued by the idea that I could become an outcast among my own people for helping to add succour to a political system which openly denigrated blacks,' he wrote in his autobiography.

Haynes's biographer Rob Steen recorded similar thoughts. The temptation for the batsman was great, no question of that. 'I was very nervous and confused about the whole thing. I had to look at the whole situation in the long run, at the prospect of securing my future . . . I felt that what was going on in South Africa was wrong but by the same token I did not believe that going there would change anything. There is so much hypocrisy in the world.'

The decision they took to refuse South Africa was a late one; up until the departure of the rebels there was some uncertainty about where Haynes, Marshall and Alleyne actually were. Some reports said that they had left Australia for Johannesburg. David Murray says that he spoke to them about meeting in Perth to fly together to South Africa. Desmond Haynes solved the mystery when he rang officials in Barbados on 13 January to let them know that he and his two friends would be flying back to the island via San Francisco. When they arrived at Grantley Adams airport they were slightly embarrassed to see cheering crowds and the chairman of the national sports council. 'I am so glad you boys have had the good sense to turn down the offer and to come home to your own people,' the politician told them. 'You will not regret this. You will be able to live with yourselves – which may not be the case for some of your countrymen.'

He wasn't joking. The same day the WICBC banned the rebels from any sort of cricket sanctioned by the board. Life bans.

*   *   *

Less than two days after landing in South Africa the West Indians were playing cricket – a 50-over game against Western Province at Newlands in Cape Town. Richard Austin in a sun hat and Alvin Greenidge in a maroon helmet walked out to open the West Indian batting. They had crossed the line. In the press box one mischievous reporter asked, 'I wonder what John Vorster is doing right now?' There were to be provincial matches and two 'Test' matches against South Africa plus six one-day games.

The second fixture of the tour, against Border, was David Murray's first. As he stood behind the wicket, the enormity of his decision was now inescapable. 'Yeah. The first ball I received in South Africa was a dismissal. A Sylvester Clarke first-ball catch, and the guys ran from first slip and all over the field. All I was thinking was *You can't play for the West Indies again once the umpire said "Play."* So, first ball of my tour and my career was finished. I shed a tear, I remember that very much. Water came down the eyes as if to say, *You can't play for your country again*. I was solemn. Very.'

*   *   *

Robin Buckley is sipping a beer in the back room of his house in Pretoria. The two family dogs are sniffing the air for the scent of snacks. In his day Robin was a fine club cricketer. Some of his trophies sit on the shelf above him. 'Just Mickey Mouse stuff,' he chuckles.

Robin saw the West Indies team play in the second 'Test' match of their first tour in Johannesburg. He couldn't wait. He watched

Collis King make a hundred and smiles when describing the way King could drive a yorker off the back foot through the covers.

'We were starved,' he says. 'We'd missed out on the West Indies of course. I remember asking friends from England, "What is Andy Roberts like? What does he *look* like? What is his style? How does he bowl?" We didn't see any of it. So when these guys came out, we were off like a shot to go and see them. People couldn't get enough of them here.'

Like a lot of white middle-class cricket lovers in South Africa, Robin Buckley was less interested in politics than he was in sport. He had a university friend who had been imprisoned for his beliefs by the regime, but his view is that meddling politicians – for and against apartheid – wrecked people's enjoyment of sport. 'These black cricketers were ambassadors. The crowds realised that they were putting their lives on the line and taking a chance, so there was support and respect for that. As for the situation we were in, that was just the law. My family was brought up to respect people; we worked with black people; I sat next to a black guy in my car every day. But that was the law. Sitting watching it all happen, there was not much you could do about it.'

He also knew that however mild the transgression, the authorities' reach – and memory – was long. As a student at Natal University he had once illegally played cricket against a local Indian XI.

After the game one of the players said, 'Did you see the police there? They were taking photographs of us all.' 'You must be kidding,' we answered. Well, 15 years later I was working as a surveyor and had a job looking at a government building in Pretoria – the Special Branch police offices or something. They assigned a chap to walk with me to make sure I didn't go anywhere I shouldn't. Along the way he showed me the room with all the files of the naughty people in it. So I gave him my card and said, 'See if you can find anything on me.' A little while later he came back and said, 'There was a photo of you when you were younger in cricket whites.' It had been taken at that game in 1971.

Politicians mess it up for the sportsmen – just let them get on and play. It made me sad that people like Viv Richards and Clive Lloyd would say, 'I will never come to your country because of what it represents.' But I also think that they didn't actually understand that there were people here who didn't think like the government. I would say that most English-speaking people here would give you roughly the same answer. If you spoke to Afrikaners, well, you'd perhaps get a different answer. I think we probably all knew that the tour was a trick, but I wasn't going to turn around and say, 'This is a government ploy; I'm not going to go and watch.' Here was an opportunity to see these guys, and we knew the people playing against them and we wanted to see cricket. It might come with a bit of a taint to it but we weren't going to miss it. What you have to understand is that nobody could foresee when apartheid would end, you know?

*   *   *

Essop Pahad is sitting in the shade on the back deck of his house in Johannesburg. At his feet are some of his grandchildren's toys. On the wall by the front door are two framed pictures, one of Muhammad Ali and one of Nelson Mandela looking on while Chris Hani, once the leader of the South African Communist Party, gives a speech.

'What you must understand', Essop insists,

is that white South Africans would say of these black cricketers, 'Ah, but they are different. They aren't like the black people who cut our lawns. Our blacks can't play cricket, they aren't any good.' Because if they admitted that we were all the same and that we had skills which were as good as theirs, then you were admitting there had to be a change. And they were refusing to change. No one could turn a blind eye like a white South African could in those days. Liberals and others.

Pahad is a cricket-lover, a sports lover born in the Transvaal just before the Second World War. As a teenaged member of the Indian Youth Congress he campaigned against Frank Worrell bringing a cricket side to South Africa. He became a communist and later, an African National Congress politician. He didn't see much cricket in the 1980s though, because he was exiled in Iron Curtain Czechoslovakia. After apartheid had been dismantled, he served in the government of his student friend, President Thabo Mbeki.

The pair studied at the University of Sussex together, where Pahad combined his academic life with political agitation. In 1965, he went to Lord's to meet the MCC Secretary, 'Billy' Griffith. 'Wow. We're sitting in the Long Room,' said his companion, Dennis Brutus. Brutus was a poet and anti-apartheid sporting activist. They were hoping to persuade MCC not to let the South Africa side tour England that summer. Griffith granted them an audience in the famous pavilion where women were not yet allowed (even though the wedding reception of Griffith's own daughter had been held there) to listen to the pair's arguments in favour of sporting boycotts.

'He gave us a typical conservative English answer about politics and sport not being mixed,' remembers Pahad. Before long the student was arrested on St John's Wood Road for putting up stickers protesting against the tour. He laughs. '"Don't worry," a friend told me as I was being taken away. "They're not like the South African police."'

'I think it is fair to say', he goes on,

that the anti-apartheid movement had its origins in England, and it became the most powerful solidarity movement the world has ever seen. We had spent 18 years building this organisation up, and by 1983, when nobody wanted to touch apartheid South Africa, you get these black cricketers coming here, a huge, huge disappointment. For the regime it was a great success. They had broken the boycott, or so they thought.

I regarded these black men as traitors. Traitors to the cause. Because it was treachery of the highest order – and treachery for what? They didn't come here to develop cricket, they came here because they were offered a lot of money. It's understandable of course because most cricketers in the West Indies weren't being paid very much at all. But they were making a fast buck on the back of somebody else's oppression. They gave respectability to a pariah state. Giving solace and comfort to the fountainhead of world racism.

Of course those who went to South Africa disagreed – publicly, at least. They had a variety of reasons for going. Some were unemployed; others recognised that, given the strength of the 1980s West Indies side, they would never play Test cricket; some who had played Test cricket before knew they never would again. Sylvester Clarke, for instance, was a superbly destructive fast bowler but probably sixth or seventh in line to take the new ball for Clive Lloyd's side. Lawrence Rowe and Alvin Kallicharran knew exactly what it took to play Test cricket – they had 96 caps between them – but were distressed by the way their careers had ended. Both thought they had been unfairly dropped from the side, and in a manner that was disrespectful of their service. Professionally at least, they felt they had nothing to lose by playing cricket in South Africa.

For Colin Croft the decision was also about where he had come from and where he wanted to go. 'I had hopes and aspirations of getting a degree in engineering. I had hopes and aspirations of becoming an airline pilot way back in 1979 when I was an air traffic controller. So the possibility presented itself during WSC to get some money.'

And now, five years later, another opportunity had arisen.

I can recall some names that I know from when I was in high school – Basil Butcher, Joe Solomon, Roy Fredericks. They all played for Guyana and the West Indies and they got nothing out of it, absolutely nothing. I'd had a tough life so anything I have accumulated since I played cricket for the West Indies is a bonus. I came from a very poor background, so for me to put on a suit like this or to be dressed up or driving a car is, to use a modern circumstance, 'elevation'.

You say to a man, 'Well, you mustn't go to South Africa.' But you don't provide anything else for him, so what is he supposed to do? How is he supposed to feed his kids? Is he supposed to go to the grocer and say, 'My name is Colin Croft; I played for the West Indies. I need two baskets full of groceries.' It doesn't work that way.

When Collis King was interviewed by the CNN journalist Don Riddell for a 2013 documentary called *Branded a Rebel*, he said it was dissatisfaction with the West Indies' cricket authorities that helped him make his decision. 'I wasn't getting treated right as far as the West Indies were concerned. I was still scoring runs yet I wasn't on the team. And I said to myself, *Well, cricket is my job. You're not picking me; I'll go to play cricket someplace where people will see proper cricket.* And that's why I went.'

And there was the cash. 'It's true to say', mentioned one of the squad once he had arrived in South Africa, 'that I'm getting more money from this short tour than I can earn in Jamaica in a year. I'm just trying to secure my financial future.'

'Well, money is everybody's god, let's be honest,' is how Colin Croft puts it.

An official programme recorded that 'for the majority of the players the principal motive for making the tour has been the financial angle. The words of one of the players – Richard Austin – may well be echoed by all. "I cannot feed myself and my family on principles." The lot of the West Indian cricket professional who is not counted among the few top stars is far from easy.'

'How do you become a mercenary?' asks Croft. 'Simply because you are paid to play the same sport that you've been paid to play before? I had played for the West Indies and had been paid. Was I not a mercenary then? When I played World Series Cricket was I not a mercenary? But if I go to South Africa and I'm being paid, I'm a mercenary now? I'm not sure I know what the difference is.'

A decade after the tour, speaking to Michelle McDonald from the website caribbeancricket.com, Lawrence Rowe explained why he had accepted the captaincy of rebel team: 'By going I didn't believe we could have made it any worse for the [non-white] South Africans. The second thing was, by going, there was just a possibility that we might have a little opening, and especially if I went and we won, it would have been a victory for the black people. Number three, money was involved.' The money was about 60 times as much as he was getting paid for playing for Jamaica. 'And most of the guys were pissed off with the West Indies board.'

Rowe believed that after the runs he scored against England in 1980–81 he should have been selected for the tour to Australia. Instead, he and Alvin Kallicharran were 'thrown through the window' and dropped.

So here is an offer, 60 times more. You have your family, and for some people like Everton Mattis these people didn't own a car, had four or five children, didn't have a house, didn't have anything. The people of influence would have passed them on the road. If you were leaving a Jamaica match you had to go get the bus carrying your own bag. How do you tell a man in a position like that not to accept $100,000 to go play five months of cricket over the two tours?

Rowe's notion that a West Indian side playing cricket in apartheid South Africa was 'a victory for the black people' which could bring hope for the future irritates Essop Pahad.

This idea – that sport during that time in South Africa could bring people together – it's absolute rubbish. There is not one single black person in South Africa, except the ones that were already sell-outs, who would make that argument. It didn't prove anything. We already knew that Sobers, Richards, Roberts, Kanhai were some of the best cricketers the world had seen. We didn't need to discover that blacks could play cricket too. The whole thing was designed to placate the whites in South Africa that all was not lost. They were being herded into their *laager* and fed the illusion that actually *We are in control of the situation.*

Neither does the former politician think that West Indian cricketers were historically ignorant of apartheid.

In 1966 I was in Brighton with Thabo Mbeki. One day he would become president of South Africa. We're doing our masters degrees together at Sussex University and the West Indies were touring. They came to play Sussex at Hove. I had a nice little house in Spring Street and Thabo said, 'Let's invite the team there.' And so they all came and spent the evening – Hall, Griffith, Kanhai, Sobers. A lot of drinks, a lot of food. We talked about apartheid and the hope of a boycott. There was cricket conversation, talk about the sanctions, about the importance of isolating apartheid South Africa. So they were not unaware. I remember that we spoke to them about the importance of demonstrating the capacity of blacks. And for us, those West Indies cricketers were the epitome of that. So for those of us who loved cricket, this tour in '83 was especially crushing because we thought the West Indies were the greatest team.

*   *   *

'We made these decisions in our life, rightly or wrongly,' says Alvin Kallicharran. 'But we weren't involved with the whites alone. We went into townships. We went into Soweto, we went into Coloured and Indian areas. What people were seeing for the first time was blacks against whites, and that opened up lots of avenues for black cricketers in South Africa. People have to look at the plusses too.'

Kallicharran's supporters at the time wrote that by playing in South Africa he would help to break down barriers between black and white a lot faster than politicians could. Some black sports administrators inside South Africa were less sure. Krish Mackerdhuj, who would later become the first non-white president of a South Africa cricket board, told the *Sydney Morning Herald* in 1982, 'Sure, there will be certain black sportsmen who would welcome Kallicharran. But the majority detest his presence because he is non-committal to their struggle for non-racialism in sport.'

Kallicharran was disgusted by spectators who heckled him and said that if they carried on he would not be able to sympathise with their cause. 'I will play the game, regardless of what any person or organisation has to say about me or my choice,' quoted the *Herald*. 'I am a professional cricketer. Like a doctor or a teacher trained to do a particular job, I am best at cricket. I earn my living from playing and coaching cricket, and I don't think anybody has the right to stop me from doing this.'

What was obvious was that almost all of Transvaal's cricket supporters – that is their white fans – adored Kallicharran. The warmth of the applause he received when he scored his first hundred for the side made him cry.

'The loudest cheer I ever heard for any cricketer at the Wanderers was for Alvin Kallicharran in his last innings there,' remembers Robin Buckley. 'These guys left their mark here. People shouting anti-apartheid things at sport is stupid, absolutely crazy, because that's where you get to influence people – you get inside the *laager* mentality and have a chance to make people change. The best thing was to play sport together. Let these South Africans see what the rest of the world is all about.'

* * *

To see what South Africa was about, the rebel side of 1983 had to go through a curious transformation. They had to become 'honorary whites'. This was less a process of signing documents or carrying a piece of paper than an existential change of status. The argument was that any black person *invited* to South Africa automatically became an honorary white. Practically, this allowed Rowe and his team to go to places – restaurants, hotels – or to travel in taxis forbidden to black South Africans by law.

'I remember thinking, *These guys have sold out*,' says Michael Holding, 'and I suppose having now accepted the term 'honorary white', if they paid them enough money they would even accept chains on their ankles. I remember saying that. Now, looking back on it, perhaps that was a little bit harsh, but that is just the way I felt at the time.' The insult of being granted such a status was too much for Vivian Richards. It was 'as low as you can get in selling your soul'. He says he would rather have died than lost his dignity in such a way. 'How can a black man be a honorary white man?' he asks. 'No money in this world would get me to go to South Africa if I had to give them my natural status. I was going to sit anywhere on a train I wanted to sit. I was going to go anywhere that I wanted to go. That is the privilege of human beings.'

'What is wrong with the colour of my skin?' wonders Holding. 'What is wrong with my ethnicity? Why should anyone tell me that I should be an honorary anything apart from what I am? If I am black, I am black – I am proud of it. Why would a white man want to go to a black country or where black people rule and say that he is an honorary black? That is absolute rubbish. There is no way I would accept that.'

Lawrence Rowe is sure he never signed a piece of paper to become an honorary white. Colin Croft is certain he didn't either. 'This story where they said we were given white status or some crap like that, that was very, very wrong. You see, it was not so. None of us were given white status – that's crap. But politically it was expedient for them to say that.'

When Croft returned to South Africa later in the year to fulfil his contract, he took a train journey. The conductor of the train certainly saw him as nothing other than black.

I was asked to remove myself from a train carriage because it was for whites only. It became an international incident because people wanted to make a big thing out of probably what was a big thing. The conductor told me I was sitting in the wrong carriage. Fine, I was prepared to move. Politically you're saying to me, 'Because my skin is black I can't sit in this carriage.' That's not fine but that's what the law says. Another man in the carriage made a noise about it. I managed eventually to get to Cape Town without moving. Again the newspapers had it wrong because they said we'd moved and we didn't.

The man who had 'made the noise' was called Raymond Roos. He recalled that his Christian duty had prevented him from watching Croft being harangued by the conductor. In his version of the story he and Croft went and sat on the benches in an inferior carriage together with black passengers. Whatever took place, it was deeply awkward for the promoters of the tour.

'It's such a pity in this day and age', lamented Joe Pamensky, 'that such an embarrassing situation should arise and that one of our esteemed international visitors should be the victim of a system that so many of us in South Africa are attempting to change.'

'I couldn't have handled that,' says Clive Lloyd,

and I would never have put myself in that position. It's ludicrous. But that's what these boys had to do in South Africa; they were made honorary whites for the duration. It was demeaning. Think about the things we experienced in England in the 1950s – NO DOGS, NO BLACKS, NO IRISH on the guest-house doors. We experienced bad things in America, prejudices that we had to overcome. The worst thing is for someone to tell you that you are a lesser person because of your colour. I can't accept that.

A decade before the West Indians flew in, the black Guyanese novelist E. R. Braithwaite had visited South Africa. He had been given a visa and granted honorary white status. *Honorary White* became the title of his next book. After the sanitised sightseeing trips, which had been carefully provided by the Ministry of Information to show South Africa at its best, he managed to unravel a conflicting story. Black acquaintances among the urban poor explained the misery of their lives in the Johannesburg townships of Soweto and Alexandra. They also impressed upon him the preposterous reality of his own temporary privileged status.

Braithwaite concluded, 'the "Honorary White" thing was no better than a kick in the ass. The intention was the same. To humiliate the black visitor; to deny him the dignity of his blackness; to remind him in that society he had no identity except that which they, the Whites, chose to let him have. As a Black I was invisible, not there, not to them. To be seen and heard, I needed an overlay on my invisibility.'

Lawrence Rowe's side were certainly seen and heard by plenty of people. Much of the cricket they played was broadcast live on television, and during the first tour the grounds were full. Some of the matches were undoubtedly exciting. For South Africa their stunted Test greats – Richards, Pollock, Procter – all showed the skills that had never come to full bloom in international cricket. For the West Indies XI Sylvester Clarke in particular announced himself as a bowler of frightening power. He won the second 'Test' almost by himself. Collis King made thrilling runs. The crowds were delighted by the contests. But who was watching?

'The first thing is all of the venues were sold out. *All* of the venues were sold out,' stresses Colin Croft. 'I remember the first day we played at Cape Town they had so many people they had to bring in the boundary to 60 meters, and not keep it at 75 or they couldn't get the people in the ground. At least one third, I would say, maybe a half of the patrons were black.'

Lewis Manthata is a teacher and historian of black cricket. He was born and brought up in Soweto. He was living there as a young boy when the rebel cricketers came. In his neighbourhood at least he says there was little interest in cricket.

The first thing you have to know is that you cannot even quantify in percentages the number of black people in Soweto in the 1980s who would have played and enjoyed cricket. It was tiny. Absolutely tiny. You're talking about possibly 20 people who played cricket at the time in Soweto. I can name those families if you like, because cricket was not a community-based sport. It was known largely as an elitist sport played by English-speaking people from the Eastern Cape. Soccer was the game. To play soccer was almost to take part in a political act. It was seen as the sport which allowed people to relieve their frustrations against the apartheid system.

If there were hardly any black cricketers in the townships, does it follow that there would be hardly any black spectators at the games?

I wonder. It's unlikely that in Johannesburg for example many black people at the time would *freely* have watched these matches. If they did, it's very likely that they would have been mine workers put under pressure by mine owners to be there. But the sight of buses and buses full of black people turning up to watch cricket at the Wanderers in 1983 would be surprising. Those days were the height of organised oppression. We lived more or less in a police state. P. W. Botha was in power.

Yet David Murray tells the story of Ali Bacher coming into the dressing room at Berea Park in Pretoria and weeping with joy at the sight of the sold-out stadium. 'So many black people came to watch the game, and Ali Bacher said, you know, "We turned away thousands more – in the heart of Pretoria." He cried and said, "You have made it here."'

*   *   *

The first Caribbean tour of South Africa lasted just a month. It was over by the middle of February 1983. The second tour at the end of the year was twice as long. It began in November and lasted until the end of January 1984. The novelty that had been part of the first series was missing the second time around. There were rows between the players and the organisers about money, and on some occasions there were fewer spectators in the stands.

Someone who did want to see the cricket was the husband of Margaret Thatcher – the British prime minister. Dennis Thatcher had business interests in South Africa connected to his directorship of the motor parts firm Quinton Hazell. In January 1984 he planned to visit the Ford and Volkswagen factories in Port Elizabeth and the Toyota plant in Durban. At the invitation of the Transvaal Cricket Council, he also hoped to catch a couple of days of the game against the West Indies. It was a nice thought, but attending the match could cause difficulties.

'Mr Thatcher has told me', wrote the prime minister's private secretary in a confidential letter to the Foreign Office at the beginning of January 1984, 'that he is conscious that, if the press show interest in his visit, he is likely to be questioned about the wages paid to black employees of his company in South Africa – he is therefore setting in hand some research on this matter.'

The invitation caused a flutter at the Foreign Office. Within days, the foreign secretary Geoffrey Howe had set out reasons why the kindness of the Transvaal Cricket Council should be rejected. His reservations were passed back to Downing Street, where it was left to the private secretary to break the regrettable news to Mr Thatcher's wife.

'Prime Minister', he wrote in a briefing note at the end of the week, 'I am awfully sorry to raise this point, but I think it would be better if Mr Thatcher did not attend the cricket matches between South Africa and the West Indian touring team . . . I can well see some British newspapers and the Opposition in Parliament setting out to embarrass you if Mr Thatcher does go to these events.

'You may like to discuss this with Mr Thatcher over the weekend,' he suggested gently.

Graeme Pollock would make 41 on the first day at the Wanderers, and Ezra Moseley and Hartley Alleyne would get four wickets each, but Dennis Thatcher wasn't there to see them. On this occasion at least the prime minister took her foreign secretary's advice.

* * *

Ali Bacher wanted the 1983–84 West Indian tourists to be as attractive a team as possible, and so there were changes from the first squad. Three men were told they were no longer needed – Richard Austin, Herbert Chang and Ray Wynter – they were replaced by Hartley Alleyne, Faoud Bacchus and the Surrey batsman Monte Lynch. Bacher had tried to get even better-known players to join the side. He had sensed how close Malcolm Marshall had appeared to be to signing for him the first time, and he was apparently also interested in Gordon Greenidge, Vivian Richards and Joel Garner.

Marshall had agreed to meet Bacher again during the English county season of 1983; he was curious about how the rebels had been received in South Africa. Among those who he spoke to when they got back the general view seemed to be that they had been very well looked after and had enjoyed the honorary white lifestyle, but few would contemplate returning by choice. Marshall's final meeting with Ali Bacher was at a cheap cafe on the London Road in Southampton early one morning. Around them sat dockers from the night shift tucking into fried breakfasts and slurping large mugs of tea.

By now there was only one question that Marshall needed answering, and that was 'How much?' Quietly Bacher responded with a figure that he thought the bowler would have to yield to: one million US dollars.

A million dollars for a two-month tour plus a contract with Transvaal? Marshall was only temporarily dumbfounded. 'I looked him straight in the eye,' he wrote. '"No thanks," I told him. Now it was his turn to be staggered. He spilled his coffee down his shirt-front in shock. Recovering his poise and wiping down his shirt, he could scarcely contain his disbelief at my audacity. "Malcolm Marshall," he said. "You are a very good cricketer but a foolish young man." With that he excused himself and we left the dock workers to their breakfasts.'

That morning shaped the rest of Marshall's career. By saying no to Ali Bacher, he would go on to play another 64 Test matches for the West Indies, becoming probably the best fast bowler the side had ever had. That was not a possibility for Sylvester Clarke or Franklyn Stephenson. For them big cricket ended in the apartheid republic. Only one rebel – Ezra Moseley – would wear a real maroon cap again. After the players' life bans were lifted in 1989, he would be chosen to play against England in two Tests the following year.

* * *

The last game the rebels played together ended on 31 January 1984. The West Indian side beat South Africa by six wickets at St George's Park in Port Elizabeth. Alvin Kallicharran and Collis King were there, not out at the end. Kallicharran would continue to play cricket in South Africa with Transvaal, then Orange Free State. King had a deal to play with Natal, as did Alleyne. Bacchus, Moseley and Clarke also took part in South Africa's regional tournament, the Currie Cup. The contracts were welcome because going back to the Caribbean after visiting South Africa was not straightforward. Colin Croft and Lawrence Rowe both headed for the USA and settled in Florida.

'I suppose in retrospect it was not a good decision,' says Croft.

Maybe from naivety, maybe from singularity I may have made a mistake there, I could understand that. I take whatever comes with it. A lot people will say, 'Well look, in some sense he might have embarrassed the Caribbean.' I would agree with that perhaps, I might just agree with that. But you see the West Indies is a very small place and the minds are small. Very small-minded. I went to the US. I lived there for a while and I've come back to the Caribbean, and life goes on. It was a mistake. It happened. Done.

Others who ended up back in the West Indies found life there very difficult. After spending time in Australia, David Murray went home to Barbados to live with his grandmother.

Woah! I came back here, and I'm telling you it was like you were outcast. The government got very drastic and said, 'Hey, you can't play when you return home on local pastures.' It was a life ban – it was not nice at all. People looking scornful that you're not a Barbadian, you're alien. It was amazing. Barbados is a very serious society; they don't give you a second chance. It was demoralising, sad at the time. It wasn't easy, it wasn't easy at all. I don't know how to describe it. I still feel it up to now, you know, and this was more than 30 years ago.

Murray was now without his wife and his child, who had stayed in Australia. The money he had earned from playing in South Africa was gone. Drugs, which had been a part of his life for many years, now took him over. For months at a time he was homeless. He resembled one of the Bridgetown scavengers he had seen on those early-morning training runs when he had been working to become the best cricketer he could.

'Their reception back in the Caribbean varied from island to island,' says Michael Holding. 'In Jamaica they were total outcasts. When they came back here they were in shock because they did not believe that they would be treated as poorly as they were. A lot of them got affected mentally. Some of those guys right now at this moment are not stable mentally. I'll call names. Richard Austin walked the streets of Jamaica. Very unfortunate, very sad. Herbert Chang, another one. Very unfortunate, very sad. They just were, as everyone will say, naive.'

Austin was known locally in Kingston as Danny Germs. He ended up living on the streets around New Kingston and Cross Roads and sleeping in a bus shelter. A quarter of a century after the tour he was still homeless, often high on crack and living under a bush in a hotel car park. Despite the efforts of his family and his local cricket club, Kensington, which had allowed him to play in the Senior Cup competition after the life ban was lifted, he always seemed to slip back into drugs and crime. 'I made the street my friend and my home,' he once said. He died aged 60 in 2015.

'My greatest innings,' says Vivian Richards,

rather than the ones at Lord's or at the Rec in Antigua, was having said no to the apartheid regime. Not going. That to me is worth more than any triple century, double century, the fastest century, whatever. It was a crucial decision in my life. There was little temptation for me. It wasn't hard to make the decision. Why should I be paid all this money that could be used to uplift people elsewhere just for a game of cricket? I couldn't see myself being part of that. I would have let a lot of people down, but that wasn't the point. It was about me. I couldn't be part of something that was so obviously discriminatory. No. To me that was selling out in a big way. Everyone had their own explanation for why they went.

I'm not going to judge them one bit. They took the decision and they have to live with it.

When a BBC documentary crew found Herbert Chang several years after he returned from South Africa, he was sleeping in a shed near the wharves in the Greenwich Town area of Kingston. He was barefoot, incoherent and taking food handouts from people who lived in the yard with him. His job as Jamaica's youth cricket coach had long gone. His wife and children had left him. 'He is emotionally disturbed,' his brother told the documentary team, 'withdrawn and unable to relate to other people. You can't get to him no more.'

Sympathy for Chang and Austin was very limited, at least from the cricket authorities in Jamaica. Rex Fennell, the island's board president at the time, said going on the rebel tour was like 'murdering your brother. It was like putting a knife into the back of the South African people.'

'I'm sorry to hear they're not well,' said the former WICBC president Allan Rae when asked about the health of Austin and Chang in 1991. 'To use a loose and unpleasant phrase, I wouldn't like to see any of them in the gutter. But apart from that, I would say that's where my interest would end.'

'I talked to some of the West Indians who went on that tour,' says Vivian Richards, 'and some not only felt humiliated but were also utterly ashamed of themselves.'

'I think that any judgement made on these men must be tempered by some understanding of the dilemma they faced,' reflects Ronald Austin.

On one hand, they made a fundamental error in believing that a visiting cricketing team could have any major impact on the internal dynamics of the apartheid system or soften the hearts of those who governed it. On the other hand, it is clear that they felt excluded and forgotten. Yet again the Caribbean had neglected to create the institutions necessary to support our cricketers and to afford them a reasonable standard of living. C. L. R. James once said that if we cannot take care of our cricketers, we do not deserve them. This is still true. But the real tragedy of the whole episode is the realisation of what we lost. Sylvester Clarke was a fast bowler of unique skills; Ezra Moseley could swerve a cricket ball like no other bowler in international cricket. There has always been a poverty of ideas in the region that played a role in the eventual loss of our eminence in the game. That came because of a failure to appreciate the true value of a West Indian cricketer.

*　*　*

Nowadays, David Murray says he is no longer a drug addict. Depending on who he is talking to, he either regrets going to South Africa or he doesn't. He either expected to be banned for life or it was a shock. When he tells of his rise and fall, few lines from Caribbean literature seem so well matched to his experience as these from *The Middle Passage* by V. S. Naipaul: 'Unless the cricketer had heroic qualities, we did not want to see him, however valuable he might be. And that is why, of those stories of failure, that of the ruined cricketer was the most terrible.'

'I try to live day to day,' Murray says. 'Give things some praises and do my little exercises and try to be as spiritual as possible. I had my little lull – a few little hiccups – but I am over them now, you know what I mean?'

But when he talks, hope is often followed by sorrow.

'It's amazing how with cricket you come from love to hate. You still conscious of the cricket going on, but I think from that tour I lost a bit of love for the game, you know? Can happen, you know what I mean? It was heavy, very heavy, very heavy. Your own people look down on you like you've just murdered a dozen people. It was harsh. Eyes, cross eyes, people look on you, you know, bad looks. It heavy. They still do, up to today, I'm telling you, up to today. It's not easy.'

7

They all really could bowl with their eyes shut

A month after the first renegade side left for South Africa, the Test team were playing again, this time at home to India. It was a sign of the West Indies' strength that, despite the fracture caused by the apartheid tours, only Gus Logie in the first Test and Winston Davis in the fifth made their debuts. The team could prosper without the rebels. They would not be missed.

Since the surprising defeat to New Zealand at the beginning of 1980 Clive Lloyd's side had won three Test series as well as retaining the Frank Worrell Trophy in Australia. By the time the rebel players were counting their final krugerrands, the Test side had won two more. Five series victories. Undefeated against Pakistan, Australia and India, and the first side since Donald Bradman's Australians in 1948 not to lose a first-class game on tour in England. The West Indies were now unchallenged as the best side in cricket. What better way to confirm it than by winning the World Cup for the third time?

The 1983 competition was held in England. The West Indies had a little shock when they were beaten by India at Old Trafford in their first group game. Still, there was nothing much to worry about. India were seen as a poor side whose only other victory in three World Cups had been against the amateurs and club players of East

Africa in 1975. They had a new captain, Kapil Dev, who was quarrelling with Sunil Gavaskar, his predecessor and the team's star batsman. Gavaskar was out of form and was dropped for one of the games. India seemed underprepared. After all, they hadn't even played a one-day international game in their own country until 1981.

So there was some surprise when India also beat Australia and England to get to the final at Lord's. There they would play Clive Lloyd's team again. The West Indies hadn't lost since that first game in Manchester. Their semi-final win against Pakistan at the Oval was an easy one; even the leg spin and googlies of Abdul Qadir, which had tormented Desmond Haynes and Vivian Richards, couldn't throw them off course.

'I don't see us slipping up again,' said Lloyd the day before the final when asked if India could repeat the success of their group game. 'We're more relaxed now and playing well.' Richards was scoring runs, and the four fast bowlers – Garner, Marshall, Roberts and Holding – were either quicker or cannier than ever. Marshall even had the confidence to order a new BMW sports car, which he would pay for from his winnings after the final. Relaxed and playing very well indeed.

India batted and still had more than five overs left of their allowance of 60 when they were bowled out. They made 183, at least 40 runs short of a decent score. The young Barbadian bowler had taken two wickets; he was almost running his finger along his new walnut dashboard.

India were a side of medium-pace bowlers – a bit of seam movement here, a little wobble through the air there – nothing that the experienced West Indies feared. But wickets fell. Richards, who had been clubbing boundaries from Madan Lal, played too soon when trying to hook him to the stands. His top edge went high and over mid-wicket, but, running back, Kapil Dev took a fine over-the-shoulder catch. It was the moment of the game. The West Indies were unable to control the bowling that remained. Lloyd, with a twanged groin, was out for eight on the same score as Larry Gomes, and then the careful Jeff Dujon fell. The world champions were 124 for 8, then 126 for 9. There would be no last-wicket miracle stand from Garner and Holding. At 7.30 p.m. the final wicket fell, and to general amazement and not a little delight from many watching, India had won the World Cup. Spectators from all sides but the pavilion speedily flooded the ground. A West Indian supporter in a mustard-coloured suit lay face down on the grass, unable to watch. In the scrum and run for the dressing rooms Michael Holding injured his leg and had to have it put in plaster.

'Hordes of fans poured across the hallowed turf straight at the members' enclosure,' wrote the *Sunday Times* sketch writer, 'enabling some of the senior incumbents to relive in imagination their more alarming imperial experiences.'

With a side dependent on gritty players from the looked-down-upon north of the country rather than the traditional cricket city of Bombay, India had enjoyed the most unlikely of victories. Kapil Dev's matey captaincy had abandoned the master–pupil relationship that previous Indian sides had been expected to recognise and changed the way India has viewed its cricket ever since. The huge tremor of this win meant that in India, one-day cricket would now rule over the five-day Test, and during the next 25 years, India would become the dominant economic and political force in the world game, generating billions of dollars in television money. The win at Lord's in the 1983 World Cup was the Big Bang moment for this new universe.

In the West Indies dressing room there was a hell of a row. The bowlers blamed the batsmen, and Lloyd bawled out Andy Roberts for saying the wrong thing at the wrong time. What they had seen today was a performance of amateurs, the captain said. There was disbelief, anger and humiliation. As the recriminations went on, Lloyd had something else to add – he was resigning.

"'I have had enough," he said. "Somebody else can take over,"' is what Malcolm Marshall remembered. 'It left us still further dumb-founded. Our "father" was going to desert his "children" in their hour of need.' Lloyd made it official that evening in the Wellington Suite of the Westmorland Hotel opposite Lord's. In front of the team, WICBC members and journalists he said he'd spoken to his wife and together they had decided that it was time to go. 'West Indies cricket woke up this morning with the realisation that not only have they been dethroned as World Cup champions but that after nine years they now have to look for a new captain' said the sports lead article in the next day's *Gleaner* in Jamaica.

'We lost that World Cup because of complacency,' says Michael Holding. 'The West Indies team thought, *This is a cakewalk. We will just go out there and get the runs. If I don't get them, then five or six will get them.* We pretty much gave them the match because we thought that irrespective of how we played we would win. Clive said that he was finished because it had become so acrimonious in the dressing room. He said, "It will all fall on me. I am happy to resign and walk away from it." It was not a happy time.'

Andy Roberts disagrees: 'I do not think it was complacency; I just think we batted badly on that day. Bowlers win matches. Batsmen draw or lose us matches. Now we've bowled first and we bowled out India for 183. Our batsmen could not score us 183. After 1975, as the years go by, I study the games, and every single cup we play, we have to bat bad once. Once. And it just happened that the one time we choose to bat badly was in the final.'

For several weeks the West Indies had no captain. Eventually the

board persuaded Lloyd to change his mind, and he took the side
to India at the end of 1983. They won all five of the one-day internationals and the Test series.

*   *   *

India's win in the 1983 World Cup was such a surprise not least
because it came against the West Indies' best four fast bowlers of
the era: Roberts, Holding, Marshall and Garner. All were extremely
difficult to play against, and even the very best batsmen were appre-
hensive about facing them. But they played together in just seven
Test matches and never more than four games in a row. This was
because, as Marshall's promise was becoming increasingly obvious,
Roberts's career was ending. When the side went to India at the
end of 1983 Holding and Marshall led the attack. 'Who wants the
new ball?' asked Clive Lloyd. 'Give it to Malcolm,' said Holding
immediately. 'He's the fastest now.' Very soon afterwards Marshall
would replace Roberts, the man from whom he'd learned so much.

Deryck Murray reckons that Holding was the fastest of the bowlers
he kept wicket to, but Roberts was the best. No other bowler was
as intelligent or had such strength. His great rounded shoulders
were like cannonballs. Once, to emphasise his point of view, Roberts
lifted Dennis Lillee up by his lapels in the lobby of the Old Melbourne
Inn. He tried to make every ball he bowled different from the last,
with small variations of angle and trajectory that would unsettle a
batsman. He combined nous with extreme pace. Roberts, more so
than any other modern West Indian bowler, possessed the skills that
C. L. R. James described as being 'the result of psychological sensi-
tivity and response to a particular batsman at a particular time on
a particular wicket at a particular stage in the game'.

'I wish people would remember me for my outswinger,' says
Roberts. But he will always be best known for the cunning of those
two-speed bouncers.

'If I grip the ball here to bowl a bouncer,' says Roberts, putting his fingers across the seam of a cricket ball and not either side of it,

the ball hits the ground on the shiny side and it's not going to bounce. It's going to skid. Skid onto the batsman. If it hits the seam then it will rear. In order to bowl the two-pace bouncer, the first one I would run in and don't jump, I will go straight through and don't jump at all in my delivery stride, and the ball will come on at normal pace. Now if I run in and I jump, for me to jump I have to put in more effort to elevate to a certain height and in doing that I am also transferring that effort into the delivery, so that is where you get the difference in pace. The second one would come on to you quicker. A lot quicker.

Like most things Roberts did on a cricket field, it was carefully planned. 'I wasn't a big party man – I didn't drink – so most nights I would stay in my room and think about cricket. We didn't have laptops or DVDs of our matches, so my own memory was my computer.'

Roberts had a lot of processing power. Clive Lloyd tells the story of playing against him in the West Indies in the Shell Shield competition, Guyana versus the Combined Islands. 'He bounced me viciously. Usually he didn't say much, but he came down the pitch and went, "That's for hooking me for six in Dominica." The shot he was referring to had been played five years previously. He'd waited that long to give me his quicker bouncer.'

'I am a warrior,' say Roberts simply. 'I have a job to do, and when I go on a cricket field I have no friends; all my friends are back in the pavilion. But if a batsman gets injured it is very difficult for me to go and look at him, because if you get up to bat again, the next ball I ball to you may be another bouncer. No, the sympathy is in here, he says, tapping his chest. 'You may not see it and I can't show the batsman, but it is in here.'

Apart from bouncers, Roberts had a lesser-known skill that also confounded batsmen. Experienced players would look at the ball in the bowler's hand as he ran in. They would note which side of the ball had been polished so they could predict which way it would swing when it was bowled. But Roberts was able, after hours of practice, to flick the ball around 180 degrees in his hand in the moments before he let it go in his delivery stride. The shine was now on the other side, and many batsmen expecting the outswinger were LBW or bowled by a ball that swerved back into them.

That finesse was learned over several years. When Roberts began, he was what he calls an 'out-and-out fast man' bowling straight. Now and again he'd let go of a ball that came back into the batsman. Then he read in a newspaper that the old England fast bowler Fred Trueman thought he was good but not great. But he could be great if he brought his arms higher.

'In Australia in '75–76 I changed my action, got my arms higher at the point of the gather and learned to swing the ball away from the right hander. And that was my most regular delivery. But whatever I did, in my mind I became a batsman. I used to think what I would be able to do if a particular delivery was bowled at me. That's why the batsman was often presented with the unexpected.'

No West Indian bowler was closer to Roberts than Michael Holding.

They first met on a bench in Jamaica, twelfth men on opposite sides in a match against the Combined Islands. They chatted and became friendly. 'When I got into the West Indies team, we became room-mates and talked a lot,' recalls Holding.

I got to realise that Andy's cricket brain was brilliant. Not everyone who is great at their craft has the ability to pass that on. He taught me a lot about fast bowling, about studying batsmen, seeing their weaknesses and their strengths. I'll give you a fine example. We were in India in '83. Andy was ill and he didn't play in this Test match. Might have been Kanpur. I was out there bowling to Syed Kirmani. Andy was in the dressing room and noticed something about him. At the next water break he sent out a message with the twelfth man who said, 'Go round the wicket. Don't bowl anything short, just attack his leg stump.' I didn't know why Andy said that, but I had so much faith in him that I did what he suggested. In that same over Kirmani lost his leg stump and was walking back to the pavilion.

Like Roberts, Holding developed into an intelligent, crafty bowler. At the beginning of his career he had presented batsmen with little else than sheer speed. 'I had the advantage of being able to bowl at 90 miles per hour, but only rarely did I swing the ball a lot. In England it would go if I bowled very full, but in most countries I depended on hitting the seam regularly and getting movement that way. Whichever batsman I had to bowl to, left or right, I wanted to move the ball away from him. Doing that meant there was no second line of defence. He just had his bat and not his pad.'

Holding's great speed was enhanced by a run-up of extreme grace. Few bowlers could match it. Since being a teenager he had run well. He had been a fine long jumper and hurdler (but not the champion 400-metre runner that many think he was) so had experience of having to plant his foot in the right place every time he competed. Holding bowled very few no balls as a Test cricketer. The discipline of his youth meant that he never had to concentrate on running in smoothly. This talent was brought on by the West Indies' trainer Dennis Waight, who got all of his bowlers to practise their approach to the stumps at full speed while blindfolded. They all really could bowl with their eyes shut.

'As far as I am concerned, bowling is about action and reaction,' says Holding.

You bowl a ball; you see the reaction of the batsman. *What do I need to do now to combat that action of the batsman?* That's what I'm thinking about walking back to my mark. *OK, he did that when I pitched the ball in a particular area – what can I do?* It is a continuous process. A bowler is always thinking about what the batsman did. Remembering the last delivery. If that batsman is going to be an outstanding player, he has got to forget that last delivery and focus on the next one.

That might be difficult for Geoffrey Boycott. The England batsman will remember one particular over from Holding for the rest of his life. At the Kensington Oval in March 1981 he received six balls of such quality that many people believe it to be the best over by a fast bowler in modern cricket. Boycott had practised facing Holding, Roberts, Croft and Garner before the tour started by batting indoors in Yorkshire on a polished wooden floor to mimic the sheen, skid and speed of a Caribbean wicket, but on the second day of the third Test at the start of England's innings in Barbados, that did him little good.

Holding had been told by Clive Lloyd before the West Indies went out to field that he only wanted a short spell from him – three or four of the fastest overs he could bowl.

The first ball to Boycott was short of a length on off stump, and the batsman played it uncomfortably high off his gloves to just in front of second slip. To the next three balls he played and missed as Holding got faster and faster and the crowd got noisier. The fifth ball headed for the batsman's throat, and again only his glove saved him. Before the last ball of the over Holding decided that Boycott would be expecting another short one. He had noticed too that the batsman had deliberately been playing inside the line of the ball – not getting his bat or his feet fully towards off stump. The sixth ball was full. It moved at great speed and away a little from the straight. Boycott's off stump was jettisoned from the earth. Four slips, a gully, a wicket-keeper and short leg all danced towards the bowler in congratulation.

'Bridgetown exploded,' wrote Scyld Berry in the *Observer*. 'They had come over the walls and through the fences, they had sat on the stand roofs with such an expectation in mind. And Holding fulfilled it when, after five short deliveries he sent his off stump cartwheeling back to the wicket-keeper.'

Later that evening Frank Keating of the *Guardian* went with Boycott to the hotel room of the BBC reporter Michael Blakey, who had been editing a TV news item and had the film of the batsman's humiliation. Staring at the small portable screen, Boycott asked for the over to be replayed four or five times. 'At the end he said knowingly, "Thanks, I think I've seen all I need to see."'

According to Holding, the over has become part of cricket folk-lore because 'Geoffrey Boycott goes around the world telling people it was the greatest thing ever. People have jumped on the band-wagon.' He disagrees. It wasn't even the best over he remembers bowling. That came in a WSC match against Australia in 1979 when he got both Ian and Greg Chappell out.

* * *

If Michael Holding's greatest attribute was pace, Joel Garner's was trajectory. His height meant that the ball – full or short – was always difficult for the batsman to judge. The bounce from the length he bowled most often took the ball into the batsman's chest rather than past his waist. Such a Garner delivery was too short to drive but too full to cut. The direction – almost always straight – also took away the possibility of deflected runs either side of the wicket.

'How do I score against Garner?' Geoffrey Boycott once asked the bowler's Somerset teammate Ian Botham, the night before England were due to bat against the West Indies. 'You don't,' replied Botham: 'no one does.'

'Right. I may as well go to bed then,' announced Boycott.

Garner also became known as the owner of the world's most exquisite yorker – a full ball which landed at the batsman's toes at more than 80 miles per hour – which was extremely difficult to stop from hitting the stumps or his pads. It was taught to him by the Barbadian Test bowler Charlie Griffith, and he mastered it early in his career. Later, Vanburn Holder would teach him how to bowl the outswinger when all he had known previously was how to nip the ball back into the batsman.

The skills Joel Garner already possessed, as well as those he learned, made him possibly better than all of his fast-bowling peers except Malcolm Marshall. Garner was thought of as a supporting bowler rather than as one to lead the attack with the new ball, but alongside Holding, Roberts, Croft and Daniel, only Marshall took more wickets, bowled more Test overs and had a lower average (by three hundredths of a run) than Joel Garner. And no one went for fewer runs per over.

C. L. R. James once wrote a very brief letter to *The Times* cricket correspondent John Woodcock. It read, 'Garner is not, I repeat not, a fast bowler.' But he was. Especially towards the end of his career. After he was dropped in 1983 he came back against Australia at the end of the year, lengthened his run-up and took the new ball. He took 31 wickets in the series – a record – and had never bowled quicker. Only Marshall hit the keeper's gloves harder that year.

*   *   *

Colin Croft began as a wicket-keeper. Then he got tall and realised he could bowl fast. By 1969 he had a fearsome reputation in youth cricket in Guyana. Within a decade people felt similarly about him in Test cricket. What made Croft uniquely difficult to bat against was the angle from which he bowled the ball.

'It was not until I played for the West Indies,' he says, 'that I fully realised that I bowled from so wide of the crease. So the ball always gave the batsman the impression that it was coming in at him. They reasoned that, if the ball started so wide, it had to dart in. That's why I worked really hard at doing the opposite – bowling a leg cutter that would leave the right hander.'

Croft always preferred cut to swing.

A fast bowler has got tools. You've got an outswinger or an inswinger, but personally I don't agree with the swing bowling because the ball is only new for so long. So I liked to manipulate the ball off the pitch, which is known as cut. The ball comes in a straight line, hits the seam and then deviates towards the slips, that's a leg cutter. If it deviates into a right-handed batsmen, that's an off cutter. Now to me that's more useful because you could bowl it for longer and it happens later in the delivery. Therefore the batsmen has to think very much quicker to play the ball that cuts.

Infamously, Croft also had another weapon. The bouncer. Every fast bowler is happy for people to be afraid of him; some just hide it better than others. The former England all-rounder Vic Marks once said of the West Indies' bowlers, 'Joel didn't really want to hurt you. Michael was a gentleman. But I always got the feeling with dear Colin that he wasn't really that bothered if he caused you a great deal of pain.' Croft ran up straight and fast, almost behind the umpire, then leaped out towards the return crease while flinging down the ball with a rapid untangling of his arms.

'Now, if the batsmen can't get himself out of the way, then I genuinely think you should not be playing, because cricket is a game that goes on reflexes. You take catches as a wicket-keeper, silly point, you take reflex catches. Now here's a guy coming into bowl from 22 yards away; he's bowling at about 90 miles per hour, so it takes about one half of a second to get to you. If your reflexes are that slow, you shouldn't be playing.'

If the bouncer missed the bat and hit the man, Croft was untroubled by remorse. 'I grew up in a very different way to most people who played cricket for the West Indies.' His childhood in Guyana was very difficult. 'I've seen people kill people,' he says.

When I hit somebody, that was the end of that. I'd go back to my mark and sit down and wait until somebody else comes to bat or he gets up and I could not be bothered how hurt you were. My simple theory as a fast bowler was *I'm gonna get you out by any means necessary, so I'll either get you out legally, caught behind, bowled, or if I could knock you out, that's OK too.* I remember Alvin Kallicharran asking me one time, 'Why don't you go look at the batsman; he's on the ground?' I said, 'Well look, I know about aviation; I don't know anything about doctoring. I can't fix him. Call a doctor.' That's the end of that and I was being very, very honest. I know exactly what I planned to do. I bowl a bouncer, it hit the batsman. I was successful and therefore I don't care about the result.

Of course I'm a warrior. I'm representing millions of people. When the warrior walks out onto the field, it is not a playing field. It's a war zone. Whoever comes out of there after 50 overs or after a Test match alive, well and victorious, then good luck.

*   *   *

Malcolm Marshall won matches for both Clive Lloyd and his successor as captain, Vivian Richards. In the last 18 months of Lloyd's reign and the first year of Richards's appointment he took more than 20 wickets every time he played a Test series. That included 33 wickets at the end of 1984 in India, a place where fast bowlers had almost always been muffled and blunted by the baked-mud pitches. The bowler to whom Marshall is most often compared, Dennis Lillee, only went to the subcontinent once, to play Pakistan, and came home with three wickets from as many games.

At the beginning of his career Marshall came off the long run. Which self-respecting Caribbean quick bowler didn't? Later on he shortened his approach when he realised it didn't cause his pace to drop. Marshall was small for a West Indies fast bowler, just five feet ten inches; his Barbadian partner Joel Garner was almost a foot taller. So he didn't lope to the wicket, getting up to speed like a cargo plane heading for take-off; he scampered in like a messenger boy holding an urgent telegram. When he delivered the ball, there was great pace for sure, but the ball skidded through in a way that a taller bowler couldn't have pulled off. That made him harder to hook.

Much of Marshall's craft was learned and then perfected in county cricket. He spent 14 summers with Hampshire. He wasn't instantly brilliant. Mark Nicholas, a teammate and later his county captain, remembers him arriving in 1979, already a Test cricketer. 'He was whippy and awkward to play, but not much more than that,' says Nicholas. 'That season he bowled outswing exclusively. We saw talent but not a world-beater. His first game was at the end of April in Derby. It was so cold there may even have been snow. Anyway he arrived in a pair of sandals and just wanted to snuggle up to the radiator. We had to help him buy socks and shoes and a big jumper.'

Marshall learned quickly about bowling fast in England. He improved almost by the hour, says Nicholas. When he came back in 1980 he was a much better bowler, but neither he nor Gordon Greenidge were with the county for long because of the West Indies tour of England. In 1981 he was very good and by 1982 he was extraordinary, taking 134 wickets in the county championship, more than 40 ahead of the next-best bowler. And it was the top batsmen he damaged most. Just 14 of those wickets were the numbers nine, ten and eleven in the opposition batting order.

His fine speed was matched by great control. In his later Tests he learned to fold his thumb into his palm behind the ball, rather than using it to support the seam from underneath. When he splayed his fingers either side, he said he got even more control. From the 1982 season he could cut the ball by rotating the seam with his rolling wrist. After Dennis Lillee once confounded him with a ball that pitched on his legs but passed the outside edge of his bat, he asked him how it was done. Lillee showed him the leg cutter and he in turn passed on the secret to Imran Khan. Lillee had been taught it by John Snow. The modern Test leg cutter came from Sussex and eventually returned there with Imran. But Marshall still had one more skill to master.

The start of the 1985 county season was an interesting one for Hampshire because Marshall didn't often bowl super-quick. He was teaching himself the inswinger. He'd cut back his pace to do it so he wasn't quite at his best. He'd spent hours in the nets and in matches bowled quite a few balls that batsmen didn't have to play. That was unusual. He wanted long spells – apart from doing 500 sit-ups a day, that's how he kept fit – and he'd often ask to bowl for an hour and a half without change on the first morning. Then, within about five weeks, the inswinger clicked, and he was absolutely magnificent.

'He became deadly because batsmen who thought they could line him up around off stump were getting bowled or trapped in front,' remembers Nicholas.

Lillee had retired and Malcolm was undisputedly the greatest bowler in the world. He could be breathtaking in Barbados, which was a very bouncy surface, and we know that his bouncer, like Andy Roberts's, was a shocking thing. But his greatness meant that he wasn't dependent on that sort of wicket. In fact there is an argument that he was a better bowler on wickets that kept low because of his skid and his cut. Viv always used to say that you could put a bunch of these bowlers in the hat, pull one out, and any would bowl well, but the only one he'd want to take to India was Maco.

Marshall could now swing the ball both ways, towards and away from a bat. The pace came mostly from the very fast rotation of his arm in the delivery stride. He had plenty of those fast-twitch fibres in his muscles that Dennis Waight loved so much. 'You couldn't buy 'em,' said Waight; 'you were born with 'em.' Marshall showed his chest to the batsman, letting go of the ball front on, but there was no clue from his body as to which way it would go. Sometimes, says Nicholas, he could try to do too much, use too many varieties, but at his best he could do anything he liked.

'Against Essex in a Benson and Hedges cup game he did Mark Waugh – who was a very fine batsman for Australia – with outswinger, outswinger, inswinger, the last one catching him LBW. He'd already done Gooch and John Stephenson the same way, and they were three down for hardly any.'

Marshall was not a sledger, but like all of the West Indies fast bowlers of the time his charity towards batsmen came in limited doses. And he had a vindictive streak. Some opponents were frightened by it. Mark Nicholas tells the story of how Marshall was once met by two Essex tail-enders, Ray East and David Acfield, in the car park on the morning of a Hampshire county game. Marshall was wondering why the old pros were offering to carry his bags to the dressing room. On the way there, they explained. If Mr Marshall would be good enough to bowl them straight half-volleys when they came in – no short stuff – they would both happily let the ball take out middle stump straight away.

'He didn't like Essex,' says Nicholas. 'Always went very hard at Essex. He found the playfulness of people like East and Acfield irritating – he took cricket very seriously – and he would bowl more nastily to a joker down the order than one who fought him.'

Marshall especially disliked the Indian batsman Dilip Vengsarkar, whose many appeals he believed had contributed to him being wrongly given out in his first Test match in Bangalore in 1978. With Vengsarkar he would often switch to bowl around the wicket, giving the Indian less space to move against his fastest and most testing short-pitched balls. The favourite wicket of his career was having Vengsarkar caught on the boundary in Antigua six runs short of a hundred. Four years later, in 1987, Marshall still hadn't forgiven him. In a match at Lord's to celebrate 200 years of MCC, as soon as Vengsarkar appeared from the pavilion Marshall went around the wicket and skidded short balls towards his throat. 'There've been rumours that Vengsarkar and Marshall might not get on all that well,' Richie Benaud informed television viewers as the Indian desperately got his bat in front of his face only to see Graham Gooch catch him at third slip.

And there were a couple of others who irked Malcolm, recalls Mark Nicholas.

Once, before a game at Bournemouth, Zaheer Abbas of Gloucestershire said something like, 'We can look after each other here. You keep it nice and full to me and I'll block it and score my runs off the others.' Well that sent Malcolm into an orbital fury. And there was this guy called Rehan Alikhan who played a bit for Sussex and Surrey. Now, with respect, he was tremendously gutsy but not the best of players. Whenever he turned up, Malcolm just couldn't get him out. And despite his lack of class, Rehan had a little bit of a swagger which always made Malcolm mad. In fact he's the only batsman I've ever heard him sledge. Rehan Alikhan almost drove him to drink. Always brandy of course. He also had a bit of a thing about Graham Roope for some reason.

If Marshall had one limitation – in county cricket at least – it was that he bowled less well to left-handers. 'He wasn't as good when they were batting,' believes Nicholas. 'I mean, all of this is relative of course because he was probably the best in the world around this time, but there was less authority against left-handers. Chris Broad would drive him nuts. He played Malcolm well. It wasn't helped by Broady's manner. He would say little irritating things. Some people shrugged them off as being irrelevant, while others latched on to them and could only reply, "Broady, you're a tosser." Malcolm was one of those who latched on.'

8

'You get bouncers, very good bouncers and brilliant bouncers'

'If I do that,' says Andy Lloyd, covering his left eye with his left hand, 'and look at your nose, I can't see the right side of your face. Not even blurred – it's just not there.' It is shortly before Christmas 2014, and the former England Test batsman is sitting in a pub in Stratford-upon-Avon, four miles or so away from the stud farm in Warwickshire that he now runs. 'I've lost 35 per cent of the vision in my right eye. And that's why I was never as good a player afterwards. When you're playing top sport any edge that you lose is the difference. I knew I wasn't as sharp. I was missing balls that I used to be able to hit for four. I was 15 per cent inferior, which at the highest level of the game is a massive margin.'

Andy Lloyd was picked to open the batting for England against the visiting West Indians in the Test series of 1984. By the first months of that year the evolution of Clive Lloyd's team from a brittle talent in the mid-70s to a supremely forged side was almost complete. Their batsmen, their bowlers, their fielders were the world's best. A single Test match lost in four years. Before arriving in England they had beaten Australia in the Caribbean three–nil. They didn't lose a second innings wicket in any of the five Tests.

'I was ready for it,' says Andy Lloyd. 'I'm not a nervous type. Never been particularly afraid of anything. You get nervous when you're not sure of yourself. I knew how I was going to play. Whether or not it would be good enough to get a lot of runs, I didn't know.'

Lloyd was in good shape. He had never played Test cricket but did well enough in the three one-day internationals that came before the series and England needed some new opening batsmen. Geoffrey Boycott was still scoring runs for Yorkshire but was serving a three-year ban for playing with the English rebel side in South Africa. Graham Gooch couldn't be picked for the same reason. The truth was that England had little idea who should be in their best side. The captain David Gower and the all-rounder Ian Botham were the only obvious choices. Usually, the Test and County Cricket Board kept 18 colour portrait photos on file to promote the picked team in magazines and brochures; this season they had more than 30 mug shots.

Lloyd's county was Warwickshire. He had been born a Shropshire lad, spotted and sent to Edgbaston in 1976 when he was 19. That summer he threw countless half-volleys at Dennis Amiss, who was remodelling his batting after being hit on the head by Michael Holding at the beginning of the season. Amiss would now take a more open stance, and his first movement would be back and to the off side. The change worked. After a summer of hard work and throw-downs from young Lloyd, Amiss got back into the England side and made a double century against Holding and the West Indians in the final Test of 1976 at the Oval.

Eight years later it was Lloyd's turn to play for England, and he had his own methods. He was a good player of fast bowling and had often taken on Marshall, Garner and Holding in county cricket. The previous season against Surrey, Lloyd had carried his bat for a century facing a 'terrifying' Sylvester Clarke on an underdone Oval wicket. Only Lloyd survived the innings as Clarke tore into Warwickshire with 7 for 53.

'Facing fast bowling was not complicated,' he says.

I knew exactly how I was going to play. The first thing is that you look to play back. But you're always looking for the up ball, the full ball. The one that gets you out is the up ball, but it was also your run ball. You had to get your weight going forward for that one, flick it off your hip if it was straightish or if it was wide, twat it square. When you drove, you *had* to drive straight as a left hander because if you didn't, there were four slips and a gully waiting. The ball was always coming across me. You didn't hook against the West Indies – there was no point – because sooner or later due to the speed you'd be late on it and hit one up in the air. You might get 20 – well done. Great. What use it that? You've got to get 120. There were very few people who could take the attack to them; you had to wait until they bowled in your areas. They were clever, intelligent bowlers. Proper bowlers. They never just banged it in short, non-stop.

The first Test of the summer was to be played at Andy Lloyd's home ground in Birmingham. Some English press men were optimistic.

'In theory, the West Indies should be entering a vulnerable phase,' John Woodcock had written in *The Times*. 'Clive Lloyd will be 40 in August; Richards, now aged 32, is not quite the player he was; Holding, at 30, and Garner, at 31, are not as fit as they were, and in the middle of the order, there will be batsmen who have yet to make a real mark in Test cricket.' Woodcock also mentioned the 'monotony' of watching West Indian speed, unrelieved by spin, for hour after hour and day after day. When the variety of the game was reduced, so was its charm, he thought. In captaining the side, Clive Lloyd had to do no more than keep his team's heavy guns firing, often pitching as short as the umpire allowed. Leading the West Indies was a sinecure compared with leading a side against them.

The eight-team photo at Lord's before the start of the 1979 World Cup competition. Some were told to wear blazers, others chose for themselves – with mixed results. From l-r: Sri Lanka, Pakistan, West Indies, England, Australia, New Zealand, India and Canada.

'You been
drinking rum?'

'Brandy.'

Vivian Richards in a mid-pitch discussion with Collis King during their match-winning stand in the 1979 World Cup final.

Joel Garner, Colin Croft, Andy Roberts and Michael Holding in the dressing room at Adelaide about to bowl against Australia on the 1979–80 tour.

An infamous moment in West Indian cricket. Michael Holding kicks down the stumps in Dunedin on the 1979-80 tour of New Zealand.

'The leg over the waist and past the shoulder then the head. Stumps flying. Fantastic. Ballet teachers throughout the world furious with envy.'

Bernard Julien warms up in front of an almost entirely white crowd at Durban before a one-day game on the renegade tour of South Africa in February 1983.

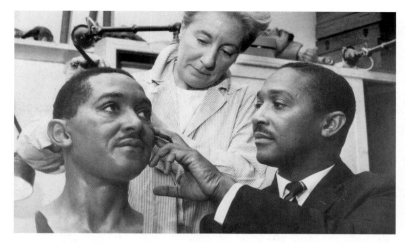

Frank Worrell in August 1963, checking on the progress of his waxwork at Madame Tussaud's. The first black official Test captain of the West Indies became one of the most influential men in the Caribbean.

West Indians watching Frank Worrell's side during the 1963 tour of England.

'He knows
everything?'
C. L. R. James
once asked
Frank Worrell.
'Everything,'
Worrell replied.

Garry Sobers sits behind the gleaming Wisden Trophy at the end of the tour of England in 1966. He was the greatest all-rounder cricket had seen.

The West Indians at Worcester in May 1984. All but six of the squad had played county cricket and England held no fears for them.

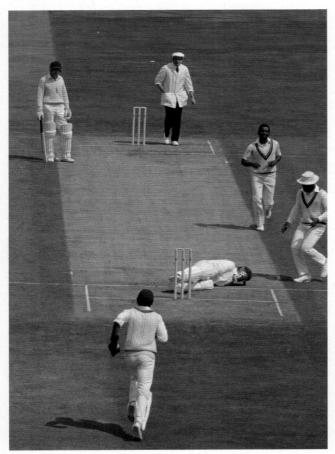

'I should have played it better, but even now, every time I go through in my mind how I could have played it, it still hits me.'

The end of Andy Lloyd's Test career at Edgbaston in 1984.

Vivian Richards batting with 'extreme prejudice' at Old Trafford during his 189 not out in the 1984 one-day international.

A missed chance? It may have been, given the looks on the faces of (l-r) Joel Garner, Gordon Greenidge, Roger Harper, Vivian Richards and Clive Lloyd. The slip cordon for the third Test at Headingley during the 1984 tour of England.

The 1984 Blackwash in England. Five-nil to the West Indies. 'In the 1980s', says the writer Colin Babb, 'the Test ground was a point of assembly... It was the only time in my life where I stood in an open public arena with lots of other people like me.'

'He has moulded the most successful team in the history of the game. He and his men have expanded the horizons of cricket... he has shown us how and has taken us to the mountain top.'

He understood the West Indian psyche. Clive Lloyd – the captain who taught his cricket team how to win.

'Clive was more like the father figure, Viv was more the sergeant major,' says Desmond Haynes – who was captained by both men. Richards played the game to represent his people. He played to prove that the creators of the game were no better than the people who had learned it from them.

Colin Croft: 'When the warrior walks out on to the field, it's a war zone.'

Malcolm Marshall of Barbados. Possibly the best fast bowler the West Indies have ever had?

'How do I score against Joel Garner?' Geoffrey Boycott once asked Ian Botham. 'You don't. No one does', was the reply.

Andy Roberts wasn't a big party man. 'I didn't drink, so most nights I would stay in my room and think about cricket.'

The man leading the side against them, David Gower, won the toss and decided that England would bat. Andy Lloyd was ready to make his debut for his country. 'This'll be good for you, Lloydy,' said the other opener, Graeme Fowler. 'You'll get involved straight away.' And off they went to face the two best fast bowlers in the world, Malcolm Marshall and Joel Garner.

Lloyd did better than Fowler, who was back in the dressing room within minutes, caught behind for nothing from a Garner ball. His successor, Derek Randall, didn't last long either, also caught for a duck. England were five for two, but Lloyd was hanging around.

'I'm sure I must have played and missed,' he recalls, 'but I'm sure too that I hadn't given a chance. I was quite relaxed and had been in for the best part of half an hour. Felt fine. Fowler and Randall had come and gone and I was still there. At the end of what must have been the sixth over Gower came down and we chatted in the middle and he said something like, "Well done, mate. You're looking good, keep going."'

It would be the last mid-pitch conversation the two would have. Malcolm Marshall began the seventh over from the City End.

'It was a short ball, but not very short,' remembers Lloyd. 'Malcolm, as we know, had a very quick arm action. I saw it all the way and I'm thinking, *The ball is going to pass here* – past my left shoulder. On my off side. I'm watching it, and it just straightened off the pitch after it bounced and it swung a little bit towards me. I was trying to get out of the way, but it followed me and it hit me here.' He touches his right temple an inch from his eye. 'I'd faced many quicker balls. It wasn't especially sharp, it was just a bloody good ball. You get bouncers, very good bouncers and brilliant bouncers. This was a brilliant bouncer. Came back at me a bit and cleaned me up.'

'Oh dear me,' said Richie Benaud on the BBC television comment-ary. 'Oh, I didn't like the look of that at all.' Lloyd fell straight to the ground and lay on his side. He put his hands to his head then didn't move. Desmond Haynes at short leg went immediately to him and crouched down. Jeff Dujon, the wicket-keeper, ran quickly to Lloyd, as did Roger Harper from third slip.

Graeme Fowler was watching in the dressing room. 'There was a locked door between us and the players' area and another closed door between us and the pitch. The telly was on with the sound turned down. The ball didn't get up as much as Andy thought it would and it walloped him on the temple guard of his helmet. I heard the crack through those two doors, and I was 80 yards away. "That's hospital," we said to each other straight away.'

In the middle, after a minute or two Andy Lloyd sat up. The physiotherapist Bernard Thomas had run out to treat him with the England twelfth man, Neil Foster.

'There was no pain,' says Lloyd.

I felt OK. Sounds stupid, doesn't it? Bernard said, 'Take your time and tell me how many fingers I'm holding up.' I said two, then he did it again and I said four. They were the right answers both times. But then I looked beyond his fingers to the boundary, and there was an advertising hoarding by a company called Rediffusion. You could rent your TV off them. And I was looking at this board and I couldn't really read it. Heavily blurred. Bernard said, 'I think you should come off,' and I looked at the advert again and I said, 'Yeah, OK.' That's when I knew something was wrong.

Within half an hour Lloyd was being examined, still in his whites, at the Queen Elizabeth Hospital in Birmingham. 'The bones around my eye socket were fractured. There was no real worry about brain damage; it was the working of the eye they were concerned about.' He pauses for a moment and looks away towards the back wall of the pub. 'I should have played it better. But even now, every time I go through in my mind how I *could* have played it, it still hits me.'

Lloyd's Test career had lasted 17 balls and barely half an hour. He retired hurt on ten. He would never play for England again. He is the only England opening batsman never to have been dismissed in the history of Test cricket.

After nine nights in hospital Lloyd was allowed to go home to his flat in Moseley, but he had to be careful. He was unable to tie his own shoelaces for a month because the doctors told him he had to keep his head still. No sudden movements. But he wanted to play cricket. By the end of July Warwickshire had reached the final of the Benson and Hedges Cup and Lloyd wanted to bat in it.

'I tried to do the *Roy of the Rovers* thing before the final by putting my pads on and having a net, but I was nowhere near. Couldn't bat properly. I had to make a decision about whether or not to keep playing cricket. I could have picked up £60,000 or so as an insurance payout, but I'd have to stop playing professionally. Thing is, I knew I would be captain of Warwickshire one day, and I knew I had a benefit year coming within five seasons. So I decided to go on.'

Lloyd wouldn't play again that year, but there was some tentative batting on an English Counties XI tour of Zimbabwe in the beginning of 1985. When the next county season came around he was back for Warwickshire. For his first game at Edgbaston, on the pitch where Malcolm Marshall had ended his Test career, he had to face Greg Thomas of Glamorgan, one of the country's fastest bowlers. He did well.

I got 160 or something, so everyone thought I was OK. Most bowlers that season made a big mistake: they tried to bounce me thinking I'd be scared. But the balls I couldn't play, the ones I really struggled with, were the full balls – half-volleys and yorkers. And the reason was this: I found it very difficult to judge distance and speed. The bouncer did two things – it went down and then up. That was OK, but the good-length ball just kept coming on the same path. That's why fielding was a nightmare. I was in a lot of trouble from a ball hit flat and hard straight at me. As for batting, there was a guy at Lancashire called David Makinson. Left arm medium pace, absolutely nothing special. Couldn't have played more than 30-odd first-class games and I doubt he got to a hundred wickets. Anyhow, he always pitched it up, and I couldn't get a run against him, and he kept getting me out bowled or LBW. I think after that I knew I'd never play for England.

His damaged eyesight had recovered as much as it would. There would be no more improvement. Freed from the constant pressure felt by the elite cricketer – the expectation of playing for your country – Lloyd changed the way he batted.

I was a completely different player now. I started smashing it a bit because I knew I would never be in the top rank again. Psychologically it was interesting too because up to 1985, my whole career – ten years – had been all about me. Improving, improving, challenges, getting runs, focusing on nothing other than playing for England. That was my professional existence. After Malcolm hit me and I realised I had no chance of getting back with England, I changed my focus entirely – my reason for being a cricketer – and it became all about my team, Warwickshire.

I never felt that I was a victim of the West Indian fast bowling.

It was fair dos. The fast bowler is not complete without a bouncer, and cricket wouldn't be right without it. The West Indies overdid the short-pitched stuff – they stretched the limit of the regulations – but it was their way of winning, and they always played within the laws. Always. And I would have done exactly what they did if it had been up to me.

* * *

Andy Lloyd was still in hospital while the West Indies were making 606 in the Edgbaston Test. They didn't have to bat again. They won the game by an innings and 180 runs. The second Test was at Lord's, and it was England's turn to declare in the hope of a win on the last day. Graeme Fowler had got a hundred in the first innings, and Allan Lamb did the same in the second. They set West Indies 342 in just under three sessions of cricket.

Gordon Greenidge opened the West Indies' second innings. He had been batting at the top of the order for almost ten years and was as important to the team as any fast bowler. Again and again that morning he hit the run of small boards put up next to the boundary ropes on both the Grandstand and Mound Stand sides of the ground. Greenidge clipped decisively off his legs and cut so swiftly to the off that his bat circled with momentum above his head with each four. He made his 50 when the team had scored only 77.

Greenidge probably knew England and the English better than any of his teammates. His first encounters had come not as Gordon Greenidge but as an uncertain teenager called Cuthbert Lavine. Until 1965 Cuthbert had lived in Barbados with his grandmother, whom he adored, while his mother sent home as much of her wages from a London bakery as she could. When Cuthbert was 14, she sent for him, and he left the village of Black Bess in the north of the island. He was leaving behind his friends, as well as swimming in the sea, fishing after school, kite flying and berry picking. He moved to Berkshire into a gardenless terraced house with his mother and her new husband, whose name was Greenidge. In a grim street he experienced the drabness of 1960s Reading. It was, he said, like setting foot in hell.

'I was going into something completely new, something I knew nothing about,' he recalls. 'It was a totally new dawn. Despite the joyful experience of being in the company of my mother again, it was very frightening, I have to say.'

If Reading itself was bad, school was worse. His thick and speedy Barbadian accent was ridiculed, but that was nothing compared to his astonishment at being racially abused. He remembers that 'black bastard' was the least of the taunts he suffered. His bewilderment was compounded by Caribbean pupils from different islands, who regarded him with almost the same suspicion and animosity as the white bullies who punched him in the face.

At 15 he was out of school and working. Unqualified and unskilled, he shifted sacks of seed and soil for a local agricultural merchant. He cared little for cricket and was better at rugby. He was a lonely, hesitant teenager, and his only dream was that he might one day become a preacher. Then an opportunity came along: in his last year at school he had been chosen for the Berkshire young cricket side, although Greenidge is convinced that the only reason he had been picked was that he was a West Indian. He hit the ball hard yet had no concentration, but he must have had some talent because the next season he was asked to play again and made a hundred against Wiltshire. His name was then mentioned to Hampshire, a first-class county. For the first time since he came to England, there was something to look forward to. Things had changed for the better. So had his name. Cuthbert Gordon Lavine was now Gordon Greenidge.

* * *

At Lord's on the last day of the 1984 Test Greenidge batted on. After lunch he faced England's fast bowlers not in a helmet but a cap. Bob Willis was driven; Derek Pringle was clubbed. Desmond Haynes had been run out, but Greenidge was joined by Larry Gomes with his unobtrusive, considered play. Meanwhile, a man was racing home across London to watch the rest of the match on his television. Harold Blackman was a bus driver from Harrow and, like Gordon Greenidge, a member of a powerful cricket team full of West Indians. Not quite Test standard, it's true, but good enough to lick most sides that came their way.

'Ah yes, the feller Gomes. We called him the carpet sweeper,' chortles Harold in his chair at his family home in Barbados. He is retired and on his 'long holiday'. He will be back in England next year, but not until winter is gone and the clocks go forward. 'Yes, we call Gomes the carpet sweeper because he bat like an Englishman sweeping a room, prodding about, not attractive. Never hit the ball in the air. But the point is, he fold in nicely with the other West Indies players. We have a lot of attacking players. We have Gordon, we have Viv, we have Clive. So we liked somebody like Gomes to steady the ship. Sometimes we in trouble and Gomes comes out, prods here, prods there, make a hundred.'

Harold Blackman had been watching the Test match on his television that morning but had to run an errand from Harrow to Charing Cross station.

'The game could only be a draw, only a draw. I had to do this delivery so I say, "No more cricket; I'll do this job." I set off and go to Charing Cross, finish the delivery a couple of hours later and then this feller at the station say, "Greenidge and Gomes are murdering England." Well, first thing I run for the train to Harrow to get back to the house and see if we can win.'

Harold had arrived in England two years before Gordon Greenidge. He too was Barbadian and, like Greenidge, was an opening batsman.

I had been a bricklayer in 1963, 18 years old, helping to build the new Queen Elizabeth Hospital in Bridgetown. Anyhow, London Transport came recruiting. They wanted people for the buses and trains. I put my name down and I got a letter one day – I'd been selected with a batch of 20 boys with a chance to go to England. We had to do exams first and they said if I was successful, I'd be going in three weeks' time. So I had my injections and all that and we had to go to the polytechnic by Kensington Oval three nights a week. Now, we had dollars and cents in Barbados, and because I was going to be a bus conductor and collect the fares in London, I had to learn pounds, shillings, pence and farthings. This was a nightmare. But fortunately I was not too long out of school so it clicked quite quickly.

The final exam was on a Sunday morning in May 1963. Harold cycled to the test because he had to get to a game of cricket in the afternoon. 'I was anxious not to miss that match. So I did the exam – pounds, shillings and pence – and then I had to write an essay about what to do if there was an accident on the bus. They told us the results immediately. And they said to me, "You're passed to go to England and you're off next week." So I cycled to that cricket match knowing it would be my last in Barbados.'

Harold had never left the island before. He flew to Jamaica and then caught a cargo boat to England. 'The bus company paid two weeks' rent in advance and put you in a house where there were eight or ten other men living – 112 Hindes Road, Harrow. I'll never forget it. Three to a room in bunk beds. It wasn't easy. But one good thing, they were all Barbadians, and I knew two men there because we'd played cricket together at home.'

A few miles to the south, as Harold was settling in during that spring of 1963, the West Indies were at Lord's, scrapping with England in one of the most exciting Test matches in years. Frank Worrell, Wes Hall, Colin Cowdrey with his arm in plaster, all four results possible. But Harold Blackman didn't see the thrilling draw. What he wanted to do was play himself. It wasn't difficult. Every bus garage in London had a side and a pitch. Harold's was Harrow Weald. He made his debut – kit-less – within weeks. In his navy-blue conductor's trousers he was told to bat at ten. For his next game his fortunes improved.

We played the hardest team in the division, Mortlake. They always won the Kingsbury League. This time the captain said, 'Young Blackie, everybody now tells me you can bat. You can open.' I said to him, 'This is a big jump from number ten to number one, Captain!' The opening bowler came from a long way off. Big run. I was on the front foot very early, and he bowled, and the ball still haven't get to me yet. *This is not like Barbados*, I thought, so I decided then to play off the back foot, see it off the wicket. Next ball, overpitch. I hit it back past him for four: everybody like it and shout. And the bowler look at me and I say, 'You can't bowl fast.' And he say, 'Blackman?' And I say, 'Tudor??' Well, turns out this feller and I used to play in the same league at home! I played for Lords, he played for Three Stars. Anyhow, I bat right through, get 68. They beat us by one wicket. But the news get around that a boy called Blackman was in the league!

Harold soon had a permanent spot in the Harrow Weald garage side and eventually became a valued regular in the London Transport XI, known as Central Road Services, a strong representative team chosen from all 48 London bus garages.

We had two white fellers in our garage team. That was about the same balance in all the garage sides. But when I first got to play for CRS, the captain had to be white. First time I see him bat, we lost. He was only captain because he was white! Oh yes, yes, yes. We still had that. He work for the buses but in the office. Once, I seen him try to make two runs to win a game. He couldn't even do that. 'We got to get a proper captain,' we said. We took it in our stride though because we were in England.

Along the south coast, young Gordon Greenidge was also trying to work out English ways. By 1967 he had played for the Hampshire second XI and had done well enough to be offered a two-year contract. At the County Ground in Southampton he painted the benches, picked up litter and swept the pavilion. When his chores were done, he was allowed to practise playing cricket. He scored some runs but was desperately lonely. He had few friends and lived in a YMCA hostel. Greenidge would pass the hours away from cricket playing snooker or table football, wary of those travellers in the hostel who would pick on him because of his colour. As he needed to qualify for the county by residence, he had to live there not just for the cricket season but for the winter too.

'That doomed me to the strange twilight world of the YMCA for some of the longest months of my life,' he wrote. 'I used to sit in my cramped and suffocating little room dreaming of the golden days of summer as the rain beat unceasingly against the windows.'

When his second season as a Hampshire cricketer started in 1968 he was hoping that life with the other junior players would be different to his dreary days in the YMCA. A few weeks into the season he and some other second XI staff were told to paint the creases for the start of a county game the following day. Instead, the other juniors decided to pin Greenidge down and paint him with whitewash. Only when they tried to whitewash his genitals was Greenidge able to break free. Made furious by his humiliation, he grabbed a spade and threatened to break it over their heads if they came any closer. 'They must have sensed this was no idle threat and they backed off hastily,' he recalled. 'Never again did I become the butt of racial jokes or of misguided horseplay at Hampshire.' He had stuck up for himself, but his sense of isolation from his teammates had never been more apparent.

'Because of the treatment you had to cope with, you had to find a way of releasing all that built-up anger,' he says now.

I felt that to go at my cricket forcefully, to attack, was a way of letting out that anger. I can't take it out on another human being because it wouldn't be right – although I felt like it at times – but I'm sure gonna take it out on five and a half ounces of leather cricket ball. I wasn't always a touch player that applied a lot of finesse. Maybe the word to describe how I go after the ball on the field of play was 'brutal'. Maybe it was a way of expressing myself and releasing that anger that had built up inside of me.

Greenidge's experiences would not have surprised Harold Blackman, who by now worked the 140 bus route from Mill Hill Broadway to Heathrow Airport.

I can tell you it wasn't easy. Things often happened. I would collect the money on the bus and I would have people who didn't want to touch my black hands. One woman held the coins high in the air and dropped them to me – went all over the floor of the bus. Now, if that had happened later in my career I would have just let the coins roll, not a problem. But I was new. I didn't want to lose my job so I was there on my hands and knees picking up this woman's pennies. It was humiliating. Not very nice. That's one incident. There were plenty more. They would call you a black bastard. Later on, when I was a driver, people would spit on you. It wasn't fun, but we take it, we take it. You had to work it out for yourself. You could either get in trouble – I had friends who ended up in court for that – or you could walk away. My thing on the bus was not to talk to nobody. That way worked for me. But there are some things that were done to me that will stick in my mind until I die. When people ask me how can I stay on the buses for 48 years, I say, 'Only God knows.'

And it made me angry – and I'll tell you why. When I went to those evening-class lessons in Barbados before I got selected to be a conductor, they told us a lot of lies. They told us, 'The English people are the nicest people in the world.' First day I walked to the Harrow garage, we said, 'Good morning,' to everyone we passed – like we did in Barbados – and not one person answered. Why didn't they tell us the truth?

We walked home at night in the early days, got followed by a group of Teddy boys with chains. Well, we made it to the Wealdstone police station and there were two policemen outside. We asked for help and you know what they said? They said, 'I'll tell you the best thing to do – why don't you go back home where you belong?' And you wonder why there were problems with the police in later years? They had the same hate in them as those Teddy boys.

*   *   *

At Lord's in 1984 Bob Willis ran in from the Pavilion End to bowl. The ball was short, and Gordon Greenidge cut it square. It didn't go for four, just a one to deep cover, but it was enough to bring the batsman a hundred.

'Up goes the bat, up go the arms – a super hundred this,' said the TV commentator Jim Laker. 'He really has played exceptionally well. A hundred out of 149 for 1. He's really set West Indies on their way.'

The West Indies supporters in the stands blew on creamy pink conch shells, rang hand bells and pumped portable radio sets up and down above their heads. Greenidge was their man, a batting hero of the best sort – dependable, experienced and exciting. But it had not always been this way.

'Go home, Englishman! Who the hell are you?' the fans had hooted. It was the beginning of 1973 and Greenidge was walking off the field at the famous Kensington Oval in Bridgetown having failed again for Barbados. The previous summer he had done well for Hampshire and had been given his county cap. This was much more than just a piece of cheap cloth; for Greenidge its award brought the sense of belonging and status, the legitimacy he had yearned for. It was recognition of his efforts. It made all those dreadful nights in the hostel worthwhile. With his Hampshire cap on his head, he felt less of an outsider. But now, months later, he was once again bewildered and confused. Barbados had asked him to play for the island. Perhaps this was a sign that he was being considered for the West Indies. Greenidge thought he was coming home, but he was in for a stunning let-down. What he calls a 'hate campaign' unnerved him so much that he seriously considered returning early to England.

It was very strange. I was encountering behaviour very similar to what I encountered when I first moved away. Up until this day I don't think I am accepted as a Barbadian. I mean they still call me an Englishman, and that's a fact. That made me very angry, as well as the reception that I received on coming back to the Caribbean. It was unexpected, so maybe I felt more anger towards the people behaving like that than what I felt towards the English guys who were calling me names when I first moved to England.

Greenidge worked out that the resentment was caused by the belief that he was taking the place of local cricketers in the Barbados team, the 'home-grown' players, that somehow his time in England had made him privileged and wealthy. Apart from his family on the island, few people welcomed him. Yet again he was an outsider. It didn't help that he couldn't make big scores on Caribbean wickets.

The skills he had learned in England – playing late, watching the ball off a deviating pitch against medium-pace swing – were no use to him here. The West Indies regional bowlers were faster, the wickets much quicker and the glare from the sun made Greenidge's eyes water. To make matters worse, he wasn't selected for the West Indies side to tour England in 1973 despite there being no obvious talent to accompany Roy Fredericks at the top of the batting order. Back in Hampshire that summer, Greenidge was quietly asked if he might be prepared to play for England. After all, he had lived in the country for long enough. He was flattered and gave it some serious thought. If he didn't get picked for the West Indies in the next year or two, then yes, playing for England was very likely.

In the end the West Indies selectors made the decision for him. Greenidge was chosen for the tour of India, Pakistan and Sri Lanka in the winter of 1974–5. He was one of many young players under the new captain, Clive Lloyd. In his first Test he made 90 and a hundred. A century on his debut for the West Indies – like George Headley, like Conrad Hunte and only five other men. It was a wonderful start to a very long international career, yet for all his successes Greenidge never seemed entirely soothed by a great innings. He was easily disturbed by his failures and had a tendency to sulk. Being dropped as an opening batsman in Australia the following season angered and humiliated him. Had his experiences as a young man taught him always to expect misfortune? Yet his determination to get even, to fight back, was equally strong. He was hugely competitive within the West Indies line-up. It's likely that he felt his batting wasn't recognised and applauded in the same way as that of the more gregarious members of the team such as Richards and Lloyd.

'I have often wondered if my life would have been easier had I been bred and discovered on one of the Caribbean islands,' he wrote in his 1980 autobiography. 'I am the only member of the West Indies party who has come to the top via another route and there are still moments when I feel like an outsider in the West Indies dressing room.' That feeling of separation was not helped by other remarks in the book. He made it clear that he did not think Clive Lloyd would go down in history as an inspirational leader. A marvellous and instinctive cricketer, for sure, but not a man whose shrewd captaincy changed the course of matches.

'I think Gordon felt that he didn't get what he really deserved in the side,' says Tony Cozier.

He craved recognition. But the fact is he is right up there with the best West Indian opening batsmen there have ever been. Him and Conrad Hunte. And actually Greenidge was a fortunate batsman. He was fortunate to have Desmond Haynes as a partner. Roy Fredericks and Hunte had something like 13 different batting partners; Greenidge had Haynes and Fredericks. A big advantage. He had physical power matched by mental strength. He was a very serious man who I've no doubt didn't entirely fit in to the West Indies dressing room, which was usually a place of fun and laughter. After all, they were West Indians. There was a lot of leg-pulling. But Gordon must have been strong because the one thing Caribbean cricket watchers can do immediately is detect any sort of psychological flaw, any weakness in a player. On the pitch Gordon didn't have those flaws.

Certainly not on that day in 1984 at Lord's. By the middle of the afternoon he was still there and had gone past 150. Less than a hundred to win now. Derek Pringle came back on to bowl. With beauty and power Greenidge put him over mid-wicket for four. Greenidge's followers now honked with delight. 'There's the old Bajan sea shell,' noted Jim Laker, before adding after a pause, 'I've blown a few of those in my time.' Off the next ball Greenidge nearly killed umpire Barry Meyer with a waist-high straight drive that would have ricocheted around the pavilion had it not been stopped by the dainty whitewashed fence guarding the front door.

'It was unbelievable,' recalls Graeme Fowler. 'Allan Lamb was at cover; I was at backward point, and Greenidge was giving himself room and smacking it past us for four. The closer we got, the harder he would hit it one side or the other – he was playing games with us. We didn't blame the bowlers though. It just got to a stage where it became inevitable. We couldn't stop him.'

With a hook to long leg, Greenidge took Neil Foster for a six into the Edrich Stand. Now he had made two hundred. Only eight other men had done that at Lord's since Test cricket began. His first reaction was to punch the base of his bat hard into the wicket as if planting a flag on a conquered peak. It had been a brilliant match-winning innings. Not long after, the defeated England fast bowler Ian Botham pottered up off four paces and bowled a fluttery off break which Larry Gomes, now on 88 and surely the finest carpet sweeper in the land, cut for four. Spectators fought for the ball at deep extra cover. Greenidge with a purloined stump in his hand, ran for the pavilion. It was half past five, and the West Indies had won by a mile.

It was one of the great West Indian innings of modern cricket, although Greenidge himself believes that his 134 (out of 211) at Old Trafford in 1976 was a more important score because it enabled his side to win a game they would otherwise have lost. Greenidge had showed himself to be supremely organised, a punisher who in the words of his captain batted 'with the interests of West Indian cricket at heart'.

His opening partner, Desmond Haynes, had sat and watched most of Greenidge's innings from the dressing-room balcony. They hadn't shown it that day, but they were the most successful front two batsmen the West Indies would ever have. Sixteen times they put on more than a hundred together; four times they scored more than 200. For 13 years they stayed together.

'My role was the supporting one,' says Haynes. 'I would never try to outdo Gordon. I wanted to make sure that our batting partnership was a long one. I don't mean the number of runs we put on in an innings; I mean the number of Tests we played. If he made 89 and I got 11, then it was a hundred partnership and I would be picked in the next game. I was happy to play second fiddle. I always thought that Gordon was better than I was. He was a more complete player.'

England were now two–nil down in the five-match series. The loss at Lord's was particularly embarrassing for the new England captain, David Gower. On the fourth evening his side had been in a very solid position, heading towards a good total. Then they came off the pitch in poor light when the braver thing to do might have been to stay on and make more runs to take the game away from the West Indies. Time had been lost.

Such a decision had been 'psychologically weak and tactically timid', wrote John Woodcock. *The Times* also questioned how hard Gower's England had prepared to play the world's best team. 'There is one fairly gruesome story doing the rounds,' revealed Woodcock. 'It tells of how before the Lord's Test West Indies practised hard from 10 o'clock in the morning until two o'clock in the afternoon while England, due at three o'clock, arrived late and were soon gone. Clive Lloyd insisted that Garner, against his wishes, should have a proper bat, helmet and all, in case he should have to go in with 10 to win.'

Not since 1948 had an England captain declared his second innings and lost.

'It was a mighty humbling day to be in the field against that,' admits David Gower. 'They won with nearly 12 overs of the last 20 left. To use a colloquial expression, all the wheels came off. The chairman of selectors, Peter May, was keen that we declared early. By the mathematics of the 1960s, that made sense; by the mathematics practised by the West Indies, it was a bit ambitious.'

'It wasn't the done thing to go on batting,' says Graeme Fowler. 'And that was the trouble. We were stuck in the 1960s, and the West Indies were playing twenty-first-century cricket in 1984.'

'You see, your problem in England was flair,' says Harold Blackman, who had made it back to Harrow to catch the last half-hour of the Test match on television.

Gordon was a flair man. A power man. A beater of the ball. Now you had no players with flair, well not many. Gower, he had a touch. 'Lord' Ted Dexter, he even batted like a West Indian. Colin Milburn. There was a feller we liked. We liked to see players hitting the ball. You also had a great player by the name of Ken Barrington, but we couldn't stand him! He could prod around all day. A killer of the game! Peter May, he wasn't bad, but the flair wasn't there. The flair wasn't there.

∗   ∗   ∗

On the first morning of the third Test at Headingley Malcolm Marshall fractured his left thumb in two places. He had been fielding at gully and was hit trying to stop the ball. He left the ground and

went to hospital, where his hand was set in plaster and the exam-
ining doctor told him he would not be able to play cricket for ten
days. Marshall returned to the ground to watch England bat. The
following day he saw his own team's reply.

Larry Gomes again went well for the West Indies and on the
third morning was nearing a hundred having got the side past
England's score of 270. The trouble was, he was running out of
batting partners. When Joel Garner was out with Gomes on 96, it
seemed that the innings would have to be closed. Only Marshall
was left. But in the dressing room what had begun as a light-hearted
tease – 'Get your pads on Maco and go and help Larry' – hurriedly
became a serious plan. Garner was nearly back at the top of the
pavilion steps when Marshall was seen trotting out wearing hastily
fastened pads and throwing a batting glove back to his teammates.
He was to admit on television that evening that he had still been
'in his civvies' when Garner was given out.

When he got to the middle he realised he couldn't hold the bat
in two hands because of his rigid plaster cast. 'What shall I do?'
he asked Gomes. 'Just try to block it, I guess,' replied the batsman.
With Marshall at the non-striker's end, Gomes sprinted for two
into the leg side and then, when the field came in to stop him
getting the strike for the next over, he slogged Bob Willis back past
his head for four to make his hundred.

That wasn't the end of the innings. Marshall stayed with Gomes
and faced eight balls of his own. He played and missed with a huge
swipe that made him laugh, and then to the delight of the West
Indies supporters on the terrace got up on his toes to glide a fast
ball from Paul Allott wide of the slips. He'd hit a boundary with
one hand, and before he was out his team had gone past 300.

Back in the dressing room Marshall realised that he was not in
a huge amount of pain. He thought he might be able to bowl. England

may have tolerated the light relief of him batting, but seeing him join the West Indies on the field to take the new ball was as serious as it was unexpected. England had scored only ten when he got his first wicket – Chris Broad caught at leg gully fending off a perfect short, fast and straight ball. After complaints were made that the England batsmen might be distracted by the flashing white plaster of Marshall's cast – which had been signed by the West Indies team – his arm was wrapped in pink tape by Dennis Waight. He then took six more wickets, including a caught-and-bowled to dismiss Graeme Fowler, and destroyed England single-handedly.

Before three o'clock the following afternoon the West Indies had won the match by chasing a target of 128. They were now three up with two Tests to play and had once again defended the Wisden Trophy. English hands hadn't raised it since 1969. 'I had a certain feeling of helplessness,' confesses David Gower. 'It was now a question of the margin.' He says he was trying to deal with his emotions both as a captain and as a player. 'We'd been beaten badly, and whatever I said when I made an attempt to build or maintain an aura of confidence in the dressing room felt a bit hollow.'

By the time the series was complete, Gower had tried to gee up 20 different players. In four of the Tests he had had to inspire men who'd never played for England before. 'These guys were having to make their debuts against one of the strongest sides they'd ever play in their lives,' remembers Desmond Haynes. 'C'mon! This was such juicy prey for our fast bowlers.'

At Old Trafford for the fourth Test the West Indies found yet another way of winning. Again they only had to bat once because Gordon Greenidge made another double century. In their second innings England had to score 221 just to make the West Indies bat again. They got nowhere near and were bowled out for 156 – not by Garner, Holding, Winston Davis or Eldine Baptise, but by Roger

Harper the off-spinner, who took 6 for 57. John Woodcock remarked that the appearance of a slow bowler in a West Indies line-up was 'as rare a sighting as an olive-backed pipit in Longparish in December'.

*　　*　　*

The West Indies had a squad of 17 players for the 1984 series in England. Harper was one of six who hadn't played any county cricket. In the previous English season just Northamptonshire, Sussex, Nottinghamshire and Yorkshire (who only took players born in the county) didn't have a West Indian on their books. Those West Indians who played for the other 13 counties all played Test cricket in 1983. Several of the sides also had young British West Indian players – either born in England or who had moved to the country as children. At Middlesex, for instance, there was Wilf Slack, Roland Butcher, Norman Cowans and Neil Williams.

The importance of county cricket to the development of the West Indies team cannot be overstated. 'Big time. It made a huge difference,' says Alvin Kallicharran, who had 19 seasons playing for Warwickshire.

We became professional cricketers, and it became a way of life for us. For a young man to go to England and then to bat every day, to bowl every day – surprise, surprise you become a better player. Your capacity improves; you're now a thinking person, thinking professionally. Because of England, I learned to keep my eyes on the ball, to play late, to remain focused in an innings and to concentrate for a long time. I learned discipline, I learned the etiquette of cricket. I felt I could combat any batting situation. So when we came to England as the West Indies later on, it was like batting in your backyard.

In 1968 the rules on overseas cricketers playing for counties had been reformed. Sides could employ a single foreign cricketer immediately and another after three seasons. Nowhere else in the world could a man play so many games of professional cricket in a season. The county championship programme of 1967 consisted of 238 fixtures, much more than the total of all first-class matches played that year in all other cricketing countries combined.

By the late 1960s Clive Lloyd had begun playing at Lancashire, Keith Boyce was at Essex, Garry Sobers was with Nottinghamshire and Lance Gibbs played at Warwickshire. Lloyd helped Lancashire to become the best one-day side of the time. In 1972 Warwickshire won the county title with four West Indians – Gibbs, Kallicharran, Deryck Murray and Rohan Kanhai – Murray and Kanhai could play because they qualified through owning property in England.

These players were developing the tradition begun by men such as Learie Constantine, the three Ws, Sonny Ramadhin, Collie Smith, Conrad Hunte and Basil Butcher. All these great West Indians had played English cricket in the Lancashire leagues, where they had gained a sense of responsibility. After all, they were carrying their teams. They were well paid so it was in their interests to develop not only their main skills but their subsidiary abilities too – fielding and batting if they were a bowler, catching and bowling if they were a batsman. To succeed they very quickly had to develop a sense of professionalism because the way they carried themselves in those little towns was noticed. Upright living was expected of them. These useful and important character traits would have been observed by and passed down to the players of later generations, building up to 1968, when the overseas player could flourish fully for the first time in county cricket. When Garry Sobers played at Derby that season, the county took more gate money than ever before in its history. These players were now sharing the experiences and challenges of those many voyagers who had left the Caribbean since the war to try to better themselves in England.

'The league professional has a tremendous burden to shoulder,' wrote Frank Worrell in *Cricket Punch*, 'and it is a good thing for any cricketer who aspires to international fame to learn how to shoulder tremendous burdens. It sharpens him up, makes him realise that whereas cricket is a delightful game, it is also a difficult game if you are going to be at the top in the top class.'

'They became stronger people,' says Tony Cozier. 'They went overseas, often for the first time, often alone. Their behaviour had consequences now. To put it another way, they did their own laundry for the first time. It made them into men.' (Clive Lloyd was perhaps an exception on the laundry front. During his early seasons at Lancashire, the washing of his underwear was generously overseen by the wife of the county captain, Jack Bond.)

Migration to England made the West Indies Test side better. Domestic cricket in Australia and the Caribbean was only semi-professional, and there was not a great deal of it. You couldn't earn much. So playing for a county meant good money and lots of cricket experience. 'In the 1970s,' says the cricket author Stephen Chalke, 'there was nothing better than spending four months of a year when there was not much cricket going on anywhere else in the world, fine-tuning your skills within the rich variety of pitches and match conditions that English county cricket offered.'

Batting was done on uncovered pitches so there were always different surfaces created by wet or dry weather that helped the ball to spin, seam or swing. A young West Indian who had learned his cricket in Barbados or Trinidad had to tighten his technique considerably. The ball did very different things in England. Greenidge, Fredericks, Lloyd, Richards and Kallicharran all became more complete players because they batted in England a lot. In fact Richards and Greenidge served the bulk of their apprenticeships on English wickets. All would still have become great players, but their English experience taught them to adjust to different circumstances more quickly.

Bowling in England was always done best by the most intelligent cricketers. You had to think to bowl well on English pitches. Malcolm Marshall was a good example. During his great season of 1982, in all matches in England he bowled 1,008 overs and took 160 wickets. County cricket gave him the hours he needed to become brilliant. He could rehearse without fear. When he was perfecting his inswinger in 1985 it took him two months of net bowling and competitive matches to get the delivery to a standard with which he was happy. That meant at least 18 first-class and one-day matches. Had he been playing only for Barbados it could have taken him two seasons to build the confidence to use the inswinger in big cricket.

County cricket helped the West Indians more than it did any other foreign Test side. They were able to hone their skills and retain their competitive edge. Their sides of the 1950s and early 1960s had had some successes but lacked the consistency of professional cricket. Batting collapses were quite common, and the West Indies never stayed at the heights for long. Without the experience of English cricket, their great teams could not have advanced in the way that they did under Lloyd. County cricket made the Test side much harder to beat.

Perhaps the culmination of this shared experience was the team that excelled during Packer's World Series Cricket. There is a connection. Here was a supreme travelling independent side, playing against all types of players on different types of pitches. At last they knew they could look after themselves.

* * *

At the fifth Test at the Oval in August 1984 the West Indies had the chance to make cricketing history. No team had won every Test of a five-match series in England before. Marshall was back and got five wickets in the first innings. Holding, reverting to his long run-up of '76, did the same in the second. Lloyd saved the West Indies with an undefeated 60 when they batted first, and Haynes got a hundred when they went out for a second time. At one minute past midday on the last afternoon, Tuesday 14 August, the England swing bowler Richard Ellison nicked a catch to Joel Garner in the gully. The last of England's 97 wickets to fall that summer had gone, and the West Indies had won every Test. Five–nil. Not a whitewash, a blackwash.

'Everyone knows of our association with the British,' says Viv Richards, 'and everyone knows the standard that the British had set as far as cricket was concerned. So beating them felt like we had come a long way. They adore Test match cricket. I heard someone say, way back when, that England would rather lose a battleship than lose a game of Test match cricket.' He laughs. 'Now I don't know how true that statement is, but hearing it like that, then you know how serious the English appreciate Test matches.'

Since the beginning of Test cricket such a complete result had only been recorded by four other teams. Australia had managed it twice, between the wars. England did it against India in 1959, and the West Indies beat India five–nil in 1961–62. By winning at the Oval, Clive Lloyd's side had also equalled the all-time record of eight successive Test match wins. They hadn't lost now for 23 matches. One defeat in 39 Tests.

'We never expected to win five–nil,' says Lloyd. 'I must be honest and say that we didn't expect to lose, but the margin of victory was a bonus. By now we were formidable. I think we were largely respected wherever we went, certainly by other cricketers, and people spoke about West Indian cricket with admiration.'

Up to a point.

While other players may have appreciated the West Indians' craft, there was undisguised displeasure regarding their bowling by some in the English media. Writing in the *Sunday Times*, Robin Marlar stated that 'as the umpires seemed neither to count nor to care how many balls pitch closer to the bowlers than the batsmen, we can expect the plague of short stuff to continue. The beautiful game will die of such brutality but you cannot get a West Indian to agree with that proposition.' The only thing that gave Marlar any joy on the Saturday of the final Test was listening to one of Mozart's horn concertos in his car as he drove to the Oval.

Ideas were also being formulated to blunt West Indies tactics. Two former England captains, Sir Leonard Hutton and Ted Dexter, had specific plans. Dexter wanted the pitch to be made longer so the ball took longer to reach the batsman. (Such a change would have killed off slow bowling at a stroke.) Hutton wanted a white line to be placed across the wicket halfway down. If the ball pitched on the bowler's side of it, it would be an illegal delivery. The editor of *The Cricketer* magazine, Christopher Martin-Jenkins, endorsed Sir Leonard's thoughts. He suggested trialling the line for a season of first-class cricket across the world so as to prepare teams for its use in Test matches. 'It would be so much better to deal with the problem now rather than when someone has been killed,' he wrote.

By now the view had formed that the West Indies were somehow tarnishing the spirit of cricket, that the way they played the game with four fast bowlers was underhand, unfair even. In the words of Marlar, 'most people on whose support English cricket depends, believe monotonous fast bowling to be both brutalising the game and boring to watch'. To accompany the 1984 Test series in the *Wisden Cricketers' Almanack*, its editor John Woodcock printed a photograph of the England night watchman Pat Pocock, 'ducking for his life' to get under a bouncer from Malcolm Marshall. The picture was captioned, 'The unacceptable face of Test cricket'.

'Unacceptable?' asks Graeme Fowler. 'Was it hell. We never thought that. We just knew we were involved in a monstrous battle. We never thought this was against the spirit of the game. Our only thought was that if you can't handle it, then don't do it. Just get stuck in. The West Indies were found guilty of nothing more than being superb.'

Matthew Engel covered the 1984 tour for the *Guardian*.

As the possibility of the blackwash built, the series actually became more and more vivid. The extent of it enhanced the drama. And I don't think monotony played any part in it. Monotony is trundling medium-pacers of the sort England quite often put out. The sense you had was that you were witnessing something extraordinary. Vivid, on the borderline of what we conceive as cricket, but never monotonous.

The West Indies were supposedly dull to watch, yet advance ticket sales for the third Test at Headingley (when England were already two–nil down) were a record £130,000. Gate receipts at Lord's – £507,000 – were also a record. The boundary on the Grandstand side of the ground had to be shortened to 65 yards to accommodate extra spectators on the grass.

It was often repeated that summer that dreadfully slow over rates drained all the excitement from the game, yet when the unused playing time from 1984 is added up, it totals 15 two-hour sessions not including time lost to shorter weather delays. That would have been enough time to play another complete five-day Test. 'If they'd have liked,' says Clive Lloyd, 'we could have won all our matches a lot quicker. I wonder what the people who counted the money in the tills would have thought of that.' As for the depressing homogeneity of fast bowling, Woodcock suggested in *The Times* that there could be a scenario for the second Test where England might be better off picking four pace bowlers: Richard Ellison, Derek Pringle, Bob Willis and Neil Foster – as well as the fast-medium Ian Botham.

West Indian fast bowling was supposedly dangerous and unedifying. *Wisden*, in its review of the 1984 season, complained that umpires had allowed bowlers to resort 'ever more frequently to the thuggery of the bouncer'. But others seemed to like it. At the end of May, when the West Indies had played Glamorgan, *The Times* had reported that after a delay for rain the weather and the play were more enjoyable. 'There was a purple passage when Winston Davis [playing for Glamorgan] attempted several bouncers at [Richie] Richardson, a miniature war, as it were, between the Windward and Leeward islands. Those that Richardson could reach were hooked, pulled and driven for five fours.' Black bowlers bouncing black batsmen seemed to be perfectly entertaining to some critics. Only in Test matches against England were bouncers apparently unpleasant.

In the series before the West Indies came to England they had hosted Australia. In one phase of the fifth Test in Jamaica the Australia fast bowler Rodney Hogg bowled 12 bouncers in a row (two complete overs) at the throats of West Indies' openers Desmond Haynes and Gordon Greenidge. In the first innings Greenidge made 127 and Haynes scored 60. In the second innings both were not out, making the 55 runs the West Indies needed to win the game by ten wickets. Far from being intimidated by Hogg's extraordinary bowling, they took it on and subdued it. It is interesting to wonder what the reaction would have been had Michael Holding bowled 12 bouncers in a row to a pair of England batsmen.

'It's so beautiful to see the hook shot played well,' says Desmond Haynes. 'I wanted people to bowl short at me. It was like a half-volley, a four ball. I always expected to get a short ball from a good bowler.'

'The criticism has to be rooted in jealousy. Why else would people complain?' reflects Joel Garner.

And the answer is very simple. You play to your strengths. It wasn't intimidation. If you take short-pitched bowling away, how many fewer runs would Clive Lloyd, Alvin Kallicharran, Viv Richards and Gordon Greenidge have scored? They conquered the bouncer. Take away the short-pitched ball and you take away one of the joys of cricket. It's such a nonsense because when we were on the end of it we never complained. The way I see it, we didn't bowl excessive bouncers, we attacked people who had a weakness.

The reaction to West Indian fast bowling was troubled by inconsistency. It seemed to perturb journalists much more than it bothered the players and the spectators. Even those who called for its supposed unpleasantness to be tamed by legislation – such as *The Cricketer* – couldn't decide whether fast bowling should be shunned or supported. Perhaps it depended on where the bowlers came from. In 1983, the season before the West Indies arrived, the magazine ran a nationwide competition: Find a Fast Bowler for England. Its quest was supported by Alf Gover and the England selector Alec Bedser. The winner, whom the two men chose from a group of 16 finalists, was a 19-year-old teenager from Paddington in west London called Junior Clifford. His parents were from Jamaica.

*   *   *

For the Oval Test in 1984, the last of the series, the press box was not in its usual place, but in a temporary building on the Harleyford Road side of the ground opposite the famous gasometers. To get to it, journalists had to make their way through the West Indian supporters. One reporter recalled that the atmosphere was different to anything he had experienced before. 'The crowd was hostile,' he said.

> There was lots of dope, not mellow dope. There was no doubt they were in the majority. I guess this was getting to the peak of West Indian cricket watching in England. It was by no means dangerous, but I felt uncomfortable. But was it any more intimidating than moments I'd had with Yorkshire supporters on the Western Terrace at Headingley? Probably not. I think that more than ever most of these young people saw that West Indian cricket team as an expression of their frustrations. It was a solution. Given what had happened in inner-city England in recent years, was that surprising?

In 1981 there had been serious riots in Brixton, just a couple of miles from the Oval. Plenty of people in the blackwash cricket crowd would have experienced that trouble, and they would witness further riots in the same suburb the following year, which began after the police shot and paralysed a black woman in her home while searching for her son, who was suspected of an armed robbery.

Professor Paul Gilroy, who has written widely about black British culture, was in the 1984 Oval crowd.

> For lots of young people there was a sort of Manichean purity to the confrontation that summer. The pulse of the 1976 cricket had been very strong and it radiated outwards for years. These victories,

condensed into this sporting encounter, were symbolic reparations for their sufferings in England. There was, I think, one resonance for the Caribbean migrant and another distinct sensation for those who were born here, those people whom the government called rather memorably 'the coloured school-leavers'. They had an extra dimension of bitterness.

'In the 1980s,' says the cricket writer Colin Babb, 'the Test ground was a point of assembly. It was a place you went to meet people who were like you, to connect with them and to celebrate. Yes, there were local sports grounds, the odd bar where you could sit, perhaps an annual carnival in your city, but the cricket ground was the place. When I went to the Oval it was the only time in my life where I stood in an open public arena with lots of other people like me.'

*   *   *

By the start of the 1980s the relationship between the police and many of the people who lived in Brixton had deteriorated badly. At the beginning of 1981 a fire at a house party in New Cross, a few miles to the east, had killed 13 people. There was a widespread local view that there was orchestrated indifference to the tragedy (on the part of the newspapers and the police) because the victims were young and black and that the party had somehow been considered a sinister event. Six weeks later, at the beginning of March 1981, between 6,000 and 20,000 people (the reports vary) walked through London to protest against the authorities' reaction to the fire.

Less than a month later a police initiative called Operation Swamp took place in Brixton. It was part of a campaign against burglary and robbery which the Metropolitan force was carrying out across London. In six days 120 plain-clothes officers stopped nearly a thousand people. Given that the suburb contained the country's largest number of British West Indians, almost all the people stopped were black. In a part of London where suspicion of the police was already profound, the operation caused remarkable animosity. The name Swamp had apparently been taken from comments made by the prime minister, Margaret Thatcher, when she was leader of the opposition in 1978. She predicted that by 2000 there would be four million immigrants from 'Pakistan and the new commonwealth' in Britain. 'That is an awful lot, and I think it means that people are really rather afraid that this country might be swamped by people of a different culture. The British character has done so much for democracy, for law, and done so much throughout the world that if there is any fear that it might be swamped, then people are going to be rather hostile to those coming in.'

The head of the local CID described the 118 arrests made by his officers during Operation Swamp as a resounding success. Within days of its ending, tens of millions of pounds' worth of damage had been caused to Brixton by rioters.

*　　*　　*

Steve Stephenson is sitting in an armchair in his house in Bedford. Around him is the evidence of his deep involvement in West Indian sport in Britain: photographs of him with players, posters advertising charity games, black-tie dinners, community matches for football and cricket. For 40 years he has been a confidant, fixer, supporter *in loco parentis* and adviser to Caribbean cricketers who come to England to play for a county or in the leagues. And his wife has been their chef. If it was egg and chips on the menu yet again in Bristol, Leicester or Swansea, Steve would rescue the West Indies by driving over with a car boot full of rice and peas and chicken patties, or ackee and saltfish with dumplings.

'You remember that famous banner at the 1975 World Cup final?' he asks. 'You see it on the TV. The one with the kangaroo? That was painted by my younger brother Harvey. He was an A-level student at the time. He didn't come to the game himself, but I was there. The banner got taken away from us and passed around the crowd.' Harvey's painted artwork had shown a marsupial bound with rope being pulled along by a black cricketer in whites and pads. It read, WEST INDIES – WORLD CHAMPION, WILL TIE THE KANGAROO DOWN.

Steve's father was one of the first Jamaican immigrants to come to Luton in the early 1950s. He had cycled around Kingston selling tobacco from his bike, but in Bedfordshire he worked on the Vauxhall car assembly line. 'Like a lot of people of his time, he saw England as the mother country where the streets were paved with gold,' says Steve. 'He wanted a better life.'

Steve arrived from Jamaica in 1971 when he was 17. He too worked in the car factory but by 1981 was studying for a university degree in social work. The riots that year in London, Manchester and Liverpool had spread to Luton. 'I'd opened up a club with a friend of mine. The Starlight Club. We wanted to do something for the 200 or so young people, a lot of them alienated, many aspiring to be Rastafarian, most of them born here. 'Social exclusion' was the phrase they called it at the time.'

Luton was a tricky place in which to hang around at weekends in the early 1980s. There was regular trouble between supporters of Luton Town and visiting football clubs such as Chelsea and West Ham United.

'Yeah, so the point was that this club was open all day on a Saturday. Keep the boys away from the nonsense. The police bought us a pool table. All the Asian boys would come and watch the Bruce Lee kung fu movies, the white boys come in hiding their cans of lager, the Caribbean boys come in hiding a bit of spliff, but they all mixed in the club together and they were off the street.'

Steve also set up a little library at the Starlight Club.

Lots of these kids had an identity problem, just like I had in Jamaica 20 years previously. I knew about Shakespeare, I knew about *Pygmalion*, we did exams through the Cambridge board, but we didn't know the capital cities of the Caribbean islands. We knew nothing about slavery. It wasn't until I came to England and read Malcolm X that I put all the pieces together. So I started teaching these kids a bit of black history. Some of them ended up in university and, I must say, some others ended up in Bedford Prison.

Then came the 1981 riots. 'I was down there in the middle of it all trying to stop some kids destroying a snooker centre. "This is not the way it should be," I kept saying. "We can't wreck the town we live in."' The disturbances caused enormous bitterness between many people in Britain's inner cities and the police. When it was all over in Luton, Steve wanted to do something to reduce the animosity. So he organised a cricket match.

I knew that we needed to bring the communities back together. The police had a good side, but we beat them in the park. Then they played us at their headquarters. We beat them there too. The mayor came to watch, and we all had a drink afterwards. These boys got a lot of pleasure from beating the police.

The heart of the problem was that for these kids they saw a lot of racism wherever they turned. Not necessarily from the police. You'd go to interviews with your qualifications and they'd offer you a job digging holes. If you spoke in patois, they automatically assumed that you were stupid. But at the time the backdrop to all this, the thing that we had, was West Indies cricket. I have to say that cricket was the mainstay, cricket gave us our pride. Clive Lloyd, Viv Richards. They lift us to another level. It was very important and it's still important today. But there was more. Where we played cricket, the local black club we were in, the opening bowler would be a carpenter, the wicket-keeper was a car mechanic or a builder. I was the letter writer, the passport signer. And we would all help each other with our skills for our mutual benefit. It was so much more than a cricket team.

To watch the blackwash triumph of 1984 was special. 'The cricket we went to see together used to lift our self-image. It was something we could look at and say, "Look what we have achieved." We felt by winning at cricket we was having our own back. We weren't getting the jobs, we weren't getting up the ladder. I don't think we analysed it at the time, we thought about it later on. The cricket brought us pride which we weren't getting in other parts of our life.'

In 1996 Steve Stephenson was awarded an MBE for his years of service to the people of Luton. 'I went to Buckingham Palace with my wife and my two children. All dressed up. We were inside the palace near the cloakroom and this very posh English lady who was also getting an award walked straight up and, without a pause, handed my daughter her coat. My daughter said, "But I'm not working here." Racism? It's alive and well. But, you know, I'm a social worker so I'm trained to show my humanity to all people whatever the situation.'

9

'I understood the
West Indian psyche'

A microphone on a stand has been set up on the outfield of the Kensington Oval in Bridgetown. It is 26 April 1985 and the West Indies are about to begin the third Test against New Zealand in Barbados. Clive Lloyd is there but not in his cricket whites; he is wearing a short-sleeved lightweight grey safari suit. He stands waiting with his hands joined in front of him.

Vivian Richards is at the microphone, self-consciously gripping a presentation tray on which are three cut-glass drinks decanters.

'On behalf of the members and the management of the West Indies cricket team,' says Richards, 'let me say thank you very much, Clive, for the strength, power and, most of all, the winning habit. Also I hope that you will accept this little token which we have gathered here.' He briefly raises the decanters. 'Thank you very much, Clive. Well done to a champion.'

Clive Lloyd walks up to his teammate and they shake hands. They pose with the decanters for photographers. Lloyd smiles beside the man who is the new captain of the West Indies. He has retired. Richards is now in charge.

* * *

Clive Lloyd had played his last Test match in Australia four months earlier. Another series had been safely won. He had led the team in 74 Tests and lost just 12 of them. There had been 36 victories. No West Indian had played as much Test cricket. Nineteen years had passed since he sat, fearful, in the West Indies dressing room in Bombay, wondering if he had the wit to bat against the Indian spinner Bhagwat Chandrasekhar.

The *Trinidad and Tobago Review* summarised Lloyd's achievement:

He has moulded the most successful team in the history of the game. He and his men have expanded the horizons of cricket; they have played before hostile crowds with dignity and Clive Lloyd has been at the helm keeping his cool, loving and being loved by his players. He has shown us what courage and self-belief added to self-discipline and talent can achieve. He has warded off eye problems, back problems, knee problems. He has had to fight for his form; has had his battles with administration; successfully led his men in and out of the Packer affair, always coming out stronger, dignified and victorious. Devotion and decency are the qualities that come readily to mind. His place will not be easy to fill. He has shown us how and has taken us to the mountaintop. We salute him.

The recognition Lloyd received from the WICBC at the time was a little more restrained. 'The board have long memories,' recalled Lloyd years after his retirement. 'I believe that they never quite got over Packer. I think in some way they felt shamed by what happened then, by what the players did.' His conclusion was that some of the board were jealous of the money the players had begun to earn and envious of Lloyd's standing within the team. 'They saw me as the big cheese and themselves as underlings, and of course they wanted that position to be the other way around. I got rid of a lot of headaches for them. They didn't even have to think about appointing another captain for the best part of a decade.'

The undercurrent of ill will between the board and the players was perhaps inevitable. The relationship reflected the tension that existed throughout the twentieth century in the Caribbean between employers and workers. Only after the Second World War had any meaningful recourse to trades unions for employees really existed. Even in the 1970s, as the Packer affair unfolded, members of the WICBC would have been unused to their authority being questioned. And although in the years before Lloyd's retirement the board was largely made up of former players, there was, in Barbados and Trinidad particularly, a close historical association between Caribbean cricket administrators and the white elite of the sugar industry.

As Lloyd carried his three decanters from the outfield of the Kensington Oval on that Friday in April 1985 there could be no doubt that his captaincy had helped make the West Indies into a great team – not only his tactical skills, but qualities of leadership that included the gifts of humanity and perception. He was a leader of men in the fullest sense, and the man he identified with most in the tradition of West Indian cricket leadership was Frank Worrell. In the family tree of captaincy, Lloyd was separated from Worrell by two predecessors, Rohan Kanhai and Garry Sobers.

To understand Frank Worrell's captaincy, and the leadership of those who followed him, is to understand something of West Indian history. In 1959 – 126 years after the 1833 abolition of slavery in the British empire – Worrell was the first black man to be appointed full-time captain of the West Indies. Up until that time the post was seen to be safe only in the hands of a white man, although there had been two brief interruptions to this orthodoxy: Learie Constantine stood in for the injured Jackie Grant in Jamaica against England in

1935 and George Headley led the side in 1948 against England in the Barbados Test. White leadership was an inevitable legacy of colonialism, empire – and slavery.

The social, political and economic consequences of slavery saturated the Caribbean territories for 300 years. These slave islands fuelled the expansion of European empires – Spanish, Dutch, French and British. The key crop was sugar. To colonialists the English-speaking Caribbean islands existed as little more than centres of wealth production; the connection between Britain's growth throughout the eighteenth and nineteenth centuries and the production of sugar cannot be overestimated. The wealth created by slavery fired the Industrial Revolution and brought luxury to British cities. The historian Eric Williams, who would go on to be the first prime minister of Trinidad and Tobago in 1962, wrote in *Capitalism and Slavery* 'It was the slave and sugar trades which made Bristol the second city of England for the first three quarters of the eighteenth century. "There is not," wrote a local annalist, "a brick in the city but what is cemented with the blood of a slave."'

In 1939 Winston Churchill spoke in London at a banquet given for West Indian sugar planters. 'The West Indies', he said, 'gave us the strength, the support, but especially the capital, the wealth, at a time when no other European nation possessed such a reserve, which enabled us to come through the great struggle of the Napoleonic Wars, the keen competition of the eighteenth and nineteenth centuries, and enabled us . . . to lay the foundation of that commercial and financial leadership which . . . enabled us to make our great position in the world.'

That capital, and that great position in the world, had a human cost because sugar was difficult to make (as every good Marxist knows, the capital came 'dripping from head to foot, from every pore, with blood and dirt'). Sugar cane needed money up front to pay for its planting and seasoning, and it needed labour. The money came from a network of wealthy commission agents in seventeenth-century London; the labour came from captured African slaves.

Since the 1440s European powers had been sending their ships down the west coast of Africa to collect slaves. By the time of the Industrial Revolution the pattern was set: British boats packed with cloth from Lancashire, iron goods from Birmingham and brass from Bristol would set off for the coast of 'Guinea'. Once there, they would trade for humans. 'The whites did not go into the interior to procure slaves; this they left to the Africans themselves,' wrote the American historian Benjamin Quarles. 'Spurred on by the desire for European goods, one tribe raided another, seized whatever captives it could and marched them with leather thongs around their necks to coastal trading centres.'

These outposts, on the coast of what is now Ghana, were the 'door of no return' for millions of people. The British also had slave forts in Benin, the Gambia and Sierra Leone. From these buildings the biggest forced migration in history began. It was a huge industry. Over 400 years, 11 million Africans were taken. Three million slaves were packed into British boats heading for North America and the West Indies. In the last decade of the eighteenth century a slave ship heading for Africa left a British port every second day. The great beneficiaries were the aristocracy, the Church and the royal family. 'But it is scarcely an exaggeration,' writes William St Clair in his book *The Grand Slave Emporium*, 'to say that every person in the Europeanised world who put sugar in their tea or coffee, spread jam on their bread, who ate sweets, cakes, or ice-cream, who smoked or chewed tobacco, took snuff, drank rum or corn brandy, or wore coloured cotton clothes, also benefited from, and participated in, a globalised economy of tropical plantations worked by slaves brought from Africa.'

Once at work, cutting and preparing the sugar cane, the slaves' lives were truly wretched. Nearly a million were sent to Jamaica alone to sustain the sugar plantations. By the 1780s there were more than 600 sugar estates on the island, where the planters and overseers commonly inflicted obscene, bestial punishments on their slaves for the most trivial offences. One such overseer was a man called Thomas Thistlewood, who for years kept a detailed diary of his relationships with the people he owned. One entry records how one of his slaves, after being caught eating a piece of cane, was 'well flogged, then rubbed in salt pickle, lime juice and bird pepper. Also whipped Hector for losing his hoe, made new negro Joe piss in his eyes and mouth.' At times slave mortality was so high that for every three who arrived, two would die.

The making of Caribbean sugar was a vast exercise in tyranny and repression. According to the British historian Peter Fryer, 'to establish, maintain, and justify their rule over, and their exploitation of, 370 million black people, Britain's rulers needed an ideology which told them . . . that their imperial rule was in the best interests of their colonial subjects. This imperialist ideology was racism.' Long after slavery ceased in the Caribbean, this view remained undiluted in Britain. In 1865 the *Spectator* published an article whose author reflected, 'The negroes are made on purpose to serve the whites, just as the black ants are made on purpose to serve the red.'

Clive Lloyd's ancestors were slaves. Vivian Richards's ancestors were slaves. Frank Worrell's ancestors were slaves.

*   *   *

Towards the end of 2014 Vivian Richards leans back on his chair and looks towards the sea. He is considering his people's past. The water of Dickenson Bay is turquoise and the sand is white. There are palm trees. This is Antigua – his island, his rock. Slowly he massages his shaved head with his hand as he considers what took place here. When he answers he looks to the horizon.

> I have always been conscious of slavery. I think when you recognise where it is that you have come from it is easier to work out the route you would like to take. I think about the persecution we have faced as a people. When you understand your history, you can plot your own journey. And these people who carried out these things. Are they superior? I don't think so. Am I angry about it? Nah. Not today. Being angry about it won't get you anywhere – it's like trying to spin a top in the mud. What I do know for sure is that we have come on a serious journey.

The elaborate social system fostered by slavery and the sugar industry remained long after the 1833 Act of Parliament abolished the slave trade. Cricket was a central part of that society. In the early 1800s the game was already established in the West Indies; island newspapers carried the announcement of fixtures alongside information on the sales of slaves and the latest changes in the price of sugar. Cricket was played first by whites of course, often by military men garrisoned there to thwart black uprisings on land and French invasion by sea. As one Barbadian newspaper put it in 1838, 'the manly sport of cricket' was intended for 'the gratification of the soldiers as well as the sake of their health'.

Within 30 years or so elite clubs had been founded – the Wanderers and Pickwick clubs in Barbados for instance – where private games were played and watched by the plantation owners and growing numbers of white middle-class administrators, lawyers, merchants and accountants, whose influence was now superseding that of the old families as the price of sugar fell. All these men shared a common goal – the preservation of a colonial, hierarchical, capitalist society – and so West Indies cricket was born into the tradition of white authority – British authority. Cricket was a social tool to help sustain the empire.

And the black ancestors of Clive Lloyd, Vivian Richards and Frank Worrell? Where did they all fit into this arrangement? The answer is first on the fringes, and then more centrally.

Cricket, like most aspects of colonial Caribbean life, needed ancillary labour. Land needed to be maintained, pitches needed to be prepared, and balls struck from the middle needed to be retrieved from neighbouring cane fields. This was a black man's work, and in the first decades of the nineteenth century such menial tasks were the initial black connections to West Indian cricket. They are articulated by the cricket historian and author Professor Clem Seecharan: 'The ball would disappear constantly in the thick under-growth; it was the recurring task of the slave to retrieve it. To return the ball from beyond the boundary, accurately to the wicket, was a self-imposed challenge. The hurling of the ball a long way, from canepiece to playing area, was an act of freedom: it represented a fleeting presence in the central scene.'

In the Caribbean heat batting was more pleasant than bowling. White players who wanted to improve would practise against those blacks who showed an interest in, and aptitude for, bowling. Some of these bowlers became proficient all-round cricketers and began to play the game informally among themselves in the spare time that they had. And for a black slave or a freed man to master bowling to the extent that he could implicitly threaten the authority of his master by hurling the cricket ball fast and accurately became an act loaded with symbolism – what Seecharan describes as 'an embryonic countervailing power: a potentially subversive action'. Not only that, but for a young black man to become good at bowling gave him an added use. Cricket was not yet an instrument of black liberation, but it certainly became an instrument of mobility. Not though for poor Quanko Samba.

In *The Pickwick Papers* Charles Dickens lampoons the role of Samba, the servant-bowler, when a character tells Pickwick of a game of cricket he once played in the West Indies:

'It must be rather a warm pursuit in such a climate,' observed Mr Pickwick.

'Warm! Red hot – scorching – glowing. Played a match once – single wicket – friend the Colonel – Sir Thomas Blazo – who should get the greatest number of runs. Won the toss – first innings – seven o'clock a.m. – six natives to look out – went in; kept in – heat intense – natives all fainted – taken away – fresh half-dozen ordered – fainted also – Blazo bowling – supported by two natives – couldn't bowl me out – fainted too – cleared away the Colonel – wouldn't give in – a faithful attendant – Quanko Samba – last man left – sun so hot, bat in blisters, ball scorched brown – 570 runs – rather exhausted – Quanko mustered up last remaining strength – bowled me out – had a bath, and went out to dinner.'

'And what became of what's-his-name, sir?' enquired an old gentleman.

'Blazo?'

'No – the other gentleman.'

'Quanko Samba?'

'Yes, sir.'

'Poor Quanko – never recovered it – bowled on, on my account – bowled off, on his own – died, sir.'

The unquestioning Quanko Samba, the meek servant who willingly bowled himself to death for his white master, has no basis in real life. A much better example of the development of the black bowler is found in *Liberation Cricket: West Indies Cricket Culture*, edited by Hilary Beckles and Brian Stoddart. It contains the true story of Fitz Hinds, who went to England on the 1900 West Indies tour with Charles Ollivierre.

Hinds was in his late teens at the end of the nineteenth century and was a lower-class black – a painter. He had been attached to the elite Pickwick club in Barbados, where he was a groundsman and was allowed to bowl at, but not play with, the white members. He bowled well. Yet he wanted to play rather than just service others, so he left Pickwick and tried to join the Spartan club, which was a cricket team for the new black middle class. By this time black players had grown in confidence and had begun to form their own sides. This was a necessity, for whatever their talent they were not allowed to play for the all-white clubs of Wanderers or Pickwick.

However, there were those at Spartan, even though it was a black club, who opposed Hinds's membership on the grounds that he was a lowly painter. Barbados was still a society of suffocating social rigidity based on the hierarchies of the sugar industry and the carefully catalogued gradations of skin colour. Eventually Hinds was allowed to join, but at the cost of personal exclusion. Some at Spartan refused to play with him, while some at Pickwick – in whose service he had been – refused to play against him. One member of Pickwick declined to get on the boat to England in 1900 because Hinds had been chosen in the touring West Indies side. Nonetheless, he prevailed and led Spartan to some big victories as a bowler and as a batsman.

'His was a stirring achievement', wrote the sports academic Professor Brian Stoddart, 'under intense pressure which arose from the social layering of Barbadian cricket, itself produced by the island's sugar culture, which allocated all members of the community a rank in its elaborately-defined production hierarchy.'

No one has explained the stratification of colour and class within Caribbean club cricket better than C. L. R. James. His decision as a young man in the 1920s to choose one local Trinidadian team over another was a matter of excruciating mental torment and one that he later confessed had cost him much. Within James's area of Trinidad there was the Queen's Park club – private, elite, wealthy and for whites only. There was the Shamrock club for the old Catholic families and the police side Constabulary – all black but captained by a white inspector. Maple was the team of the brown-skinned middle class ('they didn't want dark-skinned people in their club'); then there was Shannon for the black lower middle class and Stingo for the black working class.

James's circumstances and education gave him a choice: Maple or Shannon. The noble decision would have been to join the latter, the club of Learie Constantine. Their style was renowned across Trinidad. 'The Shannon Club played with a spirit and relentlessness,' wrote James in *Beyond a Boundary*. 'It was not mere skill. They played as if they knew that their club represented the great mass of black people in the island. The crowd did not look at Stingo in the same way. Stingo did not have status enough. Stingo did not show that pride and impersonal ambition which distinguished Shannon. As clearly as if it was written across the sky, their play said: Here on the cricket field if nowhere else, all men in the island are equal, and we are the best men on the island.'

James knew well what it would mean to play for Shannon, but he succumbed to another impulse. 'In a West Indian colony,' he wrote, 'the surest sign of a man having arrived is the fact that he keeps company with people lighter in complexion than himself.' James chose brown-skinned Maple. At a stroke he isolated himself from a portion of the people he respected and with whom he had grown up. 'Faced with the fundamental divisions in the island, I had gone to the right and, by cutting myself off from the popular side, delayed my political development for years. But no one could see that then, least of all me.'

Frank Worrell would have been sharply aware of these tensions and how tightly club cricket was bound into local society; mistrust and ill feeling between those with differing tones of blackness were not exclusive to Trinidad. Worrell himself was from the black lower middle class. His upbringing, personality and position in Barbadian society all prepared him for the job that he would one day take.

Worrell was a tactful but forthright man, diplomatic but resolute. His qualities of leadership had matured from a youthful insistence that his voice be heard. By the time he was a teenager, he was suffering from what he would later describe as a 'persecution complex'. He would write that his school days were made dismal because 'child psychology was not a subject demanded of applicants to teachers' posts. Indeed, the majority of masters did not have the experience of raising families of their own. There was no allowance for the original point of view.'

Worrell's single-mindedness at Combermere School marked him out as difficult. But he was a gifted cricketer. He played for the island in a first-class game when he was seventeen, and six years later had batted in a Test match. Later that year, 1948, he travelled to England to play as the professional for Radcliffe in the Central Lancashire League. Everton Weekes would follow at Bacup the next season, and within three years Clyde Walcott would play at Enfield. By the time the three Barbadians had become established professionals in Lancashire they had already proved themselves as Test players for the West Indies, being part of the side that won a series in England for the first time in 1950.

If Walcott beat the bowlers into submission and Weekes dominated them with his powerful driving along the ground, Worrell – in the words of Learie Constantine – simply waved them away. 'Worrell was poetry. He was the artist. All three Ws were geniuses but Worrell had the most style and elegance. He had all the strokes and the time and capacity to use them without offence to the eye, without ever being hurried. He was never seen playing across the line. That is why he never hooked. Players and pressmen agreed that even when he ducked beneath a bouncer, he did so with a lack of panic and great dignity.'

Worrell's Test career from 1948 to 1963 coincided with increasingly strident calls for political independence in the West Indies. After the Second World War some sort of separation from Britain had become inevitable, and plans were being drawn up to create a united federation of territories. And yet the West Indies side Worrell played for was still captained by a white man. 'The whole point', wrote C. L. R. James, 'was to continue to send, to populations of white people, black or brown men under a white captain. The more brilliantly the black man played, the more it would emphasise to millions of English people: Yes, they are fine players, but funny, isn't it, they cannot be responsible for themselves – they must always have a white man to lead them.'

The West Indies cricket authorities at this time had a problem: it was becoming increasingly difficult to justify the inclusion of white players in a side at the expense of Afro- or Indo-Caribbean players who were evidently more skilled. The new politics of the region compounded the peculiarity. Articulate, charismatic, intelligent black political voices and personalities were emerging across the Caribbean, yet the West Indies cricket team was captained by a white man – John Goddard – who would finish his days with a Test batting average of 30 and never make a hundred.

There is an illuminating statistical analysis of games played by the West Indies against England, researched by Professor Maurice St Pierre and published in his contribution to *Liberation Cricket*. It shows that from 1928 – when the West Indies first played a Test match – until England's Caribbean tour of 1959–60 white members of the side (there were never fewer than six in the squad on every tour to England in these years) managed 25 half-centuries, no centuries and no double centuries. During the same period non-white West Indian batsmen scored 56 half-centuries, 29 hundreds and 7 double hundreds. Only twice did white players take at least 4 wickets in an innings in these Tests; non-whites managed it 44 times. Faced with these figures, Professor St Pierre can only conclude that 'since whites were not usually picked as bowlers and they did not perform as batsmen, then they must have been picked for some other reason'.

Learie Constantine believed he knew the answer. 'Cricket is the most obvious and apparent, some would say glaring, example of the black man being kept in his place,' he wrote. Sir Leonard Hutton didn't agree. He was England's first professional captain – the job had always been done by an amateur player before him – and led the side to the West Indies on the 1953–54 tour. He observed, 'the gradual exclusion of white folk is a bad thing for the future of West Indies cricket'. Hilary Beckles has this to say: 'The politics of the ancient plantation system, then, had determined the ideological foundations on which West Indian cricket rest.'

There is another part to this story that is sometimes overlooked. The question was not simply one of colour, but of competence – and this was vital to the aspirations of the ordinary Caribbean cricket watcher. What was plain was that a number of white captains of the West Indies side were not selected on the basis of their ability. Rolph Grant was one. He was an average player by university standards yet on the 1939 tour to England he captained a Test side that contained George Headley and Learie Constantine. Grant's selection made no sporting sense.

Socially, the years in which Rolph played were terrifically volatile throughout the West Indies. There were prolonged, serious and violent strikes and riots in several territories. Many people died. When it was over, one of the conclusions of the colonial rulers was that the British needed people of greater competence to run the islands. It was within this context that people situated the question of the black captain. It was a nonsense to have Headley and Constantine in a team which was captained by Rolph Grant – or his brother Jackie, who headed the side before him.

For many years black cricket watchers – particularly on the smaller islands (whose players weren't represented) – refused to support the West Indies cricket team. The Antiguan politician and newspaper editor Tim Hector reflected that many 'men [in Antigua] who were a library of knowledge about cricket and loved the game above all else, did not back the West Indies . . . keeping the West Indian captaincy as a fine white preserve, and excluding the small-islanders, made these very fine people into anti-nationalists . . . They relished the performance of Headley, the three Ws, Ram and Val, of G. N. Francis, Learie Constantine and Martindale, but they were against the side on which these men played – and for good reason.'

*　　*　　*

By the end of the 1950s Frank Worrell was the most obvious and the most popular candidate to become the captain of the West Indies cricket team. Not only because of his talent and knowledge of the game, but because of his temperament. There was nothing histrionic about him; by West Indian standards he was reserved. Worrell was circumspect, a man who rarely acted impulsively.

He came at the right time, but he also brought a particular set of skills that were rare across the region. Lower-middle-class

Barbadians came out of a specific social context, conditioned by their education, their adherence to Christianity and a sense of responsibility to family and neighbour. Those ingredients were more strongly evident in Barbados than in many other territories of the Caribbean. Part of the reason lay in the island's 'Englishness'. Since its colonisation in 1627 Barbados had been held only by Britain; it never changed hands. Notwithstanding the perversions of slavery, whites there had felt a certain paternalistic duty towards the blacks, and certain levels of black society had been entrusted with the administration of colonial life. Barbados was still a very closed society when it came to race, colour, class and hierarchy (Worrell pretty much left for good in his 20s because he could bear its petty constraints no longer), but the modicum of responsibility given to the black lower middle class gave them a sense of their own self-worth. There was a persona in black West Indian society that was yearning to lead – and Frank Worrell was its epitome.

Worrell was eventually appointed captain in 1959 in advance of the 1960–61 tour to Australia. He had been offered the post before but it had not been convenient for him to accept: the board had proposed pitiful sums of money to tour in the past, and he didn't want to interrupt his studies at Manchester University. The trip was a great success. West Indies lost the series two–one, but the cricket was close, exciting and played with spirit by both sides. At Brisbane the first game ended in a tie, which had never happened in Test cricket before. More importantly, Worrell led the team – which included his white predecessor Gerry Alexander – with dignity, authority and distinction.

In British Guiana the young Ronald Austin heard the series unfold on his wireless.

Listening to it late at night, Sobers and Kanhai dominating the Australian bowling – yes, we lost eventually – but there was a sense of elation and good feeling that we were the equal of the Australians. It's difficult to describe to you the intensity of those evenings. There was the time that Kanhai hit Richie Benaud for a series of boundaries, and the radio commentator Alan McGilvray said something like, 'If this is cricket, what have I been looking at for the last 20 years of my life?' The overwhelming sense was that the West Indian nation was contributing fully to something that was vital and worthwhile.

In five games of cricket halfway around the world Worrell had proved publicly that a black man could be an exceptional leader. The fact was as simple as it was significant. C. L. R. James had played a very visible role in the public campaign to see Worrell appointed. He now knew that the 'constant, vigilant, bold and shameless manipulation of players to exclude black captains that has so demoralised West Indian teams and exasperated the people was over'. What is more, he wrote, 'the intimate connection between cricket and the West Indian social and political life was established so that all except the wilfully perverse could see'.

James made plain his views in many articles and opinion pieces. When England were in the West Indies on their 1959–60 tour he had written in the *Nation*, 'I want to say clearly beforehand that the idea of [Gerry] Alexander captaining a side on which Frank Worrell is playing is to me quite revolting. I shall mobilise everything I can so that Frank should captain the team to Australia.'

The distinguished British cricket journalist Alan Ross was appalled by James's boldness. He responded in his account of that tour, *Through the Caribbean*, 'Who but a malicious xenophobe could write, during a Test match, "that the idea of Alexander captaining a side on which Frank Worrell is playing is to me quite revolting"? *Revolting* is the parlance of the irresponsible agitator. Worrell's great gifts as a player, his intelligence and charm, and no doubt his capacity for leadership, cannot benefit from such advocacy.'

* * *

It is no exaggeration to say that from 1960 to 1965 Worrell was one of the most important public figures in the Caribbean region. One of the tragedies of West Indian cricket is that he would be dead within six years of the Australia tour, killed by leukaemia at 42. But in the last years of his life he helped to make the West Indies into the best side in the world. The success of his cricket team also over-lapped with the short-lived political federation of the West Indies. Its aim was a single economic union of ten territories within the Caribbean loyal to the British monarch.

For many decades the British had being trying to pull together what C. L. R. James called 'these specks of dust'. The idea of feder-ation had been discussed since the nineteenth century. When the British knew they were going to leave the Caribbean after the Second World War, their solution was a federal arrangement in which the limited resources of these islands could be pooled. The trouble of course was that the people of the West Indies weren't neighbours; these were islands and territories scattered over a thousand miles of sea. Jamaica wasn't even involved in the first regional cricket competitions because it was too far to the north-west; for years British Guiana had hardly any contact with the other territories. The sensation of separateness, the notion of being content with existence as an island, was well known to West Indians in the same way that many people in Britain today don't quite feel European.

The federation soon came up against the fundamental reality of Caribbean insularity. Outside the West Indies cricket team and perhaps the University of the West Indies, there was no particular commitment to, or even an understanding of, regional unity. Travelling between the territories was difficult. Only a small minority of people migrated from one island to another. A continual connection from one generation to the next – which needed to exist to help build a broader sense of national identity – just wasn't there.

'This thing – the federation – was imposed from Whitehall,' says Clem Seecharan. 'It didn't have enough local or indigenous commitment or resolve to sustain it. So insularity came to the fore immediately. Each petty leader was still the king of their little land. Very quickly there were irreconcilable positions and within a matter of years it was falling apart at the seams.'

The federation was created in 1958. In 1961 Jamaicans voted in a referendum to go their own way. That pretty much caused the whole thing to collapse. The federation officially ended the next year. Frank Worrell was the captain of the West Indies cricket team for almost the whole life of the federation. It failed, but his team didn't, and a strong feeling developed in the Caribbean that Worrell's side *was* the surrogate nation and he was its leader. People could feel committed to this successful cricket side, dedicated to it without having to face the reality of dividing the spoils of Caribbean resources and trying to build a common market. There was an emotional neatness to supporting the West Indian cricket team that could never be replicated or realised in the political federation.

'Worrell was a very smart man,' reflects Seecharan.

He understood in his own quiet way that whatever people felt about federation, he represented something that got to the core of what limited unity we had. A lot of people say that they didn't feel anything like a West Indian until they came to live in Britain. If they were Trinidadian, they came to London and they had never met a Jamaican before. So when they watched Worrell, Hunte, Sobers, Butcher, Hall and Griffith play cricket at Lord's in 1963, for the first time in their lives they felt genuinely West Indian. This was no theoretical or aspirational idea. They could say, 'This is what I am and these guys are speaking for me.' They could see it in front of them.

Yet Worrell was not only a symbol of some wider unity, he was also a fine tactical captain and an astute judge of a man on and off the field. It was Worrell who first realised in the nets in Australia that Garry Sobers's seam and swing bowling could be as potent in a Test match as his off spin. Worrell understood his brilliant all-rounder, and he protected him.

Basil Butcher, who was on the 1963 tour of England, recalls the players' irritation when Worrell exempted Sobers from the 10 p.m. curfew. 'We rebelled and went to Frank to complain,' he remembers. 'We said, "Skipper, this is not right. Why is it that Garry can stay out as long as he likes and we have to go to bed at ten?" Worrell's response was this: "OK, Basil. You or the other guys give me five wickets, take two brilliant catches at short leg and score a century and I'll let you go out as long as you want to." That was the end of the meeting.'

Worrell had noticed Sobers had dreadful trouble going to sleep early; he just couldn't do it. As his captain he came up with a solution. In return, Sobers gave Worrell his best cricket.

Joe Solomon was the middle-order batsman from British Guiana who played in all but one of the Test sides led by Worrell. He recalls that his captain would sit down in the dressing room to talk before the game and always allowed the players to express their views. He never came and said, 'You will do this or that.'

'Even if he had, that would have worked with me because I'm a quiet person,' says Solomon,

but it wouldn't have worked with a lot of the team because they were such individualists. But above all you felt you could not let

Frank down. That was because we always felt that he represented something to us. He represented what cricket meant in our heads. It didn't mean money. It was all those values which went with playing this game at the highest level. Being the best that you can and understanding the people who came to watch you. Many of them were menial workers, cane cutters who had paid a few pennies to come and watch. They were very important. And, without giving you a lecture, Frank would always make sure you understood this. He always made it clear that we must know that the people looked up to us.

*　*　*

By 1964 Garry Sobers had succeeded Frank Worrell as captain of the West Indies. He was Clive Lloyd's first Test captain. At the time of Lloyd's debut in 1966 Sobers was the greatest cricketer on earth. He could bowl all the varieties of left-arm spin. He could take the new ball and bowl fast. At slip or at short leg he seemed to catch any chance, however hard. Above all, he could bat. He could hit a ball on the rise and hammer it past mid-on or mid-off, what they called in the West Indies the 'not a man move' shot. By 1958, when he was still 21, Sobers held the world record for the highest score in a Test match, 365 not out. In 1968, playing county cricket for Nottinghamshire, he scored 36 runs in one over, hitting each ball for 6. Time and again it seemed he won Test matches for the West Indies almost by himself.

C. L. R. James believed Sobers to be the fine fruit of a great tradition, the most typical West Indies cricketer that it was possible to imagine. All geniuses, wrote James, 'are merely people who carry to an extreme definitive the characteristics of the unit of civilisation to which they belong'. On the 1957 tour of England Frank Worrell had predicted to a journalist that Sobers would become the greatest player the game would know. Within three seasons Worrell was happy to let Sobers take over if he had to leave the field of play in a Test match.   *

'He knows everything?' C. L. R. James once asked Worrell.

'Everything,' Worrell replied.

Sobers's leadership and his individual greatness coincided with a period of extended post-colonial optimism in the Caribbean. Barbados and Guyana both became independent in 1966, by which time Sobers's cricket team was the best in the world, having beaten Australia, England and India. 'There is embodied in him the whole history of the British West Indies,' said James.

What James meant was that Sobers was a different man to Worrell. He was not from the aspirational middle class but from the poorest of urban black neighbourhoods in Barbados. The street where he was born in the Bay Land district of Bridgetown didn't even have a name in 1936. Sobers's father was in the Canadian merchant navy and was rarely at home. When Sobers was five, his father's boat, the *Lady Hawkins*, was torpedoed and sunk by the Germans off the coast of North Carolina. Shamont Sobers was drowned. His widow, Thelma, brought up their six children alone.

Some of Sobers's earliest memories were of playing street cricket. The bat was hacked from a branch or a piece of waste wood, the ball shaped from a lump of tar dug up from the road. Sometimes the boys used a sour orange or a small rock wrapped in cloth. Sobers grew up in poverty but there was a richness in his cricket. Aged 15, in short trousers, he bowled against West Indian Test players in a Barbados trial match. He was picked for the island XI, but first he had to be bought a pair of cricket flannels. Aged 17 he had played in a Test match. By 19 he had opened the batting for the West Indies against Australia, and two miles from where he'd been born hit Keith Miller for six fours in the fast bowler's opening two overs at the Kensington Oval.

'Sobers was a brilliant player whose skills and charm took him well beyond his poor beginnings,' wrote Brian Stoddart in *Liberation Cricket*, 'but he remained essentially a people's man. He was far less concerned with the wider social issues than Worrell and that led to some awkward moments.'

This was particularly true once Garry Sobers became captain. It was a moment as important to the development of West Indian cricket as Worrell's appointment had been. Sobers was the first 'unambiguously native West Indian' to attain that exalted position, wrote James. Sobers was what James would have called a plebeian West Indian. He had not been to a public school nor to a British university, as had all of his predecessors. His elevation from wretched poverty to the most esteemed job in the whole of the Caribbean was the triumph of the ordinary man. 'The West Indian people are very conscious of the role of their cricket in their search for a national identity,' believed James. 'They will look at Sobers's appointment as a stage in their national development.'

The author and journalist Lloyd Best saw Sobers differently. 'Competence and performance are all that count,' he wrote in the *Jamaica Gleaner*. 'He leads his colleagues by technical example and nothing else. The moment the bails are lifted, the association is done. They have clocked out.' Best also noted that even though Sobers possessed every skill the game needed and was capable of developing more, 'his class and his education are liabilities, not assets'. The paradox of Sobers's condition was that he thought like an ordinary West Indian instead of – as Worrell did – thinking *on behalf of* ordinary West Indians. 'He will play for anybody so long as the price is right,' concluded Best.

Sobers made two damaging miscalculations when he was captain of the West Indies, one sporting and one political. In the 1967–68 series against England Sobers declared the West Indian second innings in Trinidad and lost the game. He had been irritated by England's unremittingly dull play and time-wasting throughout the series. Despite his brilliance in the final Test in Guyana, the rubber was lost and the people were angry. If he hadn't considered it before, Sobers now knew that West Indian heroes could be thrown to the earth by the people as easily as they could be borne aloft.

In 1970 Sobers accepted £600 for two days' work. The fee was to play cricket in a tournament in Rhodesia, a country like South Africa where the white minority ruled. 'I asked for a couple of days to think it over,' recorded Sobers in his autobiography, 'but after delving into the matter I thought that, as a professional cricketer, there was little or nothing to stop me earning my living in what was a fun competition. I was well aware of the politics.' The decision caused Sobers an enormous amount of trouble. He was publicly criticised by Caribbean and African leaders. As Hilary Beckles pointed out, Sobers 'was not attuned to the historical and ideological nature of his location within West Indies cricket'. Sobers was the best all-rounder cricket had ever seen, the most brilliant of all cricketers. Was that not enough? Yet he did not grasp that the position of captain of the West Indies cricket team was, at its core, a political one.

Clive Lloyd was in the side that lost to England in '68 and was captained by Sobers in the Rest of the World XI at the time of the Rhodesia controversy. He observed Sobers's behaviour at close hand on both occasions and saw the consequences. Lloyd knew he could not afford to make the same sort of errors and hope to remain in charge of the West Indies.

During ten seasons of captaincy, Lloyd realised that the demands of West Indian leadership were unique in world cricket. He had understood Worrell's legacy and the importance of Sobers's individual example. He had worked out that his leadership didn't end on the pitch or in the pavilion; it extended to the hotel check-in desk and beyond. Lloyd thought carefully about which players would share rooms on tour. He often put a bowler with a batsman – 'Come on. I took your wickets today; you get me some runs tomorrow' – or a player from Jamaica with a teammate from Trinidad.

Lloyd was rooting out inter-island rivalry. The limitations of insularity – bickering between the West Indian territories – had bedevilled its cricket since the selection of the first Test XI in 1928. 'When I was first picked to play in 1963,' recalls Deryck Murray, 'I clearly remember being warned of all the animosity that I would encounter because people would feel that somebody from their island should be playing instead of me. I was from Trinidad. One of the places that was held up as the worst place to play was Jamaica because they would only support Jamaicans. As it turned out, I never found that to be the case.'

The journalist Tony Becca remembers arranging to go to dinner one evening with the former Barbadian fast bowler Wes Hall. 'He was the chairman of selectors then,' says Becca. 'I said to him, "Looking forward to tonight. What time shall we meet?" We were in Antigua staying in the same hotel. He said, "I'll see you in my room at eight." I said, "We're going to have dinner in your room?" and he replied, "Yes, we are. I'm not going down to the restaurant to face all those people." The locals, like the Jamaicans, the Trinidadians and the Bajans, always wanted to push their own man.'

What Wes Hall was trying to avoid in the dining room that evening, says Paul Gilroy, was an encounter with Sigmund Freud's theory of the narcissism of minor differences, the idea that it is precisely the small differences between people who are otherwise alike that form the basis of feelings of strangeness and hostility between them. 'The Caribbean was a region which harboured complicated stereotypes,' he explains, 'and they governed the personality, habits and inclinations of the inhabitants of the other places that were very nearby. And they were held with an increased fervour however tiny or insignificant they appeared to be to outsiders. As far as West Indian cricket was concerned, I expect that all of these things were being negotiated on some level in the form of dressing-room banter.'

'Don't ever make the mistake of thinking that there is harmony in the West Indies,' laughs the DJ and broadcaster Trevor Nelson. 'The sensitivities and clichés are everywhere. I'm a St Lucian. We are 150,000 *very* special people. Don't *ever* call me a Jamaican! There are loads of stereotypes: Jamaicans are noisy and rude, Trinidad loves to party, Barbadians speak like farmers and kiss arse to the English.'

The clear historical differences within the Caribbean were cultural and racial, but other factors, such as geography and the climate, also played into the region's feelings of separateness. Antigua is just a hundred miles square and has little rainfall. Jamaica is 1,200 miles from Barbados. Guyana is on the South American mainland and much of its vast interior can still be reached only by boat. The prime minister of Guyana, Forbes Burnham, was once supposed to have boasted that his country had islands in the mouth of its Essequibo River that were the same size as other Caribbean nations.

'Apart from a heritage in slavery and an acquired British governance,' wrote Brian Stoddart in *Liberation Cricket*, 'these states varied considerably in economic and cultural composition which, along with the weather, produced distinctive cricket traditions.' Even local termites affected the way cricket was played, said Stoddart. The example he gave was of a burrowing insect called the mole cricket. These grubs were two inches long with shovels for front legs. They ruined turf wickets in Trinidad, so heavy coconut mats were laid on the ground to thwart their digging. In the early years of the game's development on the island the mats caused local batsmen to be better at playing square of the wicket rather than driving because the ball didn't come onto the bat at pace.

By the time Clive Lloyd became captain of the West Indies, dressing-room cliques – in which 300 years of assumptions and misunderstandings had built up like sediment – were hampering team spirit. Shrewdly, Lloyd was able to strip out the damaging differences but retain those which brought competition and a desire to succeed to the team. 'I understood the West Indian psyche,' he says. 'Each West Indian comes from a particular set of circumstances – our upbringing and the way we approached life. I had to treat all these players properly, with subtlety to get the best out of them.'

Above all, Lloyd knew that history had to be appreciated in a way that burdened no other captain of a Test team. He was aware of the significance of being the black captain of a side drawn from a collection of newly independent nations that had precious little to fuse them together other than the wins that he and his cricket team provided. He understood the ego of the athlete and the aspirations of the supporter. Intellectually, he had worked out how they were connected and how he personally had to satisfy both. To a region that had been created from the human catastrophe of slavery and stunted by the humiliations of colonial servitude, Lloyd helped to bring a decade-long joy that it had not known for three centuries. This is what cricket in the West Indies meant. This was liberation. This was respect. Lloyd had the courage to carry the hopes of five million people and brought a solidarity to the team that went beyond even the bonds created by Worrell.

Learie Constantine had called lack of spirit 'the chief weakness of the West Indies team'. It had been a problem since they began playing Test cricket. When Constantine wrote, 'we have not been able to get together in the sort of spirit which says, "Look here, we are going out today against these fellows and it is war to the knife!"' he feared that this flaw might never be eradicated. In Lloyd he had his answer. Aside from all this, Clive Lloyd was a middle-order batsman of scorching brilliance who made more than 7,500 Test runs, won matches single-handedly and could make any bowler in the world despair.

Those who say Lloyd was a limited captain – who did not much more than glance at his watch from slip and change the bowling – understand little of cricket, less of leadership and nothing of the West Indies.

10

'Bless up Viv Rich. Every time, big up Viv Rich'

'I didn't want to do anything different,' says Vivian Richards. 'We had a blueprint. We knew exactly how to win and we had a formula. Clive had the patent. So all I wanted to do was to keep the engine running. It would have been nice for the moment of captaincy to come sooner, but more than that I was thankful for the opportunity. And when the time came for it to be handed over from me, I wanted to make sure that it was in the same condition I had found it. That the legacy which Clive had created was continued.'

Richards was the obvious choice to succeed Lloyd, but in the permanently fractured world of West Indian cricket selection his anointing was not a certainty. By the mid-1980s there were those who believed the off-spinner Roger Harper was the better man; some thought that the Jamaican wicket-keeper Jeff Dujon was the team's most articulate tactician. Others preferred Malcolm Marshall. When Lloyd resigned after the World Cup defeat to India in 1983, he wanted Richards as his successor. The Antiguan had been Lloyd's vice-captain for the past five years. As Richards himself wrote, 'the captaincy rightfully belonged to me'. His view was that some board members persuaded Lloyd to carry on in order to keep him away from the job. This is why he says today, with a greybeard's tact, that it would have been nice for the captaincy to have come sooner.

. But Richards prevailed. Since the English summer of 1976 there had been no one in the team who seemed to *represent* the West Indies more potently than he did. The runs he made and the innings he built were at least as important to the West Indies' success as any wickets taken by their bowlers. Many supporters felt he was making those runs for them all.

'I never felt it was a burden,' he says.

It was a responsibility. It was a duty. I had the skills to back me up, and it was that bigger thought that helped me to compete so hard. After all, I am a citizen of the West Indies, and it is a magnificent place, and this West Indies team is our one connection. I'm an Antiguan first, and that allows me to be a West Indian because Antiguans are tenacious, ambitious. We are good people. I'm happy to be part of the tree that spreads a little bit further. I was one of the guys who carried the baton and I accepted that responsibility because no one wants to be the one who drops the baton. I grew to understand the traditions of West Indies cricket, and I was happy to embrace them and to pass them on. And it helped me that the passion came through from the folks on the other side of the boundary fence.

Richards was what C. L. R. James called a 'great super batsman'. This was not just a vague superlative description, but a role – a necessity if a team was to be a winning team. Such a man was needed in the top five along with a pair of fine openers. Super batsmen were rare, believed James, and they were defined not only by the runs they made but also by their quality of being undisturbed by any bowling or any crisis. Richards fitted this description quite early on in his career.

He scored only seven runs in his first two Test innings at the end of 1974 in India, possibly the hardest place on earth for a young batsman to make a debut. But he learned quickly against the sharp spin of Bedi, Prassana and Venkat, because in his second match in Delhi he scored 192 not out, hitting sixes that travelled 40 yards into the stands. He failed against Pakistan on the tour's second leg, but his skill had been noted. More importantly, Clive Lloyd recognised a young man who possessed great mental strength, a quality not obvious to most of those in the Caribbean who thought Richards's selection for the Test team had been a surprise and a gamble.

Yes, he had been a prince in Antigua for some years, but folk from the Leeward Islands were not expected to be great West Indian cricketers. Besides, there was a better batsman called Jim Allen from Montserrat, who was sure to make runs in big cricket before long. Yet Lloyd backed Richards, particularly towards the end of the dreadful 1975–76 tour to Australia, when he asked him to open the batting in the last two Tests. Lloyd knew that Richards had confidence and fortitude. He suspected that once he started to succeed he would become a great player in his own right – a 'great super batsman'. He was right. In 1976, against Australia, India and England, Richards made scores of 44, 2, 30, 101, 50, 98, 142, 130, 20, 177, 23, 64, 232, 63, 4, 135, 66, 38 and 291. No man from any country had made more Test runs in a single year than Richards's 1,710.

The decision to allow him to open the innings in Australia was of great importance to his development. Richards had made some brilliant contributions from the middle order, but there had been some disappointing scores too. You are not to worry about your place in the side, Lloyd told him, but I want you to try to bat up the top. 'That responsibility came at the right time for me,' recalled Richards. 'The feeling that I did not have to hit every ball helped me to settle.'

Very rarely thereafter did Richards fail for long. And when he succeeded, it was often at moments when the West Indies *had* to do well. For instance, he excelled against Australia on the 1979–80 tour, when the West Indies won there for the first time. He was brilliant in the first season of Kerry Packer's World Series Cricket, when the side had cast themselves adrift of official cricket. His run total in the Super Tests was 200 more than any other batsman, and this was the hardest cricket any of them had played. Richards proved that he could make runs on any surface on all the cricket continents against any bowler. The manner of his scoring was extraordinary too. He didn't collect runs; he thrashed them out in a way that didn't just exasperate the opposition, but demoralised them. He scored at such a rate that his big totals often gave his bowlers time to take ten second-innings wickets to win a game.

This was not classical greatness, although his exaggerated (and occasionally ironic) forward defence was faultless. Rather, Richards was unorthodox power blended with beauty. The journalist and broadcaster Darcus Howe reminded viewers in his 1985 television documentary about Richards that 'a mark of a great batsman is that he can create a shot all of his own. The flip through mid-wicket is Viv's special offering.' By turning his wrists further on what would otherwise be an on drive, Richards could flail a bowler by hitting straight balls for four or six over or through mid-wicket. This was Viv's flip. It was a shot that displayed freedom from tradition and contempt for orthodoxy. Other men tried it and would be bowled or LBW because the blow required the front leg to be placed in line with the stumps and the bat swung across the line of the ball at speed. It worked for Richards because, as his father said, he had 'eyes like a pigeon'. It was 'all wrong', wrote his Somerset teammate Vic Marks, 'yet Richards made it seem the safest shot in the world'.

The former England seamer Mike Selvey bowled Richards out

for four in the Old Trafford Test of 1976. He also got his wicket –
occasionally at greater cost – in some of the many Middlesex versus
Somerset games they played against each other in the 1970s and
1980s. 'There was a theatre to Viv's batting at the beginning of an
innings,' he says.

> It was a cleverly calculated theatrical performance – an act. Viv is
> the most destructive batsman there has ever been and unquestion-
> ably the scariest. A wicket would fall, and you think no one was
> walking out but you know who it'll be. Viv would wait. Then he
> would saunter out. And the image of Viv coming out to bat is a
> very powerful one: the cap tipped exactly as it was, head just tilted
> slightly back, the patrician nose, the Viv swagger, possibly a light
> bit of windmilling with the arms. By the time he took his guard,
> you're back at the start of your run, waiting. And he would use that
> time to intimidate you. He'd cud his chewing gum and he'd look at
> you. He'd then walk down the pitch and tap it, still looking at you.
> He'd bash the top of his bat handle with his palm, then he'd be ready.

It was, says Selvey, a clever way for Richards to assess his
surroundings. 'Now I've spoken to him about this, and he's told me
it was all an act. What he was doing was sniffing the air. As for the
bowler, he told me that it didn't matter if you were fast or slow,
good or indifferent; if you didn't bowl at him from the off with
intent, like you really meant it, then he had already won. He'd be
away from you. "I could smell fear," he said to me.'

Richards also revealed to Selvey that as soon as possible he liked
to feel the ball 'sweet on the bat'.

'And of course that was your only hope of getting him out – you
had to go at him straight away because he liked to play shots from
the start. That was what you had to keep in your mind in those

first few overs. That was your chance. Of course there were days when the ball was sweet on the bat from the start, and for several hours afterwards . . . '

Richards's weaknesses as a batsman were usually kept well hidden in Test matches but were known in the Caribbean. He enjoyed the privilege of course of never having to bat against West Indies bowlers in a Test match. He did, however, have to play against Barbados. From his debut in 1972 until his last game in 1991 Richards batted for the Combined Islands and later the Leeward Islands in the West Indian regional cricket tournament, the Shell Shield. Barbados, an island of fewer than 250,000 people in the 1970s and 1980s, probably had the strongest fast bowlers during that time: Vanburn Holder, Keith Boyce, Wayne Daniel, Joel Garner, Sylvester Clarke, Malcolm Marshall, Hartley Alleyne, Ezra Moseley and Franklyn Stephenson.

In 24 first-class innings against Barbados over 19 years, Richards made only 602 runs, an average of 27.36. His one century came in the 1976–77 season. Barbados dismissed him for 20 runs or fewer 14 times. Joel Garner got his wicket five times. Even the Master Blaster himself – the world's greatest batsman – could not always master the best West Indian fast bowling.

For the West Indies, however, Richards's batting thrilled in a way that no other man could achieve with such regularity. It especially thrilled West Indies supporters in England. He scored his biggest portion of Test runs there for them. The cricket academic Hilary Beckles believes that Richards 'was sent in to do battle by villagers, not only those in Antigua, but all those from little places in this diaspora; people who have been hurling missiles at the Columbus project since it crashed into their history five hundred years and 10 million lives ago'.

Trevor Nelson, who saw him at the Oval in 1976, has a more

demotic explanation. 'Viv was the Malcolm X to Clive's Martin Luther King. He was my hero. The swagger, the walk, no helmet. Watching him get to the crease was one of the great joys of sport in my lifetime.'

Richards tells his own story of the connection he had with the diaspora. He recalls strolling through London after a West Indies win.

One guy saw me walking down Kensington High Street. He was driving a bus. He stopped the bus with all the passengers on board and he shouted to them, 'That's the man who did that to you guys! That's Vivian, man.' And the traffic was backing up and the car horns went *parp*! People were tooting horns left, right and centre trying to get this bus out of the way, and this guy just sits there in his bus saying, 'Hey, look. There's the man who did this.' This just goes to show you that sense of pride that they felt. He stopped the traffic because he was so emotionally fired up, because the people who represented them, one of the individuals was walking in the high street. That was a good indication of how some folks felt.

*   *   *

Vivian Richards captained the West Indies in a different way to Clive Lloyd. After all, they had different personalities and different challenges. When Lloyd took over from Rohan Kanhai in 1974 he inherited a young side with several unproven players. Lloyd was older than most of the team, a fact he used to his advantage. He was a captain whom the rest of the side looked up to, just as the players had looked up to Frank Worrell 15 years earlier. Lloyd trusted these young men to do well, and most of them did. They repaid his loyalty with runs and wickets. Richards was more like a general who had inherited a battle-hardened army. He had less need to

create a team and a strategy, although he did need to find replace-
ments for Michael Holding, Larry Gomes and Joel Garner within
two seasons of taking charge.

Lloyd was a more sophisticated reader of people, whereas
Richards, say some observers, was a more sophisticated reader of
the game. Richards was more obviously combative on the field. He
was also very aware of the effect his personality and reputation had
on other players and the public. It would have been out of character
for Lloyd to wear a gold neck chain with his initials hanging from
it as Richards did. Richards urged his side on aggressively, and
some of his players have said privately that they were intimidated
by his temper. There is a story told in the Caribbean that during a
one-day match in Australia Richards ordered a player named
Richard Gabriel from the field because his performance was not
up to standard, although Gabriel insists that he had to leave the
game because of an injury to his leg.

'The Antiguan psyche is very much more in-your-face,' explains
the Rastafarian elder King Frank-I, who was a young teacher at
Antigua Grammar School in the 1960s when Vivian Richards was
a pupil. He soon became a friend, mentor and sage to the cricketer.
'Even when you look at our calypsos they are much more pedagogic
– they preach to you. The Trinidadian calypsos based on simile or
metaphor have a disguised message that is less direct. So it is that
we see the Antiguans and their mentality. The African temperament.
Head on. Direct.'

'I would like to think I am a perfectionist,' says Richards. 'I believe
that maybe one of the flaws is that because of the God-given ability
and talent you have, you think everyone is blessed with the same
things and sometimes you get a little hard on individuals who don't
quite accomplish or do the things as you expect them to, but this
is all part of what it means to be competitive.'

'Clive Lloyd was a great leader of men,' says the veteran West Indian cricket journalist Tony Becca.

He understood the differences of island culture. He knew his cricket, but I don't think he knew his cricket as much as Viv Richards did. Viv read the game exceptionally well and led by example. Tactically, he was better than Clive Lloyd. But he was an authoritarian. The fellers were a little bit afraid of him, particularly the younger ones. Whereas in Lloyd's case they were largely just full of respect for him. If Lloyd went to a man and said, 'Jump over that mountain,' the guy would try his utmost just to please Clive. If Viv asked the same, the guy would do it because he'd be afraid of the consequences if he didn't.

'One was cool and calm, the other intense,' says Tony Cozier.

In all the years that I was around the team I certainly didn't hear Lloyd raise his voice very often. And that is unusual for West Indians. When we get excited we tend to raise our voices. But Richards was very different. He wouldn't stand for foolishness in any way, particularly on the field. He would glare at players. And it was all very explicable because Richards knew that he had come in to succeed Lloyd, and if things went downhill all of a sudden, people would blame it on him. Then the fact that he was from a small island. All of his recent predecessors had been from the established cricket territories. Some would have noted that. So he had a very obvious need to keep the success going.

And he did. Unlike Lloyd, Vivian Richards never lost a series in his six years as captain of the West Indies, although his proportion of lost matches to victories was greater.

Desmond Haynes was captained by both Lloyd and Richards.

Clive was more like the father figure, Viv was more the sergeant major. Everything's come natural to Viv so Viv feels it should come natural to everybody. He wasn't the guy who's gonna say, 'Let's wait until after the game and let's have a chat about it,' he's gonna tell you exactly how he feel about you right there and then. Very frank. And he can use all the language as well, from good to bad – everything – but that was his style, you know. He was a guy who played with his heart and soul, and he wanted the best from everybody. He was a guy who didn't want to lose. Playing to win was very, very important.

There was one more nuance between the two men. While both were motivated by the same historical concerns and the conviction that they were the equal of any man, Richards voiced his beliefs more stridently. 'I believe very strongly in the black man asserting himself in this world,' he would write in his autobiography, 'and over the years I have leaned towards many movements that follow this basic cause.'

'Viv's coming into the game in this way represented the full flowering of Caribbean strength and identity,' says King Frank-I.

Not only did he come from the small islands which had been kept out and seen as a lower class of Caribbean cricket, but he also came out of that black power sentiment and time. So he was a direct contradiction to the blue-eyed aristocratic leader that had been foisted on Caribbean people. To me he represented the apex of what Learie Constantine expressed when he said that our cricket could only feel its full impact when a black captain had been installed. I would take Learie's impressions even further. I would suggest that the fullness of Caribbean-ness could only be expressed when the formerly discriminated Leewards were bought into the fold through

Viv. Both Lloyd and Worrell would have been too diffident to express this in its full blackness and full African-ness.

The former editor of the *Wisden Cricketers' Almanack* Matthew Engel has this interpretation:

In the 1960s, particularly in England and Australia, people had got to like the West Indies because they were fun. Then they became serious. There was another change when Viv took over from Clive, which had an effect on the press and possibly the public. Clive was perhaps more rooted in the old West Indies – approachable, essentially an entertainer, even though he presided over the strategy of great success via the four fast bowlers. Whereas Viv emphatically wasn't approachable. There was what one might call at times a visceral enmity. No quarter was given. It wasn't for show, it was for real. What one sensed was the anger. He was always an angry cricketer.

'The message that I sent', says Richards, 'was that I would rather die out there. A lot of people took me seriously, and I was serious about it. A lot of them looked at it as a sport, but it was a step beyond sport, where there were a whole lot of things needed defending, rather than the cricket ball itself.' Richards the Test cricketer played the game to represent his people. He played to prove that the creators of the game were no better than the people who had learned it from them. He was conscious of where he came from and from where his ancestors came. He couldn't separate his past and his people's heritage from his athleticism.

At the 1968 Mexico Olympic Games, when Richards was 16 years old, the USA sprinter Tommie Smith won the 200 metres final. His teammate John Carlos came third. When their medals were presented they each raised a fist on which they wore a black leather glove. It was a human rights salute, they said. It was also an overtly political statement by two black athletes which had a profound effect on the teenaged Richards.

'I watched the American runners and I could identify with them, more than anything else, as a black person,' he says. 'I could identify myself with Tommie Smith. So you had people who you felt had the same beliefs as you. Fighting that same cause. People like Stokely Carmichael, Eldridge Cleaver. These guys were part of a movement, the Black Panther Party. And while we were here in Antigua as young boys, we would try and associate ourselves with that particular side of things.'

When he is asked if it was only in retrospect that he painted his cricketing achievements with the wash of the pan-African cause, he denies it flatly.

No. This is something I've been thinking about since I was a little boy. I have always thought about African history. The Zulu Wars. Malcolm X got me fired up, the Black Panthers – all these things these guys were doing. And I remember realising what was going on in the southern United States in particular, what people had to put up with just to survive. I was pretty much motivated from an early age and was looking for the necessary stuff to help me in this area as an Afro-Caribbean person.

By the early 1980s Richards was probably the most attractive and recognisable cricketer in the world. It was at this time that he began wearing sweatbands on the field in red, gold and green, the colours of Rastafari. 'It was how I related to Africa,' he says. 'For us as people Africa is the starting point. Red meant the blood that was shed, yellow for the gold that was taken away, the green for Mother Nature and the greenery of African land itself. Then there was another colour, the black. Now you had the black, yellow, green and red. The black for the black folks in that part of the world. That is my representation of those particular colours and what it meant to me.'

Richards was not a Rastafarian, but he sympathised with some of the values of its followers. The movement had begun in Jamaica in the 1930s. It promoted a return to Africa, specifically Ethiopia, where Haile Selassie (Ras Tafari) was emperor. Rastafarians were nonconformists and regarded with much suspicion in colonial Jamaica. Some of them were beaten and imprisoned. They were seen as a threat to order and a bad example to the masses, but they gathered and survived in rural areas and the poorest neighbourhoods of Kingston. It was from such ghettos that reggae music would be first developed 30 years later.

'Some of us were still lingering, one foot in, one foot out, as to who we were as people,' reflects Richards. 'Rastafari sent out that message in terms of appearance, their ideology, basic thoughts on your lifestyle rather than anyone imposing how you should live. You know they had that side of things covered, and I respect that. So wearing that band itself had so many meanings to me.'

Richards was not only influenced by the politics of black liberation, but by music. He listened to the reggae of Dennis Brown, the ska and rock steady of Toots and the Maytals and the calypso-soca blend of Byron Lee and the Dragonaires.

I liked all of this stuff. And then when I played in the Shell Shield I went to Jamaica for the first time. I was already listening to the Wailers, Gregory Isaacs, Burning Spear, Culture. Coming from a small island, it was always one of my dreams to see them. A little later I had the honour of going to the studio to physically stand there while Bob Marley was recording. I would go to Hope Road, where Bob used to live. I knew Bunny Wailer from the band – I knew him best. But to meet Bob, Bunny and the other Wailers was the same sort of feeling that I guess other people may have got from meeting Bob Dylan or the Rolling Stones.

While he was playing for Somerset in 1975, Richards made a point of taking a night off to get to London to see Bob Marley on the Natty Dread tour at the Lyceum. When he went on cricket tours he took Marley's tapes with him, calling them his 'consciousness stuff'. In the BMW that he drove in Antigua Richards had a picture of Haile Selassie on the steering wheel and one of Bob Marley in the window.

'You know Bob Marley's "Get up, Stand up". All these tunes were totally inspiring stuff. You could call it your battlefield music, you know. He sang about the rights of human beings. When you heard those lyrics, it was like a poem that you recited on so many occasions. When you leave your hotel with your headphones on and then you walk onto the field.'

Richards starts to sing.

'I feel so strong when you get those lyrics, and it's totally embedded in your mind. You feel very, very powerful. Knowing that there's someone out there who feels the same way that you do. Bob did a magnificent job, and I like to think I did OK with my bat.'

'This music, these black ideologies, were now permeating West Indian society, explains Clem Seecharan.

They shaped attitudes, perceptions and behaviour when these men and women were at an impressionable age. These were major shifts in perspectives in the region. The whole cultural, political, ideological frame of reference had changed. And whether or not these cricketers were directly conscious of it or not, they were products of this more radical framework. The cricket was now infused with something that was more radically black-American than a continuation of a British tradition. And as for Viv, I would say that all of this would have been powerfully aided by the music he was listening to. I would say that was the lightning rod.

In England there was a slightly different cultural reading of Bob Marley from many of the younger West Indies' supporters.

'Every black household would have a Bob Marley album,' says Trevor Nelson,

but by 1976 we were starting to make our own music, and where I lived in Hackney it was a hotbed for a new style of reggae called lovers' rock. Most of the singers were second-generation British West Indians, and many of them were women. It went hand in hand with the little blues parties that went on. Black people didn't go up the West End to go to clubs, they had parties in houses – a shebeen – and the music played almost exclusively was lovers' rock. So Bob Marley was for radio, for the overall picture. Within a few years there was a tendency to think that he'd gone from the community a bit because he was so global, a little over-produced, but I wouldn't call him a sell-out.

'We thought Bob was a sell-out,' says Paul Gilroy. 'I don't buy him as the avatar of the rebel outlook, and I don't see him as the most important of the musical stars. British West Indians didn't need large doses of Bob Marley to come to our political senses in the summer of 1976. Certainly in London, someone like Dennis Bovell, who was involved with the sound systems and lovers' rock, was much more part of the moment.'

*   *   *

'A lot of people see Bob Marley with a ball and thinks that Bob Marley only know how to play soccer,' says Bunny Wailer. 'But Bob also knows how to play cricket. Bob was really a good cricketer. He used to bowl some great balls.'

Bunny had known Bob Marley since they were both young boys. In the late 1950s Marley and his mother moved into his family house in the ghetto of Trench Town in Kingston. A few blocks away lived Peter Tosh. Together, the three neighbours would form the most famous reggae band in the world, Bob Marley and the Wailers.

'Yes. Bob bowled the off-spinner, he bowled the leg-spinner, he bowled the googly, he bowled the Chinaman. And he had one that, you know, he called it the magic one; he didn't even give it a proper name. That one is strange. Because somehow he used that one to get the batsman whether he's getting caught or leg before or clean bowled, but when he bowls the magic one then he gets the result.'

Vivian Richards's fame in the late 1970s coincided with that of the Wailers. They sought each other out. 'When he comes to Jamaica to play cricket he always find himself in the company of the Wailers,' remembers Bunny. 'We would go for him at the hotel and take him into the communities of the ghetto, where he finds more relaxation. He gets some real soul food and the people around him are warm and receptive and loving and kind to him, making him feel at home. The people are excited because Viv Richards is in the community. Everybody wants to get a talk; everybody can get a touch. Because he's their star, you know what I mean?'

Bunny Wailer also suggests that it was Richards's connection to the band and to the people he met in Jamaica that inspired him to wear the red, green and gold sweatband.

He was a kind of character that really had some kind of respect for his roots. And when he came among us Rastafarians he really took to listening and adopting the ways and customs. He wore that armband – which sometimes was not appropriate to the authorities – but him being the person he is, a strong character, he stands up for what he believes in. He didn't back down in establishing that he was Rastarised. So bless up Viv Rich. Every time, big up Viv Rich, great cricketer, great individual. He's a leader for African people overall, so big time respect to Vivian Richards, the champion of cricket.

* * *

Not everybody has been so enthusiastic about Richards's identification with pan-Africanism and Rastafari. In 1984, when Richards wore his sweatband throughout the blackwash series, David Frith was the editor of *Wisden Cricket Monthly*, a magazine he had created in 1979. Previously Frith had been editor of *The Cricketer* magazine. He was a respected journalist whose upbringing in both England and Australia had given him a deep understanding of the cricket played in both countries.

Frith used to adore the West Indians. He'd first seen them from high up in the Sheridan Stand at Sydney on the 1951–52 tour. Frank Worrell coming out to bat in his maroon cap with his immaculate white shirtsleeves folded halfway up the forearm was one of the most enchanting visions of the young Frith's life. But by 1984 his view of West Indian cricket had altered. Their image was so different.

'I was watching them in England and I was watching them in the Caribbean, and it seemed that cricket had been transformed into something really ugly,' he says. The principal reason was the four fast bowlers around which the West Indian strategy revolved. 'The summer game, it had become something else. It had lost its romance, it had lost its sportsmanship, it had lost its lovely edge; it was now a place where people got frightened.'

At the beginning of the 1984 tour Vivian Richards had made one of the most breathtaking scores of recent years. At Old Trafford in the first one-day international against England his side had made little more than a hundred by lunch and lost seven wickets. England sat down to eat with the applause of the crowd fresh in their ears; their bowlers thought the game was won. But Richards was still there. At 166 for 9 Michael Holding joined him at the wicket. Last man in. Richards made 93 runs during that stand while Holding scored 12. Richards ended up with 189 not out.

'Viv didn't say much, but his body language shouted loud,' recalls Derek Pringle, who had to bowl against him that afternoon. 'You knew you were up against someone who intended to do you maximum harm. It's like that exchange in *Apocalypse Now* when they tell Martin Sheen to terminate Kurtz's command with extreme prejudice. That was Viv. He was a batsman who wanted to hurt you with extreme prejudice.'

'When Viv walked out with his Rasta sweatband what did people think it meant?' asks Paul Gilroy.

I would read Viv's hundred that day as an extraordinary act of insubordination. All of us who saw it were gleeful. And this was not a glee that resonated only with 'muggers and layabouts', the people who were being criminalised so actively due to the encroachment of the police into their lives. This was not just about politically minded individuals reading the game at a distance. It was one of those moments of solidarity and enthusiasm and appreciation recognised by the crowd as the spectacle was unfolding.

The rest of the West Indian team made 73 runs between them that day in a total of 272. In reply England made all of 168, less than Richards had scored by himself. 'Any of us will be lucky if we see anything quite like it in our lifetime,' wrote Matthew Engel from the press box.

A few days later David Frith met Vivian Richards at a function. 'He was feeling pretty good,' recalls Frith,

and that's the evening that I asked him about the Rastafarian wristband and asked if it should be used in a Test match. He got quite agitated and he was talking about what I thought were all sorts of quite unrelated matters like the slave trade. And he said, 'Dave, don't you know your history, man?' And I said, 'I know what you're going on about, but why are you attacking me in this way? I've got no ancestry involved in the slave trade and I think it's irrelevant.' And then I realised that this is one of his forces of motivation and that nothing I could say would dissuade him from carrying this conviction and that perhaps if you made 8,000 runs, 4,000 came from this fury at what had happened to some of his people a long time ago.

David Gower played five Test series against the West Indies and captained England in two of them.

If you've got a region like the Caribbean, it doesn't take much to work out that there was a lot of history going back to the slave-trade days that you can't just ignore. It goes down through the generations. Now, if you are you are an international sportsman from Antigua or Jamaica or Trinidad, you want to establish your own sense of pride in your nation. You might not be thinking about the history of the region when you are walking out to bat or marking out your run-up, but it's there. They will look into these things, analyse these things and encourage others to think about these things. It would be far too naive to suggest that the political history of the Caribbean means nothing to the cricket – it's a driving force. Pride in one's nationality, pride, dare I say, in one's colour, pride in oneself. These are all driving forces.

'All of a sudden I could remember a guy by the name of David Frith or whatever and he confronted me one night,' remembers Richards. 'And he said, "What do those colours red, gold and green that I wear on the cricket field mean?" And before I could answer he was telling me. He said it was a black power symbol. So I am saying, "In my opinion, it's not." We had a big argument about the whole stuff.'

Frith believes that any aggression felt by international cricketers on the field should end in a drink with the opposition in the bar.

For me that should be the limit of aggression in Test cricket, but now we are in very serious times and all sorts of things are motivating people – religious belief and racial conviction – and most of all these resentments. And I think it's rather sad if you need a resentment like that to fire you up. You should glory in the gift that you've been given. I mean, he was a born athlete, Viv Richards. He surely could have gone out there and done just as well and retained his cool. I wish he didn't get angry so often because I believed in him. But after that evening I was left quite worried, I thought, *Well, he's talking to young kids, and if he preaches that sort of stuff, the world's not going to be a very peaceful place*. He's a very influential man. And still is. So that was a cardinal moment. It changed my life really; it opened my eyes. I realised some cricketers are fired up by the most amazing drives of force from unexpected places.

*   *   *

Richards led his team to seven wins in their first nine Test matches under his captaincy. He had not dropped the baton and he had kept the engine running. England arrived in the Caribbean at the beginning of 1986 to face the West Indies for the first time since the blackwash humiliation of 1984. They were in for further punishment. By the time the sides reached Antigua for the final Test, the score was four–nil to the West Indies. On the fourth day of the game, in front of people who had known him since he was a child, Richards battered the fastest hundred that Test cricket had seen. After reaching his century in 56 balls, he declared in order to allow his team enough time to bowl England out for the tenth time in the series. Five–nil again. A second blackwash. The Test match score in the 1980s between the two sides now stood at thirteen–nil to the West Indies.

'Infancy has matured into manhood,' wrote Adlai Carrott on the sports page of Antigua's radical newspaper *Outlet*, 'and West Indies cricket reigns supreme with no worthy rival in sight. It is our golden age that we now enjoy and the English, ancient masters of the game, can find no counter on the field of play.'

The subjugation of England, in particular the method of victory, displeased others. Writing during the series, David Frith warned that 'the escalation of their fast bowlers has reached a murderous crescendo which shrieks remorselessly throughout the innings. The thrilling and permissively dangerous one-to-one joust has been replaced by a protracted gang mugging.' The chivalry and variety of the past had disappeared, believed Frith, to be replaced by something modern and sinister. 'In the streets, bars and fields of Barbados and Jamaica there are hordes of six-footers who rejoice in their strength and agility, get their "fix" by propelling a ball fast and eliciting admiration, and eye the advantages that cricket can bring with the same eagerness that impelled the unemployed in the Depression to don boxing gloves.'

The metaphor of a criminal inner-city youth now terrorising the cricket field was rejected outright by Adlai Carrott. 'Now in the age of West Indian dominance, their excuses range from the petty to the ridiculous. "Too many life-threatening bouncers," they scream, so we West Indians are to spare a thought for David Gower's men as they "face physical danger alien to cricket's birth right". Of course they have forgotten Typhoon Tyson, fearsome Trueman, who made Easton McMorris spit blood on the Sabina Park pitch after a consistent battering. Of course too, we did not complain and say, "It isn't cricket."' Never mind the English reporters, Carrott continued. Since their team cannot attain greatness, they revenge themselves by railing at West Indian excellence. 'As our cricket advances towards perfection, the spate of English press criticism advances with equal pace. In no sport has one nation so dominated another. In no other sport has one nation ruled so supremely for so long. Therein lies the motive for the slander and distortions of the English press.'

Fast bowling was very intimidating, says Clem Seecharan.

It was dangerous. To see these big black men – not one but four – I'm sure consciously or subconsciously that image would have been very intimidating. And you need to remember at that time in England, the 1980s, there was a political activism, militancy, parts of which Viv Richards clearly identified with. Now to some people that whole package would seem very threatening: 'The black power brigade are here, man.' Worse than that, they're at Lord's, watching cricket, playing cricket. These men had now appropriated something that wasn't theirs to take. What you must understand is that people such as Clyde Walcott and Frank Worrell were black Englishmen.

Of course they were proud of their background, but they were totally within the British colonial frame of reference: the education, the Church, the values which had been very congruent with values held by people in England.

*   *   *

After the second blackwash came Test matches in Pakistan, New Zealand and India, where the West Indies could not be beaten. New bowlers were introduced such as Patrick Patterson and Kenny Benjamin. Others who had first proved themselves in Clive Lloyd's time, such as Courtney Walsh, became better and better. The batsman Carl Hooper from Guyana made his debut against India at Mumbai in 1987; he would play another 101 Tests. Holding and Garner had now retired, but Curtly Ambrose from Antigua looked as if he could be as good a fast bowler as either of them. Against England in 1988 the score was just four–nil (the first Test was drawn) as the English endured a chaotic summer by combining a spanking from the West Indies with fielding four different captains. West Indies seventeen, England nil.

Yet with more success came more criticism. After Curtly Ambrose broke the jaw of the bowler Geoff Lawson at Perth in December 1988 a reporter wrote in the *Australian*, 'I will not concede that a cricket regime of black brutality, brinkmanship and boorishness which is destroying a beautiful game does credit to anybody. Not to those who perpetrate it, not to those who retaliate and especially not to those administrators too weak-kneed to put an end to it – those who would rather wait for a fatality before scuttling from the bar to the committee room.'

Tony Cozier covered that tour as a West Indian broadcaster and journalist. He had already formed the view that the 'defamation' of the team had become more strident and vitriolic with each West Indian triumph. In 1986 he had written in the *West*

Indies Cricket Annual that there had been an 'orchestrated campaign of unwarranted slander' against West Indies cricket, its press and its administrators. To try to discredit the record of the modern West Indian sides, he said, the critics dwelt on alleged time-wasting (the slow over rate) and intimidatory bowling. Cozier was also certain that the repeated calls to change the laws of the game were aimed at countering the West Indian bowling strategy.

At a meeting of the International Cricket Conference in 1982 a proposal to shorten the run-ups of fast bowlers had been outvoted, but there were regular petitions to restrict the number of bouncers a bowler could send down in one over. By the middle of 1991 delegations to the ICC had succeeded in persuading the organisation to allow only one bouncer per over in Test cricket. Three years later this ruling was relaxed to allow two per over. None of this had much effect on the way the West Indies played their cricket. The authors of the 1995 study on fast bowling *Real Quick* worked out that while the one-bouncer rule was in operation Richards's side played 15 Tests, won eight and lost two.

'There will always be obstacles in your way wherever you go' says Richards today. 'I felt that the changes to the laws of the game – reducing the numbers of bouncers – were targeted at the West Indies because we had a pretty fine line-up of fast bowlers both in quality and quantity. And I guess there were a few journalists who would have been pissed off about this bowling that was "designed to kill" and all that sort of stuff.'

The former England bowler Mike Selvey believes that there was something in the West Indies' psyche that was rather bemused by all of the criticism. 'Because actually this was the way they had always played their cricket – on club grounds, in the Shell Shield, in Test matches. They bounced each other, they hooked each other, they took it on – that's what they did. Culturally, they weren't doing anything to others that they hadn't done to themselves. It may have been at odds with the Corinthian spirit, but that's how it was.'

After he became a television commentator, Michael Holding was once seen shaking with laughter while watching the England all-rounder Chris Lewis prepare for an innings in the West Indies by repeatedly ducking balls thrown at his head by his teammate Robin Smith. When he was asked why he found it so funny, Holding said that if this had been a local club game, the batsman would not have been practising ducking fast bowling, but practising smashing each ball into the neighbouring parish.

The relationship between the 'West Indian brand' and how it has tested the philosophy of conservatism has long been of interest to Hilary Beckles.

The English have come from a very long tradition of political and social evolution, and there's a strong belief that some of the finest years of English culture are from the past. When you are evolving from a colonial context, your desire is to get as far away from the past as possible. You look back and you see the worst expression of the human journey. You see slavery, genocide, brutality, you see the oppression of the human spirit, the denial of human rights, so you look back and you say, 'Our agenda as a new culture is to get as far away from the past as possible.' The aim is to go aggressively into the future.

'What people didn't like, and I'm prepared to say that I believe they were envious, is that our boys stayed together for so long,' says Clive Lloyd.

They won matches and then came back four years later and won some more. These fellows who had been writing about cricket for years didn't like that the old order had changed. They found that threatening. Sport is not always played to the same system; things change. Some cricket writers looked at us and they knew that a certain kind of West Indies cricketer had died for good. They didn't like it. We were getting mammoth scores, we were bowling well, we fielded well. We paid attention to detail and were very fit. People were not accustomed to that. Some people took that hard and couldn't understand that here was a set of people who had put something special together. If you were born after 1975, you wouldn't have seen the West Indies lose in a real way until you were in your 20s.

*   *   *

Richards dealt easily with attacks on his team from outside the Caribbean: he just kept winning Test matches. But in 1990 he was criticised from within the Caribbean because of remarks he had made about the racial composition of the Test side. In an interview given to the Antiguan newspaper *Outlet* it was reported that Richards had said, 'the West Indies cricket team . . . is the only sporting team of African descent that has been able to win repeatedly against all international opposition, bringing joy and recognition to our people'.

Many people of Indian heritage living in the Caribbean said they were insulted. For some, Richards's words confirmed their belief that the exclusion of Indian players from the West Indies side was deliberate.

There had been a strong Indo-Caribbean culture in the West Indies for 150 years. Indians are the largest single ethnic group in Guyana and Trinidad. Alvin Kallicharran's family had been in Guyana for three generations, and Sonny Ramadhin's family had lived in Trinidad for at least as long. Both their fathers had been cane cutters, descendants of people who had left India since the 1830s to work on plantations after the abolition of slavery. Between 1838 and 1917 nearly 250,000 indentured labourers were brought to British Guiana from India. A further 150,000 went to Trinidad. There had been racial animosity between Indians and Africans in the Caribbean almost since their arrival; within a century this would become apparent in West Indian cricket.

Indo-Caribbean cricket fans had cheered for India when they played in the Caribbean since the 1950s, even though there were Indians in the West Indies side. In 1950 Sonny Ramadhin was the first Indo-Caribbean Test cricketer. Then came the batsmen Rohan Kanhai and Joe Solomon. But when India beat Clive Lloyd's West Indies in Trinidad in April 1976, local people ran onto the field to slap the backs of the Indian batsmen.

'It was not simply about ethnicity,' says Hilary Beckles.

It's much more than that. I believe that the Indian community in Guyana and Trinidad felt that they were given a raw deal by the black governments in the Caribbean. Forbes Burnham was in government in Guyana; Eric Williams was in government in Trinidad. These people felt that when the nation states of the Caribbean were built in the independence period, they were built as black states. These people had been in the region for some time, yet they thought that they were not treated as equally and as fairly as they deserved. One way to express their discontent of living with inequity was to forge links with the motherland and to support India.

The last great contribution to West Indian cricket from an Indo-Caribbean player had come from Alvin Kallicharran, who hadn't played Test cricket since 1981. Shiv Chanderpaul, who would be the

SIMON LISTER

next great Indo-Caribbean batsman, wouldn't make his Test debut until 1994. It seems that for many years there was no Indo-West Indian good enough to force his way into Lloyd's or Richards's best Test sides.

'I don't blame Vivian Richards for the comment he made and for which many Indians took umbrage,' says Clem Seecharan, whose book *From Ranji to Rohan* is a study of cricket and Indian identity in Guyana.

There was no Indian in the team at the time. The cricket was black cricket. It was very political. Don't forget that Viv himself had refused vast sums of money to play cricket in apartheid South Africa; I think his statement has to be seen in the light of this principled stance. That said, Viv doesn't come from Guyana where ethnic insecurities between Africans and Indians are deeply rooted.

There was violence and racial killings in the early 1960s. These insecurities festered and were aggravated by the regime of Forbes Burnham, who rigged every election between 1968 and the mid-1980s. So at the time Viv made this statement Indians in Guyana rightly felt disenfranchised. I doubt that Clive Lloyd, who is Guyanese himself of course, and is sensitive to the ethnic insecurities in that country, would have said anything similar.

Professor Seecharan's conclusion is that the Indian contribution to the development of Guyanese and Trinidadian cricket had been significant, but in Test cricket it was rather patchy and uneven.

No Indian fast bowler had made the Test team. In an area so crucial to the rise and dominance of West Indies cricket no contribution at all! Again, you would have thought that of the numerous Indo-West Indian spinners who have played for Guyana and Trinidad over the decades, a few would have established themselves in the Test team. But none replicated the example of Sonny Ramadhin in the 1950s.

And apart from three batsmen of distinction – Kanhai, Solomon and Kallicharran – there was no other Indo-West Indian cricketer who had achieved at the highest level. This is incontestable.

*   *   *

By 1991 Vivian Richards had decided to end his Test career. He was 39 and had been playing international cricket for more than 16 years. He had led the side in 12 series since 1985 and never lost. The side he brought to England in 1991 was a good one. Gordon Greenidge had retired after the home victory against Australia earlier in the year, but from the 1984 blackwash tour there was Desmond Haynes, Richards himself, Gus Logie, Richie Richardson, Jeff Dujon and Malcolm Marshall. The latest version of the bowling attack was impressive: Marshall, Walsh, Ambrose and Patterson.

Impressive, but again not universally welcome. The June 1991 editorial in *Wisden Cricket Monthly* anticipated what it called an unappetising tour. 'Another invasion is upon us by a West Indies team which is the most fearsome, the most successful, and the most unpopular in the world. Their game is founded on vengeance and violence and is fringed by arrogance.' Richards led a team, wrote David Frith, which had become embroiled in one sour series after another.

Their supporters will insist that bitterness arises from the fact that West Indies have been so steadily victorious. That may be close to the truth, but there is a vital additional factor to be identified, and that is that these matches have long since become manifestations of the racial tensions that exist in the world outside the cricket-ground gates. Just when the cricketers of both sides should be teaching ordinary folk how to co-exist and enjoy honourable sports combat, a damaging counter-image emerges.

Frith was tired of what he called the 'monotony and brutality' of slow over rates and unremitting bouncers. He professed himself to be a cricket lover who was justified in articulating his dislike of that kind of cricket.

'Mr Frith sounds a very embittered man to me,' said Vivian Richards at the time.

'I stated that in my view,' says Frith, 'the West Indian game was now based on violence, and when that was questioned I said, "Well four, five, six bouncers an over is violent cricket." There's no getting away from it. As for arrogance, Clive Lloyd said to me later, "We've got reason to be arrogant; we are beating the world," so I was right on that count too.'

David Frith says that his strong criticisms of the West Indies and their bowling tactics came from a single concern. The reason he was close to despair was that he loved the game and saw it being traduced. 'I care for cricket,' he insists,

> and any accusation that there is a racist motive for this . . . [the 1991 editorial] any accusation that this is a racist attack, is despicable, and I refute it. But it's very easy for people to hop on this racism bandwagon. I am sick to death of it; it's just become the scourge of our age. They got me wrong. I used to like those blokes and dine with them and be accepted by them. However, in 1991 – I suppose I had to expect it – Gordon Greenidge – he was a former friend – walked straight past me.

The previous spring, when England had narrowly lost in the West Indies, *Wisden Cricket Monthly* had had a heavy mailbag full of post about the West Indies' play. The editor selected five of the letters for publication. The first called for the immediate sacking of the manager Clive Lloyd and the captain, Vivian Richards. Three other letters were headed 'Murder', 'Moral Winners' and 'Unsavoury'. The fifth letter was entitled 'Voodoo?' and was from a reader in Cheshire. 'Until we can breed 7-foot monsters willing to break bones and shatter faces, we cannot compete against these threatening West Indians. Even the umpires seem to be scared that the devilish-looking Richards might put a voodoo sign on them!'

*   *   *

The 1991 series between England and the West Indies was drawn. It was the first time that the West Indies had not defeated the English in England since 1969. The four series under Richards's captaincy had finished five–nil, four–nil, two–one and two all. England were getting closer. Perhaps the potency of the West Indies was being diluted?

At the Oval, where he'd beaten the ball and the England bowlers into a dusty submission in 1976 and seen the England captain grovel on all fours in front of British West Indian supporters, Vivian Richards played his last Test match innings. He hit back-foot cover drives off David Lawrence, an England fast bowler whose parents had come to the West Country from Jamaica. He pulled Phillip DeFreitas – an England fast bowler born in Dominica – for four through mid-wicket. He square-cut Chris Lewis – an England fast bowler born in Guyana – to the boundary. After he had made 60 from them, he was caught off Lawrence at mid-on.

He walked back to the dressing room and was given a hell of an ovation. He took his famous maroon cap off his now-bald head and raised it with his bat to the crowd. But because he was Vivian Richards, his fury at playing a false shot preoccupied him.

It was over. Someone special was crossing beyond a boundary. Such men deserve to be remembered in verse. This time the calypsonian King Short Shirt sang it best.

No bowler holds a terror for Vivian Richards.
Not Thomson not Lillee, not Bedi nor Chandrasekhar.
A perfect coordination of body and mind.
That brother is really dynamite.
I tell you, pace or spin he ain't give a France what you're
    bowling him,
Fast or slowly, you're going back to the boundary.

Epilogue

'When I am playing for my country,' says Michael Holding, 'I have five million West Indians depending on me to perform at my best so they can walk the streets and be proud. I have to do my job.'

Holding's job was to bowl very fast. He needed discipline, intelligence and discernment to do it well. He also needed the old West Indian skill of bowling short.

'I am genuinely sorry when I hit a batsman. I am not bowling to hit him, and the last thing that I should wish for is for him to have to give up his innings and retire hurt. But I know that I must have him aware that the ball can be made to do something.' These are the words, not of Michael Holding but of Learie Constantine, who played Test cricket from 1928 until 1939. He knew that the 'short, flying ball' was an integral part of the fast bowler's attack. 'These are the realities of cricket,' he said. 'These things cricketers know.'

The regular bowling of the short ball was the single greatest controversy surrounding West Indian cricket. The *Wisden Cricketers' Almanack* didn't like it. West Indian bowling was 'unpleasant, not to say dangerous' was the view of *Wisden*'s editor in the 1934 edition. It seems that short-pitched bowling by black men has always troubled some cricket writers much more than the cricketers who faced it.

The England opening batsman Geoffrey Boycott, who was

undone so thoroughly by Michael Holding in that one over in Barbados in 1981, has frank views on the matter.

Why bother with spinners? Clive Lloyd just bothered with four fast bowlers and said, 'We're going to bowl you out.' I don't blame him. People say it was bad for the game – I've seen writers write about that – but any human being who tries to tell me he wouldn't have played four fast bowlers because they were winning Test matches is a liar. We'd all have done it, and I'd have been stood at mid-off or mid-on cheering them on. Just like the West Indian fielders did: 'Go on. Give him a few more, Crofty. Sit him on his backside. Yeah, get after him.' We'd have all been doing it. It's the nature of the game. If you're competitive, you want to win, and as long as you win within the rules I can't see anything wrong with that. Good luck to the West Indies. It was a part of their history which I admire and I respect.

In 2005 England won the Ashes for the first time in nearly 20 years. Their success was largely down to Steve Harmison, Simon Jones, Andrew Flintoff and Matthew Hoggard. All four were very good fast bowlers. There were few complaints about how they had won. At Lord's, when a ball from Harmison hit the Australian captain Ricky Ponting and cut his face, a great rolling roar went around the ground. When the Ashes were safe there was national rejoicing, and the players were driven through London on an open-top bus to Trafalgar Square. Ashley Giles was there. He was the England spinner and played in every Test that summer. He was part of the side's traditional 'balanced' bowling attack. Giles took 10 wickets at an average of 57.80 runs each and his best performance was 3 for 78.

In the blackwash summer of 1984, when criticism of the West Indies' fast bowling attack had never been stronger, Roger Harper was the West Indies' off-spinner. He played in all five Tests and

took 13 wickets at an average of 21.23 runs each. His best performance was 6 for 57.

'When we started to win,' reflects Michael Holding,

> people started saying, 'We have to find some way of degrading this.
> It can't be as good as they are making it out to be,' so they started
> looking for excuses. They started to say we haven't got a 'balanced'
> team; cricket was about having a 'balanced' team. Well, this is not
> a trapeze act; it is about winning a cricket match. You pick the team
> that will win you the game. Then they decided to say that fast
> bowling was intimidatory: 'It's not fair; you can't score off so many
> bouncers.' Well, we had a batsman who didn't mind if you bowled
> six bouncers at him. His name was Viv Richards. If you were good
> enough, you could score enough.

*　　*　　*

This book began with Michael Holding's tears at Sydney in 1976.
Young men don't often cry in public, especially not in front of
thousands of people with many more watching on television. So it
was a memorable moment for Holding. It was also a significant
day for his team. What they saw that afternoon closed the door on
an old world for the West Indies. They watched Ian Chappell nick
the ball to the wicket-keeper and stay at the crease knowing that
he was out. The umpire's arm remained down. This was modern
international cricket. From that day on Gordon Greenidge certainly
never walked if he edged it; let the umpire tell him he was out.

The armour plating that was to make the West Indies almost
invulnerable for the next 19 years began to form around the team
that afternoon at the SCG. 'The Australians taught us, and we took
notice of them,' said Vivian Richards.

Clive Lloyd had arrived in Australia in October 1975 telling
reporters, 'I don't like losers. If you don't think you have a chance

of winning, there is no sense in taking part.' When he left Australia at the end of the tour he was a loser. He had little going for him except his cussed spirit. Had the next series against India been lost, who knows what would have become of Lloyd? It was a close-run thing. He became a great captain and leader, but there were never any guarantees. In 1966 when Lloyd was LBW to Garry Sobers for nought in Barbados, the received wisdom in Georgetown had been that he might never play for British Guiana again. The idea of him playing for the West Indies, let alone being captain, was outlandish.

It was a close-run thing.

Lloyd knew that if he was to survive, and his team to thrive, they had to change. He knew that if he was going to lead a great side, it would not come about by accident. His team did not fall from a passing comet, fully formed, tossed up, pads buckled, ready to play. There was a strategy.

Lloyd wanted only one thing from his players – excellence. He wanted them to play as well as they could. He was not preoccupied with vengeance, payback or righting historical wrongs. He wanted his team to entertain people with the best skills they had. He wanted to win cricket matches.

The captaincy of Frank Worrell had been drenched with symbolism. Garry Sobers's leadership was inspirational because he could bat, bowl and field his team to victory by himself. The assertive captaincy of Vivian Richards combined with his batting exploits assured West Indians of their place in the world. But Lloyd's leadership was the most significant of all because of what he created. He taught the West Indies how to win. The construction of the team, the discipline, the batting and the four fast bowlers were all about winning.

They began to play cricket in a new way. They were no longer cavaliers reliant on talented individuals; this side had a fresh intelligence at its centre. That appealed to supporters of the West Indies.

Their cricket team would be successful because of what went on in the head, not just thanks to the athleticism of the body. These cricketers were serious people, tutored and drilled to win. New players were brought in to continue the pattern. This was a team that could not be patronised like those of the past. The dominance of Lloyd's men and Richards's men was achieved through hard work, discipline and technical excellence; it had very little to do with carefree, instinctive spontaneity.

When Graham Gooch was the captain of England in the early 1990s and Micky Stewart was the manager, they tried to reform English cricket with a regime of physical fitness, rigorous practice, team spirit, pride and punctuality. It was a good idea – and nothing more than what the West Indies had been doing since 1978.

Lloyd and Richards may have distilled the values of hard work, discipline and technical distinction, but they didn't invent them. To those who looked, these qualities had been developing in West Indian cricket for almost a century. They were part of the story of Charles Ollivierre's excellence.

Ollivierre was 23 when he came to England with the West Indies side in 1900. He had played three games of first-class cricket in four years before the tour, yet he scored nearly 900 runs in a foreign country on unfamiliar wickets when the sport in his own island was at a rudimentary stage. This would have been impossible had it been down to talent alone; his innings must have featured character, intelligence, aptitude and judgement. Ollivierre began the tradition of West Indian batsmanship. A hundred years later Brian Lara probably completed it through his technical competence, his stamina and stroke play, his ability to dominate bowlers, and most of all the talent to change the course of a Test match. The tradition which Lara perfected had been refined on its way to him by George Headley in the 1930s and 1940s, and after the

Second World War by players such as Frank Worrell, Everton Weekes and Clyde Walcott, and later still, by Rohan Kanhai.

In *Rites* the Barbadian poet Kamau Brathwaite describes a Walcott innings against England at the Kensington Oval in Bridgetown shortly after the war. Johnny Wardle had just been hit for four.

> 'You see dat shot?' the people was shoutin';
> 'Jesus Chrise, man, wunna see dat shot?'
> All over de groun' fellers shakin' hands wid each other
>
> as if was *they* wheelin' de willow
> as if was *them* had the power;
> one man run out pun de field wid a red fowl cock
>
> goin' quawk quawk quawk in 'e han';
> would'a give it to Clyde right then an' right there
> if a police hadn't stop 'e!

Brathwaite's Walcott was scoring his runs for a nation; those runs belonged to the people, and the people knew it. Cricketers were the only pan-Caribbean heroes.

'If a West Indian made a century at Lord's or in Australia', recalls Ronald Austin, 'it was almost like getting inspiration from Scripture. Cricket was deeply interwoven into our lives. And not just young men like myself. My mother was obsessed with the game – all the older women were. You'd go to Bourda for a Test and you'd see them there with baskets of food for the whole day; they'd all come to watch Everton Weekes or Garry Sobers. Cricket penetrated every aspect of society.'

Ronald Austin's recollection of boyhood cricket in British Guiana connects with that most famous of rhetorical questions posed in

Beyond a Boundary. 'What do they know of cricket who only cricket know?' asked C. L. R. James.

> West Indians crowding to Tests bring with them the whole past history and future hopes of the islands. English people, for example, have a conception of themselves breathed from birth. Drake and mighty Nelson, Shakespeare, Waterloo, the Charge of the Light Brigade, the few who did so much for so many, the success of parliamentary democracy, those and such as those constitute a national tradition. Underdeveloped countries have to go back centuries to rebuild one. We of the West Indies have none at all, none that we know of. To such people, the three Ws, Ram and Val wrecking English batting, help to fill a huge gap in their consciousness and in their needs.

In Georgetown and Brooklyn, Streatham and Birmingham the successes of West Indian cricketers brought great pride to the diaspora. Just ask the three bus drivers of this book: the man with the hired top hat and cane in 1950, the man who stopped the traffic on Kensington High Street for Viv, and Harold Blackman, whose London Transport XI in the 1980s were as unbeatable as the West Indies. 'We used to think, *The same thing they do, we can do.* They gave us a spurt, they gave us heart,' says Harold.

The West Indies brought a nation of cricket lovers, whose flag flew only from a pavilion roof, to its feet. Not for a tournament, not for a season or for five years, but for the best part of two decades. Their fine play allowed their people to stop apologising for being West Indian.

'There was a lot we had to overcome, and we did it,' says Andy Roberts. 'We did not complain, and here we are. We end up having one of the greatest teams in the history of sport. Several dots on the map dominating the world.'

Acknowledgements

My first thanks must go to the film director Stevan Riley. *Fire in Babylon* was his movie, and this book was his idea. Not only did Stevan suggest I should be the author, he generously handed over many hours of interviews he had collected during filming. They are the cornerstone of this book. Apart from all of that, Stevan has always been available for an easy-going word of advice and encouragement. Without him this book could not have been written.

I must also thank Ronald Austin. I first met Ronald in Georgetown, Guyana when I was researching my biography of Clive Lloyd in 2007. Ronald was my guide then and he has been again during the writing of *Fire in Babylon*. He describes himself only as 'a man who loves cricket' but he is so much more. He has a profound, analytical and deeply refined understanding of the game in the Caribbean and what it means to people who live there. I have quoted Ronald in several passages in *Fire in Babylon*, but his voice, his wisdom and his influence resonate throughout this book.

Two other friends – Simon Kuper and Paul Coupar-Hennessy – have been invaluable counsellors. When they had much better things to do, they corrected, rearranged and polished large parts of this manuscript. I cannot thank them enough for their patience and expertise.

The perspicacity of Frances Jessop and the tenacity of Charlie Brotherstone must also be mentioned. Fran is my discerning, deadline-extending editor at Yellow Jersey and Charlie is my literary agent at Ed Victor Ltd who did so much to kick this whole thing off.

I would also like to thank Laura Barraclough, Peter Biles, Stephen Bourne, David Bull, Wally Caruana, Mike Dunk, Jane Durie, Rob Durie, Cornelius Gaskin, Jack Houldsworth, Carl Hoyte, Tony Jaggs, Euel Johnson, Michelle McDonald, the National Archive of Antigua and Joe Smith.

Contributors

Martin Adrien, Ronald Austin, Colin Babb, Tony Becca, Hilary Beckles, Harold Blackman, Geoffrey Boycott, Robin Buckley, Don Cameron, Stephen Chalke, Greg Chappell, Ian Chappell, Brian Close, Jeremy Coney, Tony Cozier, Colin Croft, Matthew Engel, Graeme Fowler, King Frank-I Francis, David Frith, Paul Gilroy, Fred Goodall, David Gower, Gordon Greenidge, Desmond Haynes, Michael Holding, Geoff Howarth, Kevin Hylton, Dilip Jajodia, Alvin Kallicharran, Sam King, Tapley Lewis, Andy Lloyd, Clive Lloyd, Ashley Mallett, Lewis Manthata, Charles Maskell-Knight, Scotty Mitchell, David Murray, Deryck Murray, Trevor Nelson, Paul Newman, Essop Pahad, Trevor Phillips, Derek Pringle, Sonny Ramadhin, Vivian Richards, Andy Roberts, Austin Robertson, Clem Seecharan, Mike Selvey, Steve Stephenson, Bob Turnbull and Bunny Wailer.

The interviews in this book come from two main sources. First, the long recordings made by Stevan Riley. Inevitably, only a small part of this original testimony appeared in his film. Second, the many fresh interviews conducted by the author, who in some cases spoke to the same players for a second time. Where relevant, the author's work has been augmented by material he gathered while working on the authorised biography of Clive Lloyd. Three contributions – by Geoff Howarth, Don Cameron and Derek Pringle – first appeared in columns written by the author for the *Wisden Cricketer* magazine.

Bibliography

All these books were of great use while writing *Fire in Babylon*, but I want to draw attention to two in particular: David Tossell's *Grovel!* on the 1976 series in England and *The Cricket War* by Gideon Haigh. Both authors deserve the thanks of readers of cricket books everywhere for their industry, insight and authority.

Arlott, John, *John Arlott's Book of Cricketers* (Lutterworth Press, 1979)

Bradman to Chappell (Australian Broadcasting Commission Books, 1976)

Babb, Colin, *They Gave the Crowd Plenty Fun* (Hansib, 2012)

Barker, J. S., *Summer Spectacular* (The Sportsman's Book Club, 1965)

Beckett, Andy, *When the Lights Went Out: What Really Happened to Britain in the Seventies* (Faber and Faber, 2009)

Beckles, Hilary McD. (ed.), *A Spirit of Dominance: Cricket and Nationalism in the West Indies* (Canoe Press, 1999)

——, *The Development of West Indies Cricket Volume 1* (Pluto Press, 1999)

——, *The Development of West Indies Cricket Volume 2* (Pluto Press, 1999)

Beckles, Hilary McD. and Stoddart, Brian (eds), *Liberation Cricket: West Indies Cricket Culture* (Manchester University Press, 1995)

Bell, Carl, *A Complete Statistical Record of West Indian Test Cricketers* (MRC, 1994)

Van der Bijl, Vintcent, *Cricket in the Shadows* (Shuter and Shooter, 1985)

Birbalsingh, Frank, *Indo-Westindian Cricket* (Hansib, 1987)

——, *The Rise of Westindian Cricket* (Hansib, 1997)

Birley, Derek, *A Social History of English Cricket* (Aurum, 2000)

——, *The Willow Wand* (Aurum, 2013)

Booth, Douglas, *The Race Game: Sport and Politics in South Africa* (Cass, 1998)

Bose, Mihir, *A History of Indian Cricket* (André Deutsch, 2002)

——, *Sporting Colours* (Robson, 1993)

Braithwaite, E. R., *Honorary White* (New English Library, 1977)

Brathwaite, Kamau, *The Arrivants* (Oxford University Press, 1981)

Brearley, Mike, *The Art of Captaincy* (Channel Four Books, 2001)

Brearley, Mike and Doust, Dudley, *The Ashes Retained* (Hodder and Stoughton, 1979)

Brookes, Christopher, *His Own Man – The Life of Neville Cardus* (Methuen, 1985)

Cardus, Neville, *Second Innings* (Collins, 1950)

Caro, Andrew, *With a Straight Bat* (The Sales Machine Ltd, 1979)

Cashman, Richard, *'Ave a Go, Yer Mug!* (Collins, 1984)

Chalke, Stephen, *Micky Stewart and the Changing Face of Cricket* (Fairfield Books, 2012)

——, *Tom Cartwright: The Flame Still Burns* (Fairfield Books, 2007)

Chappell, Ian and Mallett, Ashley, *Hitting Out: The Ian Chappell Story* (Orion, 2005)

Conn, David, *The Beautiful Game? Searching for the Soul of Football* (Yellow Jersey Press, 2005)

Constantine, Learie, *Colour Bar* (Stanley Paul, 1954)

——, *Cricket and I* (Philip Allan, 1933)

——, *Cricket in the Sun* (Stanley Paul, 1946)

Corbett, Ted, *Cricket on the Run* (Stanley Paul, 1990)

Cornelissen, Scarlet and Grundlingh, Albert, *Sport Past and Present in South Africa* (Routledge, 2013)

Da Costa, Emilia Viotti, *Crowns of Glory, Tears of Blood: The Demerara Slave Rebellion of 1823* (Oxford University Press, 1997)

Cozier, Tony, *Clive Lloyd: Living for Cricket* (Star, 1983)

—— (ed.), *Wisden History of the Cricket World Cup* (Wordsmith, 2006)

Dabydeen, David (ed.), *Oxford Companion to Black British History* (Oxford University Press, 2007)

Dalrymple, Henderson, *50 Great West Indian Test Cricketers* (Hansib, 1983)

Desai, Ashwin, *Blacks in Whites: A Century of Cricket Struggles in KwaZulu-Natal* (University of KwaZulu-Natal Press, 2003)

Down, Michael, *Is it Cricket? Power, Money and Politics in Cricket since 1945* (Queen Anne Press, 1985)

Eagar, Patrick, *Test Decade: 1972–1982* (World's Work, 1982)

Fingleton, Jack, *Fingleton on Cricket* (Collins, 1972)

——, *Masters of Cricket* (Heinemann, 1958)

Foot, David, *Sunshine, Sixes and Cider* (David and Charles, 1986)

——, *Viv Richards* (World's Work, 1979)

Frindall, Bill, *Frindall's Score Book – Australia v West Indies 1975–76* (Lonsdale, 1976)

——, *Frindall's Score Book – England v West Indies 1976* (Lonsdale, 1976)

Frith, David, *Bodyline Autopsy* (Aurum, 2002)

——, *Caught England, Bowled Australia* (Eva Press, 1997)

——, *Fast Men: Two Hundred Year Cavalcade of Speed Bowlers* (Allen and Unwin, 1982)

——, *Thommo: Story of Jeff Thomson* (TBS, 1980)

Fryer, Peter, *Aspects of British Black History* (Index Books, 1993)

——, *Staying Power: The History of Black People in Britain* (Pluto Press, 1984)

Garner, Joel, *Big Bird: Flying High* (Arthur Barker, 1988)

Gemmell, Jon, *The Politics of South African Cricket* (Routledge, 2004)

Genders, Roy, *League Cricket in England* (Werner Laurie, 1952)

Gibson, Alan, *The Cricket Captains of England* (The Pavilion Library, 1979)

Gilbert, Kevin, *Because a White Man'll Never Do it* (Angus and Robertson, 2013)

——, *Living Black* (Penguin, 1978)

Gilroy, Paul, *The Black Atlantic* (Verso, 1993)

——, *Black Britain* (Saqi, 2007)

——, *There Ain't no Black in the Union Jack* (Hutchinson, 1987)

Giuseppe, Undine, *A Look at Learie Constantine* (Thomas Nelson and Sons, 1974)

Goble, Ray and Sandiford, Keith A. P., *75 years of West Indies Cricket* (Hansib, 2004)

Goodwin, Clayton, *Caribbean Cricketers: From the Pioneers to Packer* (Chambers, 1980)

——, *West Indians at the Wicket* (Macmillan, 1986)

Grant, Colin, *I & I the Natural Mystics: Marley, Tosh and Wailer* (Jonathan Cape, 2011)

Greenidge, Gordon, *The Man in the Middle* (David and Charles, 1980)

Greig, Tony, *My Story* (Hutchinson, 1980)

Guha, Ramachandra, *A Corner of a Foreign Field* (Picador, 2003)

—— (ed.), *The Picador Book of Cricket* (Picador, 2002)

Haigh, Gideon, *The Cricket War* (Text Publishing, 1993)

——, *Silent Revolutions: Writings on Cricket History* (Black Inc., 2006)

——, *The Summer Game* (ABC Books, 2006)

——, *Uncertain Corridors: Writings on Modern Cricket* (Simon and Schuster, 2014)

Holding, Michael, *No Holding Back* (Orion, 2010)

——, *Whispering Death* (André Deutsch, 1993)

James, C. L. R., *Beyond a Boundary* (Yellow Jersey Press, 2005)

——, *Cricket* (Allison and Busby, 1986)

Keating, Frank, *Another Bloody Day in Paradise!* (André Deutsch, 1981)

Kelly, Paul, *The Dismissal: Australia's Most Sensational Power Struggle* (Angus and Robertson, 1983)

Kumar, Vijay P., *Cricket Lovely Cricket* (published privately, 2000)

Kynaston, David, *Austerity Britain, 1945–1951: Tales of a New Jerusalem* (Bloomsbury, 2007)

Lamming, George, *The Emigrants* (University of Michigan, 1994)

——, *In the Castle of my Skin* (Longman, 1979)

Lapping, Brian, *Apartheid: A History* (Paladin, 1988)

Lawrence, Bridgette, *100 Great Westindian Test Cricketers from Challenor to Richards* (Hansib, 1987)

Lelyveld, Joseph, *Move your Shadow* (Abacus, 1989)

Levy, Andrea, *Small Island* (Picador, 2005)

Lillee, Dennis, *The Art of Fast Bowling* (Lutterworth Press, 1978)

——, *Menace: The Autobiography* (Headline, 2003)

Lister, Simon, *Supercat: The Authorised Biography of Clive Lloyd* (Fairfield Books, 2007)

Mahler, Jonathan, *Ladies and Gentlemen, the Bronx is Burning* (Picador, 2007)

Mallett, Ashley, *Thommo Speaks Out* (Allen and Unwin, 2010)

Manley, Michael, *A History of West Indies Cricket* (André Deutsch, 1988)

Marsh, Rod, *Gloves, Sweat and Tears* (Penguin, 1984)

——, *The Gloves of Irony* (Lansdowne, 1982)

——, *The Inside Edge* (Lansdowne, 1984)

——, *You'll Keep* (Hutchinson, 1975)

Marshall, Malcolm, *Marshall Arts* (Macdonald Queen Anne Press, 1987)

Mason, Peter, *Learie Constantine* (Macmillan Caribbean, 2007)

Mason, Tony (ed.), *Sport in Britain: A Social History* (Cambridge University Press, 2011)

May, Peter, *The Rebel Tours* (SportsBooks, 2009)

McDonald, Trevor, *Clive Lloyd: The Authorised Biography* (Granada, 1985)

——, *Viv Richards: The Authorised Biography* (Sphere, 1984)

McGregor, Craig, *Profile of Australia* (Hodder and Stoughton, 1966)

McKinstry, Leo, *Boycs: The True Story* (Partridge, 2000)

Mermelstein, David, *The Anti-Apartheid Reader* (Grove Press, 1987)

Morris, Mervyn and Carnegie, Jimmy, *Lunchtime Medley* (Ian Randle, 2008)

Moorhouse, Geoffrey, *Lord's* (Hodder and Stoughton, 1983)

Murray, Bruce K. and Merrett, Christopher, *Caught Behind: Race and Politics in Springbok Cricket* (University of KwaZulu-Natal Press, 2004)

Naipaul, V. S., *The Middle Passage* (Vintage, 2002)

Nauright, John, *Sport, Cultures and Identities in South Africa* (Leicester University Press, 1998)

Newland, Courttia (ed.), *IC3: The Penguin Book of New Black Writing in Britain* (Penguin, 2001)

Nicole, Christopher, *West Indian Cricket* (Phoenix, 1957)

Oborne, Peter, *Basil D'Oliveira: Cricket and Conspiracy, the Untold Story* (Little, Brown, 2004)

Odendaal, André, *Cricket in Isolation: The Politics of Race and Cricket in South Africa* (privately published, 1977)

Phillips, Mike and Phillips, Trevor, *Windrush: The Irresistible Rise of Multi-Racial Britain* (HarperCollins, 2009)

Pilkington, Edward, *Beyond the Mother Country: West Indians and the Notting Hill White Riots* (I. B. Tauris and Co., 1988)

Quarles, Benjamin, *The Negro in the Making of America* (Collier, 1969)

Rae, Simon, *W. G. Grace: A Life* (Faber and Faber, 1999)

Raman, Menaka et al., *From There to Here: 16 True Tales of Immigration to Britain* (Penguin, 2007)

Richards, Vivian, *Hitting Across the Line: An Autobiography* (Headline, 1991)

——, *Sir Vivian: The Definitive Autobiography* (Penguin, 2001)

Rickard, John, *Australia: A Cultural History* (Longman, 1996)

Ross, Alan, *Through the Caribbean* (The Pavilion Library, 1986)

Ross, Gordon, *A History of West Indies Cricket* (Arthur Barker, 1976)

St Clair, William, *The Grand Slave Emporium* (Profile, 2007)

Salewicz, Chris, *Bob Marley: The Untold Story* (Harper, 2010)

Savidge, Michele and McLellan, Alastair, *Real Quick* (Blandford, 1995)

Seecharan, Clem, *From Ranji to Rohan: Cricket and Indian Identity in Colonial Guyana 1890s–1960s* (Hansib, 2009)

——, *Muscular Learning: Cricket and Education in the Making of the British West Indies at the End of the Nineteenth Century* (Ian Randle, 2005)

——, *Sweetening Bitter Sugar: Jock Campbell the Booker Reformer* (Ian Randle, 2004)

Selvon, Sam, *The Lonely Londoners* (Penguin, 2006)

Sobers, Garfield, *Cricket in the Sun* (Arthur Barker, 1967)

——, *My Autobiography* (Headline, 2003)

Steen, Rob, *Floodlights and Touchlines: A History of Spectator Sport*, (Bloomsbury, 2014)

——, *Desmond Haynes: Lion of Barbados* (Weidenfeld and Nicolson, 1993)

Stoddart, Brian and Sandiford, Keith A. P. (eds), *The Imperial Game: Cricket, Culture and Society* (Manchester University Press, 1998)

Stollmeyer, Jeff, *Everything Under the Sun* (Stanley Paul, 1983)

Swanton, E. W., *Sort of a Cricket Person* (Collins, 1972)

Tennant, Ivo, *Frank Worrell: A Biography* (Lutterworth Press, 1987)

Thompson, Leonard, *A History of South Africa* (Yale University Press, 1996)

Tossell, David, *Grovel!* (Know the Score, 2007)

——, *Tony Greig: A Reappraisal of English Cricket's Most Controversial Captain* (Pitch, 2011)

Underdown, David, *Start of Play* (Allen Lane, 2000)

Walcott, Clyde, *Sixty Years on the Back Foot* (Orion, 2000)

Walsh, Courtney, *Heart of the Lion* (Lancaster, 1999)

Warner, Pelham, *Long Innings* (Harrap, 1951)

West, Peter (ed.), *Cricketers from the West Indies* (Playfair, 1950)

Wild, Rosalind Eleanor, *Black Was the Colour of our Fight. Black Power in Britain, 1955–1976* (PhD thesis, University of Sheffield, 2008)

Wilde, Simon, *Letting Rip: Fast Bowling Threat from Lillee to Waqar* (Gollancz, 1994)

Williams, Jack, *Cricket and Race* (Berg, 2001)

Wisden Anthology 1940–1963 (Macdonald Queen Anne Press, 1982)

Wisden Anthology 1963–1982 (Guild Publishing, 1986)

The Wisden Book of Cricket Records (Queen Anne Press, 1988)

The Wisden Book of Cricketers' Lives (Macdonald Queen Anne Press, 1986)

The Wisden Book of Test Cricket Volume 1 (Headline, 2010)

The Wisden Book of Test Cricket Volume 2 (Headline, 2010)

The Wisden Book of Test Cricket Volume 3 (Headline, 2010)

Wisden Cricketers' Almanack (various years)

Worrell, Frank, *Cricket Punch* (Rupa, 1959)

Wright, Graeme, *Betrayal: The Struggle for Cricket's Soul* (Witherby, 1993)

List of Illustrations

1. Ian Chappell considers walking (Patrick Eagar Collection/Getty Images); Michael Holding (Patrick Eagar)
2. Clive Lloyd and Greg Chappell at the coin toss (Patrick Eagar Collection/Getty Images); Melbourne Cricket Ground spectators (Patrick Eagar Collection/Getty Images); defeat in Australia (Patrick Eagar)
3. John Edrich and Brian Close (Patrick Eagar)
4. Vivian Richards and Roy Fredericks (Bob Thomas/Getty Images); Vivian Richards batting (Patrick Eagar); West Indian supporters (Mirrorpix)
5. West Indies v England in 1976 at the Oval (all Patrick Eagar)
6. Derbyshire XI (Popperfoto/Getty Images); Charles Ollivierre (Popperfoto/Getty Images); Learie Constantine (Hulton Archive/Getty Images)
7. Lord Kitchener and his band (Press Association); Sonny Ramadhin (Topical Press Agency/Getty Images); Kelso Cochrane's funeral (Edward Miller/Hulton Archive/Getty Images)
8. Wayne Daniel (Patrick Eagar)
9. 1979 World Cup team photo (back row, left to right: Gus Logie, Thelston Payne, Larry Gomes, Jeff Dujon, Eldine Baptiste. Middle row: Jackie Hendricks (manager), Malcolm Marshall, Desmond Haynes, Roger Harper, Courtney Walsh, Milton Small, Richie Richardson, Walter St John (assistant manager),

Dennis Waight. Front row: Joel Garner, Vivian Richards, Clive Lloyd, Gordon Greenidge, Michael Holding.); Vivian Richards and Collis King (both Patrick Eagar Collection/Getty Images)

10. Dressing room in Adelaide (Patrick Eagar); Michael Holding kicking down stumps (Getty Images); Bernard Julien (Adrian Murrell/Getty Images)

11. Frank Worrell (Ron Case/Getty Images); Garry Sobers (Douglas Miller/Getty Images); West Indian supporters in 1963 (Keystone/Getty Images)

12. 1984 team photo (Bob Thomas/Getty Images); Andy Lloyd hit at Edgbaston (Patrick Eagar Collection/Getty Images)

13. Vivian Richards batting in 1984 (Patrick Eagar); Slip cordon at Headingley (Patrick Eagar); 1984 Blackwash (Mark Leech/Getty Images)

14. Clive Lloyd (Patrick Eagar)

15. Vivian Richards (Popperfoto/Getty Images)

16. Colin Croft (Bob Thomas/Getty Images); Malcolm Marshall (Adrian Murrell/Getty Images); Joel Garner (Patrick Eagar Collection/Getty Images); Andy Roberts (Bob Thomas/Getty Images)

Index